The Book of the
HALL 4-6-0s

Part One 4900-4999
By
Ian Sixsmith

4914 CRANMORE HALL by that monumental wall at Teignmouth station with an up stopper, 13 August 1957. J. Robertson, transporttreasury

Irwell Press Ltd.

Acknowledgements

Thanks to Richard Derry, who once again took on the daunting task of arranging the tables, Eric Youldon, Nick Deacon, Brian Penney, Tony Wright, Edward Chaplin, Brian Bailey and Peter Coster. The table details were quarried from the various GW/WR records as painstakingly extracted from the National Archive by Dave Walker.

Contents

4977 WATCOMBE HALL in lined green, at Oxford on 20 June 1957. H.C. Casserley, courtesy R.M. Casserley.

A new Hall, in original state; 4931 HANBURY HALL in lined dark green, with the 'intermediate' 3,500 gallon tender. The date is not known but 4931 had this tender from new in June 1929 until September 1932. The sharpness and clarity of an early glass plate effort such as this shows up well the four feed oil box on the curved section of the running plate. It fed oil to the tops of the bogie axleboxes from where it was channelled to lubricate the horn faces. As well as this oil 'pot' under the smokebox there were others, in the rocker shaft covers – by that plate projecting from the boiler to the running plate. The ATC shoe assembly is clearly seen, also the conduit for the ATC cable attached to the valence of the platform to the cab. Note the valve for the steam lance for cleaning the tubes, on the smokebox door rim. There is no lubricating oil pipe running down the smokebox from the oil pipe cover above the hand rail on the smokebox, which is a minor mystery. The small upright object, like an oil bottle on the running plate in the middle of the forward splasher is the 'class B' vacuum pump lubricator. It supplied oil to the vacuum pump cylinder to lubricate the pump piston. They were removed – largely – under BR.

4945 MILLIGAN HALL in lined green waits at Temple Meads with a horse box; it is still with the low type of 3,500 gallon tender but the GWR roundel puts the period at the later 1930s.

Introduction
SAINTLY ORIGINS

Of all the vast fleet of British mixed traffic (almost entirely class 5 by BR days) 4-6-0s very few pre-dated the first Hall, 4900 SAINT MARTIN. The North Eastern B16 (before it was called a B16) was earlier but it wasn't quite a mixed traffic jack of all trades of the type that we came to know – like the Black 5s and B1s, say, of which there were well over a thousand. No, the lineage of the British 5MT goes back to that first Hall, a rebuild of an engine which first appeared in 1907. Almost exactly fifty years after this unlikely progenitor was built we had only lately *stopped* building the mixed traffic 4-6-0 – Doncaster's very different-looking but in essence the same 73171. (In an interesting quirk, these were the *only* 4-6-0s ever built at Doncaster). In that very year, 1958, Dr Tuplin in *Great Western Steam* (George Allen & Unwin) wrote: *with the trend in later years to make life gentler for locomotives, Collett introduced the Hall class which is (small details apart) just a Churchward Saint with 6ft wheels and these now do much of the work on which the 2-6-0s were first engaged.*

Dr Tuplin was drawing on his memories when the engines began appearing in numbers, back in 1929-30, *The Railway Gazette* announcing that: *In these days of heavy train loadings on British railways, and particularly where the 'going' is not easy, there is an increasing demand for engines of the 2-6-0 and 4-6-0 classes*

with coupled wheels so proportioned as to permit of the requisite average speeds, combined with better accelerative and grade-climbing propensities. It was for just this purpose that Collett had Saint 4-6-0 2925 SAINT MARTIN rebuilt with 6ft wheels. Various minor changes were made to accommodate these but the only other 'new' feature was a side window cab. SAINT MARTIN retained its inside steam pipes. Four years were to pass before the first 'production' Hall – so, for the first years of its existence the class wasn't even called the Halls!

It was a canny way to proceed. The combination of the higher (225lb) boiler pressure of the Saints and smaller coupled wheels in an otherwise standardised engine produced the desired results without planning out an entirely new engine with all the attendant cost of new drawings, patterns, templates, and many other things. This was the practice now being followed on the Great Western Railway, records *The Railway Gazette*: *A new series of engines, to be known as the 'Hall' class has been put in hand at Swindon works, to the sum of 80. The new engines virtually constitute a repetition of the previous 'Saint' class, which, however, had larger coupled wheels and ranked as two-cylinder express locomotives, taking their turn with the four-cylinder classes, except perhaps for the heaviest trains. In the 'Hall' class, the combination of a boiler pressure of 225lb and a smaller diameter of coupled wheel provides*

those extra tractive and accelerative powers, and the ability to maintain average speeds on up grades, which are so necessary where heavy stopping passenger trains, or those in the intermediate or semi-fast category, have to be dealt with in difficult country, or, for the matter of that, on practically any section of the main and subsidiary line. Comparison of the 'Hall' and 'Saint' classes shows that in the first-named case the tractive effort at 85 per cent of the boiler pressure is 27,275lb as against 24,395lb in the second, and this to a large extent establishes the additional utility of the smaller wheeled engines for the purpose for which they have been designed. They further represent the solution of a problem created by the fact that the 4-4-0 type of engine is no longer able to deal with the traffic conditions mentioned.

The 43XX and 53XX 2-6-0s played no part in the genesis of the Halls (as they did as 'donors' to the Granges and Manors). Collett communicated to *The Railway Gazette* that SAINT MARTIN was a 'preliminary' to the Halls and 'generally similar' to the Saints with the standard No.1 boiler. SAINT MARTIN now 'virtually conformed to the new standard' and the Halls were 'being specially constructed to take the place of 4-4-0 type engines, which are not able to deal the long and heavy trains called for under modern conditions.' This was particularly the case with heavy stopping passenger trains and semi-fast

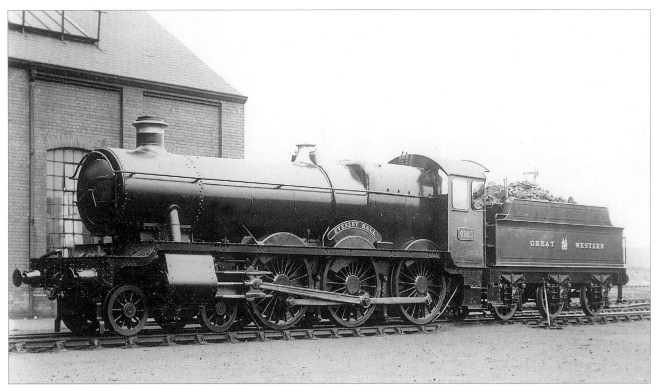

A new 4923 EVENLEY HALL; lined dark green, low-sided tender with badge and serif GREAT WESTERN.

An entertaining picture, showing an original Hall being coupled to (or perhaps uncoupled from) a Siphon gangwayed van. The eyes of the lads of course are on the operation itself, but our eyes are on the lubricator feed valve cover (just below the chimney) which for once is OPEN. See also 4926 FAIRLEIGH HALL at Hereford. transporttreasury

minute trains (over 50-60 mile stretches at least) in the early 1930s using Halls. Other Halls were taking expresses at speeds well into the 80s on the Birmingham line and such performances were being matched all over the GWR. The 'Class 5' as we came to know it was beginning to emerge; a useful second rank express engine that could show a clean pair of heels, which the next day could be on a heavy fitted freight. Halls were working the heavy Mail trains out of London and were noted performers on West of England expresses. The 4-4-0s which Collett saw them replacing could never match anything like this. The Paddington-Weymouth services continued to be exclusively worked by Halls, based at Reading, Westbury, Weymouth and Old Oak. The 'Channel Islands Boat Expresses' could run to fifteen coaches and the Halls were replaced at Weymouth only in 1958, and then by their lineal descendants, BR Class 5 4-6-0s.

By 1935, with 150 (not even half the class yet) or so at work, they were strategically placed around the Great Western, to an extent that must have near-revolutionised the working of both passenger and freight services. Nearly all the principal sheds had an established stud, though South Wales was as yet under-provided. Take Birmingham-Wolverhampton: there were Halls for freight (half a dozen at Oxley) and Halls for passenger work (another half dozen at Stafford Road) with a similar number at Tyseley for both. The Halls at all three sheds, moreover, could switch from one sort of working to the other, and did. Old Oak had the most – nearly twenty – while St Philips Marsh had several, compared to only one at Bath Road. Oxford and Reading (the GW, like

express trains over the difficult sections in the West of England.

The Halls went first to London and the West and must have been both a revelation and a revolution on any turns previously handled by 4-4-0s. They seem also to have particularly shone on the

Weymouth trains and these serve as an illustration of the mark they made back then – they were not quite yet the sort of '5MT' maids of all work of BR days but rather they were passenger engines first, behind the Castles. Weymouth shed (it had no Castles) worked mile-a-

4900 SAINT MARTIN a bit down at heel at Old Oak Common, 12 June 1949 with 'intermediate' 3,500 gallon tender 2253. In these tenders the cutaway at the front begins *level* with the bottom of the cab window while the top edge (the 'rave' or 'fender') is only as high as the middle of the cab window. W. Hermiston, transporttreasury

Tail Chasing: HALLS and the St. Martin Preserving Co. Ltd.

2925 SAINT MARTIN had been built at Swindon (Works No.2273) as a standard 'Saint' way back in September 1907. As we have seen, in December 1924 it was fitted with 6ft wheels and a modern-style cab to become the precursor of a large new class; for the time being (insofar as it was given much thought, probably) known as the 'Saint Martin' class. This would have made for confusion with the original class, though there would have been many thousands of names to choose from, though many of course were obscure in the extreme. In December 1928 SAINT MARTIN was duly renumbered 4900 to be first in line with 4901 ADDERLEY HALL onwards. A fascinating exchange took place in the columns of *The Railway Observer* in 1949. At first a few facts were established: SAINT MARTIN differed from the Halls only in certain details necessarily altered on the conversion to 6ft wheels. Externally almost the only notable difference were the inside steam pipes. 'It was therefore a great shock when some years ago' the *RO* continued when a photograph turned up of SAINT MARTIN, indisputably with outside steam pipes, passing Henley-on-Thames. Unfortunately the photographer had kept no record of the date, though it was certainly taken not later than the early 1930s. This photograph remained the only evidence, no one having 'seen or heard' of 4900 with outside steam pipes; moreover it was a matter of observed record that it had inside pipes in 1928/29 and the mid-1930s. So, as Sherlock Holmes might have said, when the impossible is eliminated whatever remains, however improbable, must be the truth... The only possible solution seemed to be that outside ones had been fitted and then removed for some unknown reason after a short time. The RO in fact got its own Holmes to examine the photograph – it *came before the incredulous eyes of an expert who had been abroad at the time. After being satisfied that it was a genuine photograph and not a joke, the expert systematically compared the photograph with photographs of SAINT MARTIN with inside steam pipes and several early Halls. These* photographs (in the case of SAINT MARTIN from 1925-1938; that is, both before and after the famous photograph) it turned out, consistently showed certain differences in detail:

Detail	SAINT MARTIN	Halls
Frame cross stay	60 degree slope at side; narrow	30 degree slope at side; wide
Rocking-lever bracket	No cover	Conspicuous cover formed like a half-splasher
Steps below cab	Rise of lower step slotted	Rises of both steps solid
Sandpipe behind wheels	Inconspicuous	Long and conspicuous
Splashers	Plain	Brass beading

In all these respects the photograph showed 'the Hall characteristics'. This meant that the photographer, a Mr Daniells, had stumbled across something even odder, a Hall carrying SAINT MARTIN nameplates. What made for the puzzle was the indecipherability of the number plate; SAINT MARTIN plates might have been fixed to a Hall in an official photograph, to demonstrate the 'Saint Martin Class' but it is unlikely; no such photograph ever surfaced and how would the engine have escaped to find its way to Henley on Thames of all places? An 'ingenious suggestion' was arrived at. A new Hall was got up as SAINT MARTIN for an official photograph and it is pointed out that (ahem!) the outside steam pipes are a giveaway and the job is cancelled, only for an urgent call from the Operating people to see it hurried into traffic before the plate is removed. This too is unlikely; the loco would not be in steam, only the photographed side would be fitted and the plate might only have a bolt pushed through to keep it upright anyway. *The Railway Observer* however favoured this explanation: *The change of name plates must have taken place when SAINT MARTIN was in shops. This was the case at the end of November, 1928, just when the first Halls were being completed and when an official photograph might be desired. And ADDERLEY HALL was noted at the same time marked as 4900. It is thus a plausible conjecture that the photograph may have been taken early in December 1928 and that the disguised engine may have been ADDERLEY HALL!* To conclude this story it can be stated that 4900 was to have been withdrawn during December 1948 under the order to cut up 4-6-0s with inside steam pipes. However it has now been decided to fit the new pattern cylinders to this engine and thus once and for all 4900 will have outside steam pipes—officially! In fact the new cylinders were *not* standard Hall castings.

Correspondent Colonel G.G. Templer thought there need be little doubt that the disguised engine had been ADDERLEY HALL, though he noted that the summary of detail differences between SAINT MARTIN and the standard Halls omitted 'the most striking and obvious difference', that the boiler of SAINT MARTIN was pitched lower than the standard Halls. When 2925 was reconstructed it was lowered by 4¼in, half the difference between the diameters of the old and new wheels. The Saint boilers sat down very low on the running plate while in the standard Halls the normal boiler centre line of 8ft 6in above rail was restored; this 4¼in raising of the boiler above the running-plate was 'most marked.'

Plymouth member Mr. R. Leitch noted the dates on which the first Halls were recorded in the West of England, on leaving Swindon after trials. 4902 had been the first to arrive at Plymouth on 24 January 1928, though it 'promptly disappeared and was not seen again until the end of March' (it was in the London Division). The only other engine to put in an appearance in 1928 was 4900, first observed on 31 December. 4901 had arrived by 5 January 1929, 4903-4906 between 10 and 17 January. 2925, as it then was, was officially allocated to Penzance for some years prior to its renumbering but 'often vanished for considerable periods, and this continued (although for shortened periods) during the early months of 1929.'

More prosaic scenarios were investigated. It was GWR practice, apparently, to make temporary changes of names for special purposes; in particular the SAINT MARTIN plates were several times temporarily fitted to the engines working the annual excursion organised for the staff of the St. Martin Preserving Co. Ltd., of Maidenhead. 4923 EVENLEY HALL and 2920 SAINT DAVID had been so interfered with. Finally the original photographer, Mr. R. E. Daniells, recalled that his photograph of the false SAINT MARTIN was taken when the engine was on a turn which worked in the summer months only suggesting that yes, it was all the fault of the St. Martin Preserving Co. Ltd.

everyone else, generally allocated new engines by the traditional 'half dozen') had twelve and six respectively which meant that there was something of a concentration of Halls in the London Division. Their greatest effect must have been felt in Devon and Cornwall, with twenty or more stationed at Newton Abbot, Laira, Truro and Penzance. A sure-footed 4-6-0 with modest wheels (the Granges coming later with 5ft 8in wheels were even more effective) must have radically improved the running of trains in Cornwall. Such an engine had to be capable of leaving in the morning

NEW SERIES 4-6-0 TYPE LOCOMOTIVES, GREAT WESTERN RAILWAY.

These Engines, to the Number of Eighty, are being Constructed in the Swindon Works, and will be known as the "Hall" Class.

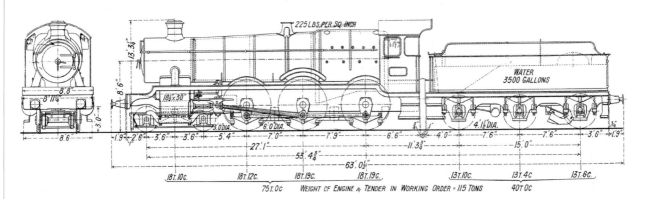

We are indebted to Mr. C. B. Collett, O.B.E., Chief Mechanical Engineer of the Great Western Railway, for a photograph, outline dimensioned drawing, and particulars relating to a new series of 4-6-0 type locomotives, the building of which is now in hand at the Swindon works. These locomotives, which will be known as the "Hall" class, are generally similar to the existing "Saint" class, except for the fact that they have coupled wheels of smaller diameter. Both of these classes are fitted with the Swindon No. 1 standard boiler and two outside cylinders.

It is of interest to note that the engine *St. Martin* was, as a preliminary to the building of the new class, fitted with the smaller diameter coupled wheels, and thus virtually conforms to the new standard. In a communication on the subject, Mr. Collett points out that the locomotives of the "Hall" class are being specially constructed to take the place of 4-4-0 type engines, which are not able to deal with the long and heavy trains called for under modern conditions, and particularly is this the case where heavy stopping passenger trains and semi-fast express trains are being worked over the difficult sections in the West of England.

The new engines have coupled wheels 6 ft. diam. and bogie wheels 3 ft. diam., the bogie, which is spring-controlled, being similar in design to the type used on engines of the "Saint" class. The boiler, as before mentioned, is of the Swindon No. 1 standard interchangeable with those on the "Stars," "Saints," and "2800" classes. It has a conical barrel and Belpaire firebox, the working pressure being 225 lb. per sq. in. The tractive effort, at 85 per cent. of the boiler pressure, is 27,275 lb., as compared with the 24,395 lb. of the "Saint" class. The cab is similar in pattern to those fitted to the "King" and "Castle" classes, being provided with side windows and extended roof.

The tender is of the standard Great Western six-wheeled pattern equipped with water pick-up apparatus. The water capacity is 3,500 gallons, and the tender carries 6 tons of coal, the weight when full being 40 tons. The weight of the engine in working order is 75 tons, of which 56 tons 10 cwt. are available for adhesion. The engine and tender in working order weigh 115 tons. Vacuum brake apparatus is fitted, this being operated by the new-pattern four-cone ejector, pressure on the blocks being equalised on all the coupled wheels.

The distributed axle weights and other leading particulars may be gathered from the outline drawing reproduced herewith. The total heating surface of the boiler is 2,104 sq. ft., and grate area 27·07 sq. ft.

A Hall in scruffy post-war condition, typical of the period; 4983 ALBERT HALL at Taunton in 1946, still with wartime so-called 'anti-glare' blank cabside. These were fitted early on; the Chargemens Log Book at Worcester Loco Factory for instance, has the following entries between 7 and 12 September 1939: *Drilling for Flack Screens Engines 6807, 5063, 4092, 5017, 5052, 5983, 4962, 4990, 4958, 4086, 6877.* The 'Flack Screens' were presumably the cab side window blanking plates so maybe they were first envisaged as protection from shrapnel! The work was a concentrated 'campaign' at Running Sheds and Factories during the early weeks of the war. ColourRail

A useful comparison of chimneys at Hereford on 13 November 1962. 5952 COGAN HALL at left has the later one which was narrower in diameter than the original of 4916 CRUMLIN HALL. ColourRail

with a fast passenger train and returning in the afternoon with fish vans for London or the West Midlands, putting a three coach local under its belt in between. The GWR, and the WR in turn, in steam days treated the section west of Plymouth more or less as a separate entity.

HALL LIVERY

The Halls got the lined GW dark green as arrived at in the 1920s; this was officially 'middle chrome' and something akin to what in BR times we called 'Great Western Green' or, erroneously, 'Brunswick Green'. Lining was black and orange (black centre lining and two outer thin orange lines) with GREAT WESTERN on the tender, either side of the coat of arms. This was the 'garter' crest which changed from 1926 to the shields of London and Bristol so a photograph with verified date is necessary for really rigorous modelling accuracy – this will not always be possible, you'd have to fear.

In 1934 the coat of arms and lettering gave way to the art deco roundel or 'shirt button' rather cleverly and pleasingly formed by 'GWR' within a circle.

In 1942 came unlined black – it was called 'wartime black' everywhere else – with a simple G/emblem/W in either block or serif on the tender.

In 1945 plain green was applied with

tender lettering unchanged. Modified Halls were lined out from 6974, new in October 1947. Original Halls were occasionally lined in 1948, the first being 4946 on 16 January.

In July 1948 5954 and 6910 were experimentally decked out in lined black with BRITISH RAILWAYS in plain lettering. In the case of 6910 this was soon replaced by the future lion-and-wheel emblem, hand painted. Transfers were not available until July 1949 by which time lined black without emblem (or lettering) had been applied for around nine months.

Lined black became standard for all Halls from about the time that 6991 was built in November 1948.

In 1956 lined black officially changed to lined green, with lining on the cylinder covers too, though 6997 was observed as early as 8 September 1955 'being painted green'. 'All 4-6-0s' were to have the lined dark green though some Halls apparently had managed to acquire it already. The 2nd emblem came in 1956.

As an aside, 6990 NEVER received the lined black; it retained its 1948 lined green until the later period of lined green – seven years!

WAR

The most remarkable thing about wartime developments in the Halls was perhaps their continued construction.

This went on uninterrupted through 1939 to the end of 1944, only to pause (for the Counties and new Castles) before resuming in 1947. In the meantime, the Modified Halls were introduced – see Part Three – with seamless continuity. The only difference was that most of the wartime engines were turned out with blank cab sides as a blackout precaution; the last would have been 6970. All side window classes were altered thus (or were supposed to have been) and the process appears to have been fairly rapid. In the first weeks of 1940 numbers of earlier Halls were noted so dealt with (the work was presumably done at sheds) while 5989 for instance (new in December 1939) was noted as 'built without side windows'. Most if not all of the other Halls had the window blanked out at some time and all were put back in order over the years from the end of the war to 1947-48. In fact the only engines *built* without side windows were 2251 0-6-0s and 6900 series Halls; a number of the former were still to be seen in this condition in the very early 1950s but the 69XXs seem to have been dealt with more expeditiously.

The wartime-built Halls, from 6916, did not carry names (it would have appeared wasteful to the public, it was felt) at first but instead had HALL CLASS painted on the splasher. The name plates were fixed as and when convenient from 1946 through to 1948. Most momentously, one Hall, 4911, was destroyed by enemy action. This was statistically unusual, and locos in this country had to be all but destroyed to warrant scrapping rather than repair/replacement. The unfortunate BOWDEN HALL received a direct hit at Keyham, Plymouth, in April 1941. This was perhaps the worst month for Plymouth when at least five intense night attacks took place. The mortal remains were moved to Swindon and eventually scrapped

CHIMNEYS

Later engines (and the Granges) had a shorter chimney though it needs the eye of faith to differentiate them; some of us find it impossible. Inevitably shorter chimneys appeared on engines that previously had taller ones and so on. As early as 1939 4963 was observed 'fitted with a short chimney similar to those fitted to later engines of this class.'

A capuchon was the order of the day with the main body of the Halls 4900s through to the 5900s but not so with the later series though it is unwise to try to pronounce upon any thing for a given engine at a given time without photographs. An edition of *The Railway Observer* late in 1953 noted that *Halls 7919, 7924 and 7927 have chimneys without capuchons and of narrower external diameter than others of their series; 7924 and possibly* *the others, carries a plate to the effect that the chimney and blast pipe have been modified to increase the steaming capacity of the boiler.* This plate was presumably in the cab or by the steps, where other companies put their 'mod plates'.

By 1958 7912 had an 'ID' stencilled on the framing to denote 'Improved Draughting' though it is unclear if this was related to the narrower chimneys on 7919, 7924 and 7927; 6917, 6934 and 6957 were noted at the same time carrying Hawksworth AK boilers 'with narrow (improved draughting) chimneys' which rather suggests it did. What happened with these chimneys is unclear, though one at least, turned up on 6979. They certainly weren't replicated on any scale.

LIGHTS

In 1947 oil burner 3904 (4972) was noted at Swindon works being fitted up with electric headlamps and cab lights, the power obtained from a small generator bolted on the right-hand side of the smokebox. A photograph in the RCTS *Locos of the Great Western Railway* shows cables draped untidily over the smokebox in a way that suggests Swindon was not exactly serious about it. In October 1949 5922 was noted similarly fitted 'with electric headlamps'

at Swindon though how long the fitments lasted (not long presumably) is unclear.

THE LOCOMOTIVE EXCHANGES

The famous Locomotive Exchanges took place in April 1948, with the GW 6990 WITHERSLACK HALL pitted against its 'mixed traffic' equivalents the LNER B1, LMS Black Five and Southern West Country Pacific. The LMS Class 5 4-6-0 was the obvious locomotive to replicate and so it came to pass, albeit with significant changes to motion and cylinder details, injectors and so on. The mixed traffic engines were worked on various passenger duties from Inverness to Plymouth but the only foreign line with clearances to suit the Hall was Marylebone-Manchester. The simple consumption results are as follows:

Mixed Traffic Engines

Engine	Coal	Water
LMS Cl.5	3.54	27.99
LNER B1	3.59	27.64
GWR Hall	3.94	29.97
SR WC	4.11	32.64

Coal and water = lbs/HP hour

The WR was not happy with this it would seem, and organised additional tests using Welsh coal, giving a figure of 3.22 for coal and 31.68 for water. The BR

Standard ship had sailed though; the tests could have no possible effect on future BR steam locomotive development, which was above all taking account of ever worsening coal quality and ever more difficult maintenance conditions.

There was a programme of testing using the Rugby plant, together with dynamometer car runs in the 1950s. WR locos (and others, including an Ivatt 43000 2-6-0) were put through their paces on the Swindon plant, with road tests using the WR dynamometer taking place between Wantage Road and Filton. 7916 MOBBERLEY HALL was evaluated in 1952, chosen because although it was one of the later examples, a Modified hall with enlarged superheater, the draught arrangements were unaltered from those of the earlier locomotives with small superheaters. It was found that, by slightly reducing the diameter of the blast pipe orifice and altering the chimney bore, an appreciably better performance was possible, and these modifications were therefore used for all the main tests. After alteration, maximum steam rates of between 22,000 and 23,000Ib per hour were attained. It is not clear if the alterations to the draughting were pursued with all the other Halls. The following figures were published:

	Hall	B1	Ivatt 4MT
Minimum water consumption, lb/drawbar horsepower	17	15.95	17.5
Minimum coal consumption, lb/drawbar horsepower	2.4	2.2	2.2

Front Lamp Iron
Was originally on the smokebox top but moved to smokebox door on engines constructed from 1933. The existing, earlier locos were so altered over the next few years.

Lubricators
The Halls had sight feed lubricators in the cab, presumably 3-glass at first; from the early 1930s 5-glass would have been used. The oil pipes passed under the boiler lagging on the right-hand side, emerging under the cover on the smokebox.

A Hall prepared for nationalised service, posed at Swindon in January 1948; 4946 MOSELEY HALL in lined green with BRITISH RAILWAYS in serif. This was the first Hall to display the new ownership; it has the little W so-called 'prefix' below the number plate and the shed code PZ (Penzance) is still stencilled above the cylinder. Smokebox shed plates were a thing of the future. The X above the cab plate indicates that the loco could haul loads in excess of those laid down. (Granges were similar – see the 'Book Of', page 119.) The route/availability disc is clear; red route for a Hall and 'D' for the power class. This GWR system remained in use until the end of steam. An interesting technical point is the positioning of the joint of the two coupling rods; here, it is *forward* of the crank pin. The coupling rod vertical flexibility on the early 4-6-0s was so provided, in front of the middle wheel bearing. A later design change saw this knuckle pin joint moved to behind the crank pin and both arrangements could be seen on different locos up until withdrawal. The reason is not clear but if it was desired to take down the forked end rod without removing the connecting rod it was much easier to remove the interference fit knuckle pin if it was clear of (behind) the big end, than if it was partly covered by the big end, in front of the crank pin. Compare 4946 for instance with 4960 at Shrewsbury. Note too the 'webbing' between the spokes at the bottom, fitted to bolster the crank pin bosses.

4925 EYNSHAM HALL parked outside the Iron Foundry at Swindon, fresh off 'AE' Shop. Lined black paintwork and original totem would indicate early 1950s period. R.J. Buckley, Initial Photographics.

4993 in Swindon's 'AE' Shop, its overhaul and repaint more or less complete. It will soon be moved forward onto the traverser to be moved out of the shop and put together with a tender. ColourRail

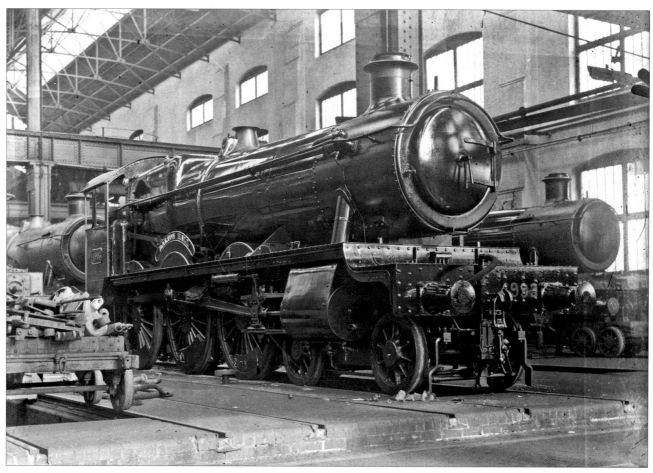

Serif **BRITISH RAILWAYS** on the tender of 4928 GATACRE HALL at Stourbridge Junction on 10 September 1949. The livery appears to be the wartime black, or plain green still. H.C. Casserley, courtesy R.M. Casserley.

Fairly new Halls together at what looks like Old Oak Common; 4996 EDEN HALL at right, with 4932 HATHERTON HALL. transporttreasury

From 7910 on, a mechanical lubricator was provided on the running plate, right-hand side behind the steam pipe.

There was further lubrication at the front; on the original locos a small reservoir sat on the sloping plate under the smokebox. Four pipes led from this to (presumably) lubricate the bogie bearing surfaces and side bearers. On the Modified Halls this was moved aside (to the right, looking at the locomotive front) to the new framing emerging at the front.

Names - 'essential that the Western be prevented from digging up any more Halls'

The reality has to be faced that most Great Western names, or at least the runs of them were, somewhat uninspiring. As early as 1948 a correspondent, Mr. R. P. Walford, wrote in *The Railway Observer* and among many points in a wide ranging review had this to say: *First, it is essential that the Western be prevented from digging up any more Halls. Another 30 threaten. Let's revive the Flowers.*

"SCORPION" took up the cudgels two or three years later; noting that 'even to this day locomotive names range from the excellent to the atrocious, it seems a good idea to try and determine some of the ingredients which go towards making a name good or bad' and selected as his starting point Mr. Walford's special bugbear, the GWR

Halls: *I doubt if anyone outside Swindon can view something over three hundred of these names with equanimity, but there are two sides to every question and it may be worth presenting the other side of this one. In the first place, the mental indigestion which these names produce is due to looking at them in a continuous list in a book; but that is not entirely a fair criterion. Names need to be considered individually and one is unlikely to see three hundred, or even thirty, 'Hall' class name plates on one day. Secondly, it has been the settled policy of Swindon since 1924 that the name of a locomotive should reveal its class. Personally, I am in entire disagreement with this policy. In the old days no one seemed to have difficulty in recognizing Queen Victoria as a 'Star' or even over the much more startling proposition that Lady Macbeth was a 'Saint'. But there we are: and the result is that if Swindon had listened to Mr. Walford's appeal we might be spared Little Something Hall, but in its place we should get — PELICAN (Hall class).*

It was certainly the main limitation of GW naming policy that after a while the supply of suitable names ran out, while the locos in a number of instances outlived the buildings, as they burnt down, were demolished or were sold off for various less than stately-home – sometimes downright embarrassing – uses. One or two seem not even to have existed, or at least Swindon got the spelling wrong; favourites are 4942 MAINDY HALL (Maindy turns out to be a suburb of Cardiff) and 5907

MARBLE HALL which, according to the RCTS *The Locomotives of the Great Western Railway* Part 14, was probably a pleasure garden demolished well over a century before the Hall emerged from Swindon. So 5907 was actually named after 'the Lambeth end of Vauxhall Bridge'.

We'll end this with Mr. J.P. Bardsley's comments subsequent to those of "SCORPION": *To close, may I make an appeal to the Railway Executive; if an engine is worthy of a name keep that engine clean. If 'Halls' and 'Granges' were less drab and dirty and the name had not to be deciphered we might take more interest in them.* Quite so.

4933 HIMLEY HALL in its earliest days, with the low-sided tender (GREAT WESTERN with badge) at Paddington. The projection on the cylinder appears to be a plug cock, used to control the supply of steam or water with one quick movement of the handle through a 90 deg arc moving the valve from fully open to fully closed. It appears to be connected into the steam chest and may have been used in the recording of steam chest pressures. It is obviously only a temporary fitting and it is surprising that the loco is in normal service with it still fitted. The open end would have a sealing cap to prevent the cock being tampered with, allowing live steam to be discharged over adjacent personnel. ColourRail

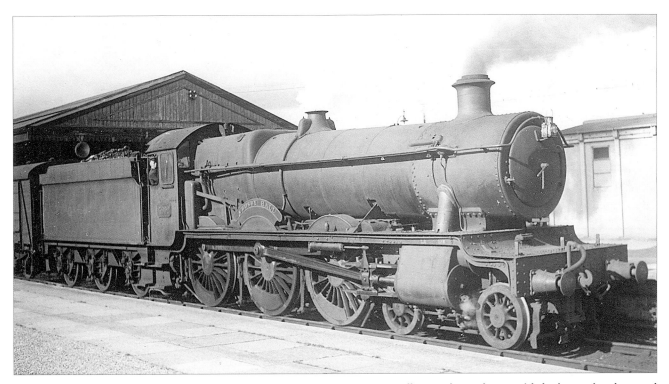

An austere wartime black 4992 CROSBY HALL at Newton Abbot; 4,000 gallon tender and GW with badge under the usual coat of grime.

4926 FAIRLEIGH HALL at Hereford shed, around 1959. It still has the first emblem on the tender. On the right-hand side most GWR 4-cylinder and 2-outside cylinder tender locomotives there was a long, prominent pipe behind the hand rail, immediately in front of the right-hand cab window. This was the 4-cone ejector, seen to advantage in this view from ground level. As with all Great Western 4-6-0s, there was a lot more going on at the right-hand side than the left. Prominent under the running plate by the front driving wheel is the vacuum pump driven off the crosshead, a more or less standard GWR feature. Note too, the reversing shaft and housing in front of cab. Hidden beneath the ejector pipe, under the cladding, are the oil pipes to the cylinders and the Swindon design of smokebox-mounted regulator in the superheater header. The concealed oil piping emerged from the boiler barrel to then enter the smokebox; the dart-shaped cover (where there were stopcocks) above the steampipe is where this piping briefly emerged. Most GW engines had hydrostatic sight feed displacement lubricators mounted in the cab, under the control of the driver. Increased/divided oil supply to valves and pistons meant there was a similar cover on the left-hand side of the smokebox. This was not always the case, however, on all classes – some exceptions can be found though not, so far, any among the 4900 Halls. J. Davenport, Initial Photographics.

9 February 1963

4900	4934	4968
4901	4935 Didcot	4969
4902 Didcot	4936 Cardiff East Dk	4970 Duffryn Yard
4903 Old Oak	4937	4971
4904 Taunton	4938	4972 Westbury
4905 St Philips Marsh	4939	4973
4906	4940	4974
4907 Hereford	4941	4975 Reading
4908 Didcot	4942 Didcot	4976 Southall
4909	4943 Pontypool Road	4977
4910 Didcot	4944	4978 Laira
4911	4945	4979 Oxford
4912	4946 Shrewsbury	4980 St Philips Marsh
4913	4947	4981 Goodwick
4914 St Philips Marsh	4948	4982
4915 Reading	4949 St Philips Marsh	4983 Duffryn Yard
4916 Hereford	4950 Didcot	4984
4917	4951 Swindon	4985 Pontypool Road
4918 Cardiff East Dock	4952	4986
4919 Swindon	4953 Cardiff East Dk	4987
4920 Laira	4954 Tyseley	4988 Llanelly
4921	4955 Pontypool Road	4989 Southall
4922 St Philips Marsh	4956 Westbury	4990
4923 Oxley	4957	4991 St Philips Marsh
4924 Swindon	4958 Pontypool Road	4992 St Philips Marsh
4925	4959 Didcot	4993 St Philips Marsh
4926	4960	4994 Didcot
4927 Llanelly	4961	4995
4928 Duffryn Yard	4962 Goodwick	4996 Taunton
4929 Gloucester	4963	4997
4930 Swindon	4964 Pontypool Road	4998 Banbury
4931	4965	4999
4932 Taunton	4966 Neath	
4933 St Philips Marsh	4967	

12 October 1964

4900	4934	4968
4901	4935	4969
4902	4936	4970
4903	4937	4971
4904	4938	4972
4905	4939	4973
4906	4940	4974
4907	4941	4975
4908	4942	4976
4909	4943	4977
4910	4944	4978
4911	4945	4979
4912	4946	4980
4913	4947	4981
4914	4948	4982
4915	4949	4983
4916	4950	4984
4917	4951	4985
4918	4952	4986
4919 Worcester	4953	4987
4920 Barrow Road	4954 Oxley	4988
4921	4955	4989 Severn Tun. Jct
4922	4956	4990
4923	4957	4991
4924	4958	4992 Barrow Road
4925	4959 Didcot	4993 Barrow Road
4926	4960	4994
4927	4961	4995
4928	4962 Didcot	4996
4929 Gloucester	4963	4997
4930	4964	4998
4931	4965	4999
4932 Neath	4966	
4933	4967	

2 November 1963

4900	4934	4968
4901	4935	4969
4902	4936 Cardiff East Dk	4970
4903 Southall	4937	4971
4904 Taunton	4938	4972 Westbury
4905 Didcot	4939	4973
4906	4940	4974
4907	4941	4975
4908	4942 Didcot	4976 Oxford
4909	4943 Pontypool Road	4977
4910 Didcot	4944	4978 Laira
4911	4945	4979 Oxford
4912	4946	4980
4913	4947	4981
4914 St Philips Marsh	4948	4982
4915	4949 St Philips Marsh	4983 Severn Tun. Jct
4916 Hereford	4950 Swindon	4984
4917	4951 Swindon	4985 Pontypool Road
4918	4952	4986
4919 Swindon	4953	4987
4920 Laira	4954 Tyseley	4988 Oxford
4921	4955	4989 Westbury
4922	4956	4990
4923 Oxley	4957	4991 Swindon
4924	4958 Pontypool Road	4992 Gloucester
4925	4959 Didcot	4993 Swindon
4926	4960	4994
4927	4961	4995
4928 Duffryn Yard	4962 Old Oak	4996
4929 Gloucester	4963	4997
4930 Swindon	4964	4998
4931	4965	4999
4932 Taunton	4966 Oxford	
4933 Tyseley	4967	

Below. Halls in their environment; Banbury shed on 26 April 1962. 4992 CROSBY HALL with Hawksworth tender at left, 7900 SAINT PETER'S HALL at right with a 2-8-2T in between. A 6900 Hall sits over on the far left. RailOnline

Left. A 5900 Hall with Hawksworth straight-sided 4,000 gallon tender, at Tyseley on 18 February 1962. RailOnline

TENDERS

4900 SAINT MARTIN and the first production batch of eighty, 4901-4980 had the low-sided 3,500 gallon tenders; the first forty-odd mostly got older ones, the next half of the batch the later ones in the series spanning Churchward and Collett's time, from the 1900s to the early 1920s. They were thus not by any means so elderly as, say, the tenders fitted to the Granges a few years later.

The twenty-six higher 3,500 gallon tenders built under Collett, 2242-2268 and familiar from the Granges, all ran with Halls at first. At first glance they look like the later familiar 4000 gallon (6 ton) type that ran behind nearly all the 4-6-0s (bar the Manors) in later years but they were only of 3,500 gallon and 5½ tons capacity. The clue to recognition is the same as for the Granges: what on the Southern, say, would be called the 'rave' ('fender' seems to have been in use with respect to GWR tenders) was lower and when coupled to a 'Grange', the rave top is in line with the middle of the cab windows, making it obvious.

The familiar high-sided Collett 4,000 gallon tenders became 'standard issue' with 5901 but a few Halls, almost all in the 4900 series, still had the low tenders even in 1948. The last of the 3,500 higher sided ones seem to have gone from the Halls by about 1947.

The new Hawksworth straight sided 4,000 gallon 6 ton capacity tenders made their appearance with 6971. All the 4,000 gallon tenders could appear on almost any engine. It is worth noting that only the thirty Hawksworth tenders for the Counties were 7 tons capacity; Hawksworth tenders built primarily for Castles and Halls were *six* tons and they were narrower than the County version.

Green coal weighing tender 4127 at Swindon in 1957; similar tender 4128 was black. Both occasionally appeared with Halls. Brian Penney writes: *When the tender (4127) arrived at Worcester I was curious to see how it operated but found that the weighing equipment was in a compartment on top of the tank, securely padlocked. I expressed my disappointment to the fitter I was working with who promptly climbed up and gave the padlock a sharp tap with his hammer. It flew open and we were able to study the weighing mechanism, a not very impressive cantilever scaled with a moveable weight. A quick tap with the hammer and the padlock was closed.*

4985 ALLESLEY HALL with low-sided tender and roundel. The location is not known but Newton Abbot seems likely; certainly it is the West Country, with Bulldog pilot coupled behind according to instructions. ColourRail

4992 CROSBY HALL with 4,000 gallon tender and roundel. ColourRail

The Great Western built two eight wheel tenders, one for **THE GREAT BEAR** and this conventional one, No.2586. Here it is attached to 5957 HUTTON HALL, at Didcot on 22 August 1951. It had been behind a Castle for a while but so far as Halls were concerned in ran in succession behind 5919, 6951, 4918, 5957, 6912 and 6905 before being withdrawn with 5904 in November 1963.

Collett 4,000 gallon tender on 4939 **LITTLETON HALL**, 'somewhere in Wales'. The tender is bare of any emblem or lining.

Churchward 4,000 gallon tender (lined green) on poor old 4946, formerly **MOSELEY HALL**, at Shrewsbury late on. That lower horizontal line of rivets is particularly apparent in nearly every view altering, often, the very way light is reflected. The framing over the tender footplate coal space was primarily fitted to prevent firemen going back into the tender to pull the coal forward. In February 1962 a Shrewsbury Fireman was electrocuted at Crewe when he climbed into the tender coal space to shovel coal forward and came into contact with the overhead 25kV wire. Elaborate precautions are now taken with present day steam workings under the wires, including a storm sheet between the cab roof and tender cab area, locking the securing chain for the fire irons, placing a cover over the coal watering pipe control valve and locking cab roof hatches or fitting a mesh over them. Tenders must be provided with a low level filling point and the back of the tender steps or ladders must have blocks or guard plates fitted to prevent access. J.L. Stevenson, courtesy Hamish Stevenson

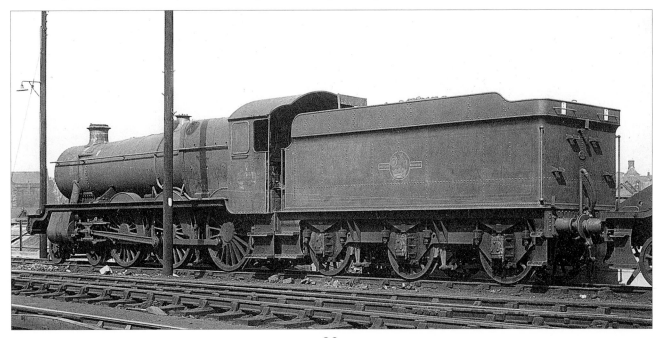

OIL

In September 1945, as the first of the (lined green!) 1000 class County 4-6-0s were coming off Swindon works and a new batch of Castles was about to be embarked upon, it was announced that six 28XX class 2-8-0s would be converted for oil burning. This was afterwards characterised as the GWR's own, independent scheme with the Government 'intervening' in 1946 to make it a national, state-directed project. This seems unlikely, given the state of GWR finances, Government control of exports/imports, direction of resources and so on. It would have been Government-prompted from the first and was of course the first stirrings of yet another famous national debacle, the Great Post-War Oil Burning Fiasco, a close rival to the Great Ground Nut Scheme. At least those given the task of implementing the oil disaster did not have to contend with lions, crocodiles and killer bees. The oil burning scheme was misunderstood in enthusiast circles, at least so far as the GW was concerned, for it is was thought that the 2-8-0s were 'an experiment' that, if successful, would mean that a 'new type of passenger locomotive' would be built.

About October 1945 Llanelly's 2872 was found to be the first of the 2-8-0s to be equipped for oil burning. Oil fuel was fed by gravity from an 1800 gallon tank on the tender to a burner fitted in the front of the firebox; there the fuel oil was atomised by a steam jet incorporated in the burner. The fuel was heavy, viscous stuff and steam heating coils were fitted to ensure that it 'flowed'. Huge 36,000 gallon storage were installed at Llanelly, from where the 2-8-0s would work and soon they would appear at sheds across the country, let alone the GWR; by the end of 1945 more and more locos were being converted. There were to be 84 Halls converted as the scheme acquired an early dizzying impetus of its own; the actual numbers were eleven (see end).

The first Hall converted was 5955 GARTH HALL, in June 1946 whereupon it worked from Swindon where it was presumably under the close eye of the works. Tentatively at first, it worked Swindon-Gloucester locals. It could hardly have performed better, the authorities said; by September it was managing nearly 1500 miles a week, 9.0a.m. Swindon to Paddington, 1.18 p.m. Paddington to Bristol and 825 p.m. Bristol to Swindon. All went well enough till economic reality set in. Despite coal shortages and its soaring expense, the country's limping economy could not afford precious dollars for oil – the same reason BR decided on steam rather than American diesels shortly afterwards. It all quietly faded away. The Irish had also got caught up in the oil burning fever and after converting some ninety engines in 1947 Coras Iompair Eireann announced early in 1948 that an improvement in the coal supply had prompted a reconversion at the rate of six engines per week – that is, as quick as possible. 'It is understood that no oil burning locomotives will be running after 26th September 1948' was the terse sentence marking the abandonment of oil burning on the Western.

The oil depot at Laira in September 1947. Ahead of us is converted 2-8-0 4808 (2834) and, lurking behind, 3904 SAINT BRIDES HALL (4972). ColourRail

OIL BURNING HALLS
From the RCTS *Locos of the Great Western Railway*:

Old	New	To Oil	To Coal
4968	3900	5/47	3/49
4971	3901	5/47	4/49
4948	3902	5/47	9/48
4907	3903	5/47	4/50
4972	3904	5/47	10/48
5955	3950	6/46	10/48
5976	3951	4/47	11/48
6957	3952	4/47	3/50
6953	3953	4/47	9/48
5986	3954	5/47	2/50
6949	3955	5/47	4/49

3900 SHOTTON HALL, 4968 that was, converted for oil burning, at Bristol Temple Meads in June 1947. That sliding shutter was introduced for all the GWR oil burners. It involved moving the cabside hand rail down a couple of inches. A further modification was the sliding ventilator (visible here) in the roof each side. G.Ellis, transporttreasury

Engine Histories

These Engine Histories follow more or less those of previous 'Book Of' volumes, derived from the Swindon Registers and other sources at The National Archive. The codes are as follows:

G General
H Heavy
I Intermediate
L Light
R Thought to be 'Running'

The relative frequencies of **L** and **R** indicate they were not recorded with consistency. Also 'Swindon Works' is often noted with no indication as to the level of work done.

WR/BR equivalents after 1948 were:
HC Heavy Casual
HG Heavy General
HI Heavy Intermediate
LC Light Casual
LI Light Intermediate
U Unclassified
C Casual
X/S is thought to stands for 'ex-store'
Cont 'Continuation' – often called 'Rectification' elsewhere. It is a brief recall to works to attend to some minor (or sometimes not so minor) fault showing up after running in following works attention.

Works Dates Compilation of the record from several sources means that dates given of works/outstation shops visits can indicate completion OR beginning of the work. **They thus indicate a period rather than a specific date in or out.**

In some cases not all the information is to hand and 'Mileages and Boilers' might not be represented, say.

Tenders. For a number of the locos, the sequence of tenders is missing.

As pointed out in other volumes of this series, railway company Engine History Cards, while containing much useful and even fascinating information, are an *indication of* what happened to the engines. A very good and complex indication – the best we will have – but not something that is 100% reliable and accurate in every instance (though it is in many). In the end they were, after all, for Accountants rather than Engineers!

A note on Disposals. The disposal dates and buyers; that is, sale dates to buyers, are normally hand written entries on the GWR/WR engine history sheets and these have been used in the book.

An Aside
The progress of larger locos through Swindon Factory, for Classified Overhauls, was as follows:

Loco arrived in sidings alongside Iron Foundry and moved into the Reception Shed where smokebox, firebox and ash pan were cleaned out, firebars and srnokebox furniture removed. Tender parted and moved to 'B' Shed for overhaul. If necessary, loco turned on turntable tor smokebox to face east.

Loco traversed into 'AE' Shop and berthed on Stripping Gang. Dismantled with boiler going to 'AV' or 'V' Shop, wheels to 'AW' Wheel Shop and motion, brake gear and all smaller components being cleaned in a caustic soda 'bosh' before being sent to specialist Shops for overhaul or renewal:
Motion parts to 'AM' and 'R' Shops,
Brasswork, injectors, ejectors, brake valves, etc. to 'T' Shop,
Pipework to 'K' Shop,
Gauges to 'O' Shop.

Frames complete with cylinders and stretchers lifted on to Reg Clarke's Frame Gang:
Cracks in frames welded,
Wasted sections renewed, Cylinders

How they ended up. 4951 formerly PENDEFORD HALL at Oxford, 14 July 1964. In just four short years steam on the Western had been reduced from near-universal supremacy to the last dregs in terms of passenger work. J.L. Stevenson, courtesy Hamish Stevenson.

renewed, re-linered, re-bored also steam chests,
Extension frames renewed,
'Zeiss' optical alignment of cylinders, frames and horns,
Discrepancies in frame alignment corrected on the Horn Grinding Machine.

Frames then lifted to Comley's gang where re-building commenced:
Boiler fitted,
Wheels fitted,
Motion bars fitted.

Engine moved across traverser on to Stan Lewington's Finishing off Gang:
Motion, brake gear, injectors, pipework, fitted.

Lifted on to Valve Setting Plant. Valves set.

Lifted back on to Finishing off pits:
Bogie or truck fitted,
Engine painted,
Remaining components fitted.

Traversed out of Shop

Run on to Weigh Table.
Engine weighed and weights adjusted.

Firebars, brick arch, smokebox furniture fitted,
Tender brought from 'B' Shed and coupled up.

Engine lit up, steam raised and static tests by Trials Gang.

Trial run to Brinkworth, Little Somerford or Dauntsey.

Back to turn table roads for any rectification work.

To Running Shed, running in turns, returned to home depot.

Two other gangs in 'AE' Shop:
(1) Light and Casual Repairs, Chargeman Harold Rayer.
West side of traverser, nearest main line, dealt with collision/derailment damage, hot boxes, rectification work off Classified Overhaul.
(2) New Works, Chargeman Bill Dando.
West side of traverser, top side of Finishing Off Gang; erected and completed all new locos and tenders.

****

A Further Aside – 'Swindon Targets'
First reproduced in The Book of the Grange 4-6-0s
A modified system of controlling the entry of engines into Swindon for heavy repairs was introduced in July 1955. The aim was to provide a more balanced flow of engines of certain types through works, calculated on the numerical strength of each class of engine in each of the nine divisions.

If a high proportion of engines of one type from any single Division required works extra 'pool' engines were needed as cover, beyond what could be accommodated within the Division. The new system was designed to reduce the numbers of any one type in a Division needing works at the same time.

Engines that could be spared in one Division were loaned to make up the shortage of engines in another. This would no longer be necessary.

When a high percentage of engines of one type arrived for heavy repairs together, a shortage of spares – most seriously boilers – could result. The non-availability of a boiler could be the worst cause of prolonged 'waiting' before a loco could complete an overhaul and the new system was intended to alleviate this. It was a most important consideration when admitting engines to works and some margins were worryingly thin. For the nine 47XX 2-8-0s there was one spare boiler, for thirty Counties and Kings five spare boilers each and for thirty Manors only two. For the Castles there were approximately six spare boilers for every thirty-four engines running.

The stock of spare boilers was not based on the number of engines utilising a particular type but was instead determined on the periodicity through works of the engines. This periodicity in turn depended on the types of engines and the duties they were intended to perform. A 2251 0-6-0 led a leisurely life and had a periodicity of forty-six months. A King on the other hand would be expected to appear every sixteen months, or after some seventy thousand miles. The shopping periods (excluding the various ex-LMS types and BR Standards now on the Western Region for which it was responsible) and expected mileages were as (right).
The new scheme involved 'target figures' for each of the nine main Divisions within the Western Region: 81A Old Oak Common, 82A Bristol Bath Road, 83A Newton Abbot, 84A Wolverhampton Stafford Road, 85A Worcester, 86A Newport Ebbw Junction, 87A Neath, 88A Cardiff, 89A

Oswestry. These tables indicate the number of engines of each type from the various Divisions likely to be found in the works. An engine '½' might seem odd but if the average overall time of repair was, say, four weeks, then it obviously could not be expected that one of the 47XX 2-8-0s would be in works for heavy repair at every visit. 'Allowances made for very good reasons' mean that not all the cross-totals add up. It was also intended that adjustments would become necessary to individual target figures; traffic requirements for instance might result in significant transfers of engines from Division to Division, making for marked alterations to Divisional type totals *(bottom)*.

Type	Class	Months	Mileage
4-6-0	60XX	16	70,000
4-6-0	4073	20	80,000
4-6-0	40XX	24	80,000
4-6-0	49XX	30	80,000
4-6-0	68XX	30	80,000
4-6-0	78XX	30	80,000
4-6-0	10XX	20	80,000
4-4-0	90XX	36	70,000
2-8-0	28XX	36	80,000
2-8-0	47XX	-	100,000
2-8-0	30XX	-	60,000
2-6-0	43XX	36	
0-6-0	22XX	46	
0-6-0	23XX	42	
2-8-2T	72XX	42	70,000
2-8-0T	42XX	36	
2-8-0T	5205	36	
2-6-2T	41XX	36	
2-6-2T	61XX	36	
2-6-2T	44XX	24	50,000
0-6-2T	56XX	36	60,000
0-6-2T	RR '30'	42	70,000
0-6-2T	RR '76'	42	70,000
0-6-2T	TV 'O'	40	
0-6-2T	TV 'A'	42	
0-6-0T	57XX	48	80,000
0-6-0T	15XX	48	70,000
0-6-0T	2021	60	70,000
0-6-0T	54XX	42	80,000
0-6-0T	64XX	36	70,000
0-6-0T	74XX	48	80,000
0-6-0T	16XX	48	80,000
0-6-0T	94XX	42	80,000
0-6-0T	'681'	60	70,000
0-4-2T	14XX	48	100,000
0-4-0T	'1142'	60	70,000

SWINDON FACTORY TARGETS

	DIVISION									
	81	82	83	84	85	86	87	88	89	Total
Class	TARGET									
Kings	1	-	1	1	-	-	-	-	-	3
Castles	3	3	2	2	1	1	1	-	-	13
Counties	-	½	½	½	-	-	½	-	-	2
70000	½	-	½	-	-	½	-	-	-	1
Halls	6	4	3	4	2	2	2	-	-	23
Grange	-	1	2	1	-	½	-	-	-	5
73000	-	½	-	1	-	-	-	-	-	1
75000	-	-	-	-	-	½	-	-	-	1
LMR 5	-	-	-	½	-	-	-	-	-	1
Manors	-	-	½	1	-	-	-	-	-	2
43XX/90XX	2	2	2	5	2	1	1	-	1	16
47XX	½	-	-	-	-	-	-	-	-	1
Totals	13	11	11	15	5	6	5	-	1	67

4900 SAINT MARTIN

Originally built as Saint 2925
Rebuilt at Swindon Works in 1924

Mileages and Boilers

9/1927	905,792	C4004
7/12/28	961,044	C4004
4/1/30	999,623	C4067
15/7/31	1,069,532	C4067
10/2/33	1,132,242	C4981
22/11/35	1,230,910	C4981
17/9/37	1,306,001	C4439
6/10/39	1,392,764	C4439
6/3/42	1,483,870	C4988
15/9/44	1,571,314	C4988
9/11/46	1,639,493	C7266
13/1/49	1,712,785	C4447
11/1/51	1,788,599	C7266
22/4/53	1,867,189	C2853
26/9/55	1,959,887	C4043

Sheds and Works

1924	Shrewsbury
6/1/25	Laira
21/3/26	Old Oak
5/9/26	Bath Road
9/1927	Swindon Works **H**
30/10/27	Penzance
22/1/28	Old Oak
13/8/28	St. Philips Marsh
13/5/28	Penzance
7/12/28	Swindon Works **H**
P/e23/12/38	Renumbered 4900
19/2/29	Swindon Works **R**
10/5/29	Swindon Works **L**
14/6/29	Penzance shops **L**
15/10/29	Penzance shops **L**
4/1/30	Swindon Works **L**
18/1/30	Old Oak
9/7/30	Old Oak **L**
27/8/30	Oxford shops **R**
15/7/31	Swindon Works **I**
1/8/31	Reading
28/7/32	Reading shops **R**
10/2/33	Swindon Works **G**
25/9/33	Swindon Works **L**
7/1933	Oxford
16/11/33	Swindon Works **L**
1/8/34	Old Oak shops **R**
30/11/34	Old Oak shops **L**
15/12/34	Old Oak
9/2/35	Oxford
17/4/35	Old Oak shops **R**
4/5/35	Old Oak
22/11/35	Swindon Works **I**
19/11/36	Swindon Works **L**
21/4/37	Swindon Works **L**
17/9/37	Swindon Works **G**
3/9/38	Wolverhampton Works **R**
5/2/38	Oxford
5/3/38	Old Oak
3/9/38	Wolverhampton Works **R**
25/4/39	Swindon Works **L**
8/7/39	Old Oak shops **R**
6/10/39	Swindon Works **I**
6/3/42	Swindon Works **G**
20/7/42	Old Oak shops **R**
2/11/43	Old Oak shed **R**
16/3/44	Newton Abbot Works **R**
24/5/44	Old Oak shed **R**
15/9/44	Swindon Works **I**
24/7/45	Swindon Works **R**
29/1/46	Swindon Works **R**
8/7/46	Swindon Works **R**
9/11/46	Swindon Works **G**
2/9/47	Old Oak shops **L**
13/11/47	Old Oak shops **L**

	Tender work only
21/4/48	Old Oak shops **R**
23/9/48	Old Oak shops **L**
	Tender work only
13/1/49	Swindon Works **HG**
26/5/50	Old Oak shops **LC**
13/7/50	Old Oak shops **U**
11/1/51	Swindon Works **HI**
27/1/51	Laira
21/4/51	Newton Abbot
11/8/51	Stafford Road
8/9/51	Banbury
30/7/52	Hereford shops **U**
9/8/52	Worcester
10/9/52	Worcester shops **U**
22/4/53	Swindon Works **HG**
24/8/54	Swindon Works **LC**
26/9/55	Swindon Works **HG**
16/6/56	Laira
6/10/56	Old Oak
17/1/57	Old Oak shops **U**
10/1/58	Swindon Works **HI**

Tenders

4/2/29	1934
18/10/29	2242
2/6/30	2243
1/12/32	2259
7/9/34	2049
25/7/36	1774
10/8/39	2684
6/10/39	2257
31/7/44	1886
16/11/48	2253
9/3/50	2030
4/12/50	2835
15/1/51	2611
26/9/55	2574
26/1/57	2623
10/1/58	2107

Final mileage 2,092,500
Withdrawn 3/4/59, Cut up 16/5/59

By 16 August 1958 there was a reversion to the low 3,500 gallon tender, now with second emblem. Poor old SAINT MARTIN (no beading on the splashers, removed in its days as a Saint, in the Great War) seems barely to have been cleaned over the years from the pictures opposite; it looks more woebegone than ever here and was indeed withdrawn less than a year later, the first to go (apart from the bombed 4911). B.K.B. Green Collection, Initial Photographics.

The Saint that was now a Hall, with 4,000 gallon tender, at Landore on 9 September 1951. 4900 was very much a hybrid and was, in its technical details, neither Saint nor Hall. When overhauled much of what it came in with it had to go out with. It caused some confusion in Worcester Factory, for instance; though officially a Hall it retained the reversing gear and motion of a Saint and its lower boiler meant that if standard Hall components were fitted the lifting arms of the weighbar shaft hit the boiler before full reverse was obtained; also the valve extension rods were of a different length. Conversely, 4900 parts caused similar trouble if fitting to a Hall was attempted. Those working on 4900 would have been glad to see the back of it and when it was withdrawn it was promptly cut up to make sure no change of mind could intervene, as had happened before. H.C. Casserley, courtesy R.M. Casserley.

4,000 gallon tender behind 4900 with first emblem, at Old Oak Common on 4 February 1956 — almost certainly the livery is lined black. Viewed from this angle, the most obvious detail difference in this former Saint, compared to the main run of Halls, was the rather lower pitch of the boiler, for when the engine was rebuilt it was lowered by 4¼ inches — as someone pointed out this was half the difference in the diameters of the old and new wheels. Peter Groom.

4901 ADDERLEY HALL

Built in 1928 to Lot no.254 at Swindon Works
To traffic 3/1/29

Mileages and Boilers
From new	4900
16/3/31	99,402 C4900
26/4/32	139,803 C4937
29/3/34	229,294 C4937
20/12/34	261,627 C4960
13/3/36	313,884 C4960
19/11/37	401,467 R2993
20/10/39	491,481 R2993
5/6/42	589,660 R2993
5/12/44	671,118 C2997
6/6/47	758,210 C7230
22/8/49	840,015 C4417
19/6/51	919,414 C4423
20/10/53	1,015,310 C9201
26/4/56	1,109,174 C9201
10/9/58	1,195,536 C4054

Sheds and Works
3/1/29	Penzance
22/7/29	Penzance shops L
16/11/29	Penzance shops L
17/3/30	Swindon Works L
15/7/30	Newton Abbot Works R
22/11/30	Penzance shops L
16/3/31	Penzance shops I
11/4/31	Tyseley
18/6/31	Wolverhampton Works L
4/7/31	Stafford Road
16/10/31	Wolverhampton Works L
26/4/32	Swindon Works G
7/5/32	Newton Abbot
1933	Laira
22/6/33	Newton Abbot Works R
26/7/33	Newton Abbot Works R
10/8/33	Newton Abbot Works R
23/12/33	Laira shops R
29/3/34	Swindon Works I
5/5/34	Penzance
6/11/34	Penzance shops R
20/12/34	Swindon Works L
9/2/35	Taunton
9/7/35	Newton Abbot Works L
9/11/35	Taunton shops R
12/3/36	Swindon Works I
4/4/36	Laira
19/11/37	Swindon Works G
11/12/37	Newton Abbot
11/10/38	Newton Abbot Works L
23/3/39	Newton Abbot Works L
20/10/39	Swindon Works I
19/7/40	Newton Abbot Works L
3/1941	Truro
28/3/41	Newton Abbot Works L
6/1941	Canton
5/6/42	Canton shops I
3/4/43	Swindon Works R
3/9/43	Swindon Works R
1/1/44	Banbury shops R
5/12/44	Swindon Works G
18/3/47	Canton shops R
6/6/47	Canton shops I
28/9/48	Ebbw Jct. Shops R
21/11/48	Canton shops R
22/8/49	Swindon Works HG
19/6/51	Swindon Works HI
2/9/52	Swindon Works LC
20/10/53	Swindon Works HG
22/12/53	Swindon Works U
19/6/54	Pontypool Road
26/1/55	Pontypool Road shops U
5/11/55	Canton
21/2/56	Old Oak shops U
26/4/56	Wolverhampton Works HI
26/1/57	Oxley
13/7/57	Carmarthen
14/9/57	Newton Abbot Works LC
5/10/57	Stafford Road
3/7/58	Stafford Road shops U
10/9/58	Swindon Works HG
1/12/59	Wolverhampton Works U
12/5/60	Tyseley shops U
16/7/60	Oxley

Tenders
Rebuilt	1649
17/3/30	2241
16/3/31	2236
26/4/32	2379
29/3/34	2261
12/8/36	2166
19/11/37	2248
20/10/39	2167
4/6/44	2701
2/9/52	2420
20/10/53	2598
8/10/55	2663
8/7/58	2890
10/9/58	2401
17/9/60	2633

Final mileage, 1,263,627
Withdrawn 16/9/60, cut up 31/12/60

4901 ADDERLEY HALL runs through Norton Fitzwarren, 8 August 1955. J. Robertson, transporttreasury

Under all that grime 4901 ADDERLEY HALL at Shrewsbury shed is wearing lined black. ColourRail

4901 ADDERLEY HALL at Kemble on 6 September 1952, with the 8.55am Cheltenham-Swindon. H.C. Casserley, courtesy R.M. Casserley.

4902 ALDENHAM HALL

Built 1928 to Lot no.254 at Swindon Works
To traffic 12/1/29

Mileages and Boilers

From new	4901
9/4/30	61,083 C4901
26/11/31	132,582 C4901
3/7/33	199,109 C2972
28/1/35	284,255 C2972
23/10/36	353,943 C4962
4/5/38	435,046 C4962
6/3/40	514,009 C4962
11/9/43	600,384 C2831
15/3/46	683,564 C2831
9/9/48	749,828 C2988
22/3/51	839,789 C4938
17/11/53	933,501 C2906
18/4/56	1,024,938 C7278
22/8/58	1,122,607 C7218
11/4/61	1,212,889 C4949

Sheds and Works

21/1/29	Penzance
20/2/29	Swindon Works **L**
14/5/29	Penzance shops **L**
17/9/29	Penzance shops **L**
3/1/30	Penzance shops **L**
9/4/30	Swindon Works **L** ATC fitted
10/5/30	Old Oak
21/1/31	Worcester shops **R**
26/11/31	Swindon Works **I**
19/12/31	Didcot
1/8/32	Didcot shops **R**
1933	Oxford
3/7/33	Swindon Works **G**
5/7/34	Oxford shops **R**
28/11/35	Swindon Works **I**
23/10/36	Swindon Works **G**
4/5/38	Oxford shops **I**
5/11/38	Swindon Works **L**
10/5/39	Oxford shops **R**
6/3/40	Swindon Works **I**
10/3/42	Oxford shops **R**
8/7/42	Old Oak shops **R**
25/7/42	Old Oak shops **R**
11/9/43	Swindon Works **G**
8/12/44	Old Oak shops **R**
15/3/46	Wolverhampton Works **I**
23/9/46	Wolverhampton Works **L**
25/11/46	Stourbridge shops **R**
21/3/47	Herford shops **R**
6/9/47	Westbury shops **R**
9/9/48	Swindon Works **G**
6/12/49	Shrewsbury shops **U**
14/1/51	Reading shops **U**
22/3/51	Swindon Works **HI**
27/2/52	Reading shops **U**
13/4/53	Old Oak shops **U**
17/11/53	Swindon Works **HG**
2/3/55	Old Oak shops **U**
23/9/55	Oxford shops **U**
18/4/56	Swindon Works **HG**
14/10/57	Old Oak shops **U**
28/8/58	Swindon Works **HG**
5/11/58	Oxford shops **U**
26/12/59	Tyseley
27/2/60	Didcot
11/4/61	Swindon Works **HI**
29/6/63	Taunton

Tenders

From new	2232
9/4/30	2151
26/11/31	2248
15/12/34	2614
28/11/35	1926
23/3/36	1772
28/10/36	2266
5/3/38	2442
4/5/38	2677
10/12/38	1906
3/2/40	2684
13/3/40	2412
11/9/43	2753
9/9/48	2803
22/3/51	2637
17/11/53	2920
26/2/55	2531
26/3/55	2714
18/4/56	2413
28/8/58	2804
11/4/61	2590

Final mileage, 1,280,358
Withdrawn 17/9/63. Sold to Cohens, Morriston 17/9/63

4902 ALDENHAM HALL awaiting a connection at Oxford on 22 June 1954. A correspondent, writing in *The Railway Observer* in 1948, recalled that 4902 had been the first Hall to penetrate as far as Plymouth, on 24 December 1928, though it 'promptly disappeared and was not seen again until the end of March'. Its official 'To Traffic' date had in fact been 12 January 1929, to Penzance. M. Robertson, transporttreasury

4902 ALDENHAM HALL at Goring with a parcels train, 21 July 1960. J. Davenport, Initial Photographics.

4903 ASTLEY HALL

Built 1928 to Lot no.254 at Swindon Works
To traffic 8/1/29

Mileages and Boilers

From new	4902
7/3/30	61,596 C4902
4/9/31	118,610 C2921
6/10/33	212,293 C2921
21/5/35	284,671 C4977
15/12/36	367,092 C4977
6/8/38	443,411 C4454
1/2/40	519,879 C4454
16/1/43	608,427 C2908
29/12/44	691,936 C2908
17/12/46	761,792 C7257
2/6/49	839,445 C4490
12/12/51	931,329 C4957
25/1/54	1,007,166 C8239
3/8/56	1,099,847 C4478
5/12/58	1,179,761 C7212
1/12/61	1,281,257 C2858

Sheds and Works history

8/1/29	Penzance
23/4/29	Penzance shops **L**
30/8/29	Penzance shops **L**
13/12/29	Penzance shops **L**
7/3/30	Swindon Works **L ATC fitted**
12/4/30	Banbury
18/5/31	Banbury shops **R**
4/9/31	Swindon Works **G**
26/9/31	Landore
20/10/31	Tondu shops **R**
9/4/32	Carmarthen shops **R**
18/11/32	Old Oak shops **R**
17/4/33	Carmarthen shops **R**
6/10/33	Swindon Works **I**
10/1933	Oxford
21/5/35	Swindon Works **G**
26/6/36	Swindon Works **L**
15/12/36	Swindon Works **I**
9/1/37	Old Oak
5/3/38	Oxford
6/8/38	Swindon Works **G**
11/8/39	Oxford shops **R**
1/2/40	Swindon Works **I**
30/7/41	Swiwndon Works **L**
16/1/43	Swindon Works **G**
29/12/44	Swindon Works **I**
17/12/46	Swindon Works **G**
28/9/47	Oxford shops **L**
19/5/48	Newton Abbot Works **L**
2/6/49	Swindon Works **HG**
15/6/50	Canton shops **U**
12/12/51	Swindon Works **HI**
5/5/52	Swindon Works **U**
25/1/54	Swindon Works **HG**
27/3/56	Tyseley shops **U**
3/8/56	Swindon Works **HI**
4/6/58	Old Oak shops **U**
5/12/58	Swindon Works **HG**
26/12/59	Old Oak
26/3/60	Reading
6/2/61	Southall shops **U**
1/12/61	Swindon Works **HG**
30/12/61	Oxley
6/10/62	Gloucester
3/11/61	Old Oak
29/6/63	Taunton
29/6/63	Southall
5/10/64	Worcester

Tenders

From new	1791
17/1/30	1790
26/6/31	1979

10/11/31	2137
17/7/33	2049
8/9/34	2259
6/11/36	2134
13/6/38	2173
6/12/39	2601
3/6/41	2577
29/3/42	1831
16/4/43	2215
29/12/45	2244
17/12/46	2405
18/1/47	1459
2/6/49	2556
17/6/50	2445
1/12/50	2410
12/12/51	2783
5/5/52	2683
28/11/53	2563
27/1/54	2393
3/8/56	2666
5/12/58	2848
6/1961	2845
7/10/61	2039
1/12/61	2661

Mileage at 28/12/63 1,340,597

Withdrawn 10/1964

Now with a 4,000 gallon tender, at Oxford shed on 15 September 1952. M. Robertson, transporttreasury

4903 ASTLEY HALL, begrimed but unbowed, at Swindon shed (even more woebegone than its steam inhabitants) in 1964, the loco's final year. That seems to be a red flag tucked in the handrail on the smokebox and what looks like the aftermath of a fish and chip supper drift sadly around the wheels. A leaking whistle valve serves as a safety valve! New EE Type 3 D6926 alongside. D.K. Jones Collection.

4904 BINNEGAR HALL
Built in 1929 to Lot no. 254 at Swindon Works
To traffic 1/1/29

Mileages and Boilers

From new	4903
18/8/31	128,440 C4903
2/2/33	194,799 C4938
7/3/34	247,473 C4476
9/11/34	273,697 C4476
12/6/36	348,101 C4921
5/4/38	438,849 C4921
28/12/39	515,721 C4491
28/9/42	601,744 C4491
14/3/44	637,424 C2966
5/4/46	709,796 C2966
8/3/48	767,541 C2973
24/1/50	830,054 C4934
16/2/51	866,957 C4934
29/1/54	955,135 C4934
14/8/56	1,041,123 C4431
21/11/58	1,132,411 C4431
27/10/61	1,220,082 C8222

Sheds and Works history

1/1/29	Penzance
2/5/29	Penzance shops **L**
9/9/29	Penzance shops **L**
21/12/29	Penzance shops **L**
25/3/30	Swindon Works **L**
	ATC fitted
12/4/30	Old Oak
18/8/31	Swindon Works **I**
29/8/31	Stafford Road
26/9/31	Oxford
9/9/32	Wolverhampton Works **L**
2/2/33	Swindon Works **G**
1933	Oxley
1/9/33	Oxley shops **R**
7/3/34	Swindon Works **L**
7/4/34	Tyseley
9/11/34	Swindon Works **I**
17/5/35	Tyseley shops **R**
12/6/36	Swindon Works **G**
8/3/37	Tyseley shops **R**
2/4/38	Stafford Road
5/4/38	Swindon Works **I**
19/4/39	Oxley
12/7/39	Chester shops **R**
28/12/39	Swindon Works **G**
2/1940	Chester
28/9/42	Swindon Works **I**
10/1942	Oxley
14/3/44	Swindon Works **L**
5/4/46	Swindon Works **I**
4/5/46	Wolverhampton Works **R**
18/12/46	Tyseley shed **R**
18/2/47	Oxley shops **R**
20/5/47	Oxford shops **R**
4/10/47	Oxley shops **R**
16/1/48	Severn Tunnel Jct. shops **L**
8/3/48	Swindon Works **G**
24/1/50	Swindon Works **HC**
25/2/50	Shrewsbury
16/2/51	Wolverhampton Works **HI**
6/9/52	St. Philips Marsh shops **U**
8/7/53	Shrewsbury shops **U**
29/1/54	Swindon Works **HI**
26/5/54	Wolverhampton Works **LC**
9/10/54	Tyseley
14/8/56	Swindon Works **HG**
13/7/57	Shrewsbury
22/1/58	Shrewsbury shops **U**
3/10/58	Stored at Shrewsbury
21/11/58	Ex-store Swindon Works **HI**
24/3/59	To store at Shrewsbury at Oxley
11/5/59	To store at Oxley
11/7/59	Laira
26/12/59	Taunton
5/4/61	Taunton shops **U**
27/10/61	Swindon works **HG**

Tenders

From new	2145
30/1/30	1993
8/1931	1940
12/5/31	1834
7/8/33	2341
2/2/34	1834
25/9/34	1704
29/4/36	2268
28/12/39	2250
4/8/42	2645
21/8/43	2839
8/3/48	2168
30/11/49	2636
29/1/54	2543
14/8/56	2734
25/1/58	2618
21/11/58	2420

Final mileage 1,288,079

Withdrawn 28/12/63

4904 BINNEGAR HALL awaiting attention at Swindon in the rain, 17 May 1931. H.C. Casserley, courtesy R.M. Casserley.

BINNEGAR HALL glints in the sun at Shrewsbury in the 1950s. The light picks out the webbing between spokes at the bottom, which add strength for the crank pin bosses. Another example of 'reversed' coupling rods – see 4946 MOSELEY HALL in the introductory notes, page 10-11. ColourRail

4905 BARTON HALL

Built in 1928 to Lot no.254 at Swindon Works
To traffic 2/1/29

Mileages and Boilers

From new	4904
5/8/31	121,027 C4904
3/11/32	171,136 C3005
24/5/34	250,034 C3005
5/11/35	315,986 C4423
7/7/37	408,031 C4423
10/1/39	488,866 C4941
16/11/40	570,511 C4941
12/10/43	666,041 C4941
26/3/45	717,543 C4961
30/1/47	787,231 C4037
28/10/49	866,589 C2852
24/12/51	925,706 C2855
18/3/53	973,761 C8219
28/4/55	1,058,263 C7234
25/7/57	1,157,748 C4447
12/11/59	1,244,502 C9200
8/3/62	1,322,321 C7248

Sheds and Works history

2/1/29	Truro
12/4/29	Truro shops **L**
14/4/29	Penzance
26/8/29	Penzance shops **L**
5/12/29	Penzance shops **L**
22/3/30	Penzance shops **L**
2/5/30	Swindon Works **L** ATC fitted
10/5/30	Laira
3/9/30	Laira shops **L**
22/11/30	Newton Abbot Works **L**
5/8/31	Swindon Works **I**
29/8/31	Leamington Spa
3/11/32	Swindon Works **G**
19/11/32	Old Oak
24/5/34	Swindon Works **I**
2/6/34	Oxford
24/10/34	Didcot shops **R**
5/11/35	Swindon Works **G**
7/7/37	Swindon Works **I**
3/5/38	Oxford shops **R**
10/1/39	Swindon Works **G**
24/11/39	Old Oak shops **R**
16/11/40	Wolverhampton Works **I**
16/1/42	Oxford shops **R**
11/6/42	Westbury shops **R**
15/7/42	Old Oak shops **R**
8/1942	Old Oak
12/10/43	Swindon Works **I**
4/1944	Swindon
13/11/44	Leamington Spa shops **R**
26/3/45	Swindon Works **G**
30/1/47	Swindon Works **I**
17/10/47	'Experimental'
16/5/48	Swindon shed Tender Work only
27/8/48	Swindon shed Tender Work only
19/12/48	Swindon shed Tender Work only
28/10/49	Swindon Works **HG**
24/6/50	To store/returned to traffic
12/8/50	Chester
21/2/51	Old Oak shed **U**
17/8/51	Chester shed **U**
24/12/51	Swindon Works **HC**
18/3/53	Swindon Works **HI**
3/10/53	Hereford
23/12/54	Worcester shops **U**
28/4/55	Swindon Works **HG**
16/6/56	Newton Abbot
25/7/57	Swindon Works **HG**
30/10/58	Old Oak shops **U**
12/11/59	Swindon Works **HG**
26/11/60	Newton Abbot Works **U**
20/3/61	Newton Abbot shed **U**
22/4/61	St. Philips Marsh
8/3/62	Swindon Works **HI**
27/6/62	Swindon Works cont **HI**
7/12/62	Caerphilly/Swindon Works **LC**
2/11/63	Didcot

Tenders

From new	1775
25/3/30	2075
4/5/31	2319
31/8/32	1739
11/4/34	2137
25/7/36	2264
5/12/38	2243
23/4/46	2389
30/1/47	2860
17/10/47	2233
27/7/49	2643
25/10/49	2394
21/11/51	2584
13/2/53	2400
24/3/55	2821
25/7/57	4101
1/11/58	2811
12/4/59	2927
8/3/62	2796

Final mileage 1,370,858

Withdrawn 13/11/63, Sold to J. Cashmore, Newport 30/1/64

Lined green 4905 BARTON HALL on the turntable just to the north of Snow Hill station, Birmingham; the date is not known but the 85C shed plate indicates the years 1953-1956, when 4905 was at Hereford. A few years earlier 4905 had figured in various tests. There is an entry in the Engine History: 'Experimental' and this refers to the period 15 April to 4 September 1947 when 4905 was run on the Swindon Test Plant and with the WR Dynamometer Car between Swindon and Stoke Gifford on cylinder lubrication tests for the Anglo-Iranian Oil Company.

4905 heading a Castle on an up train through Totnes station in the later part of the 1950s. One of the Rattery 2-6-2T bankers sits over in the siding. A. Scarsbrook, Initial Photographics.

4906 BRADFIELD HALL

Built 1928 to Lot no.254 at Swindon Works
To traffic 16/1/29

Mileages and Boilers

From new	4905
12/8/31	121,203 C4905
9/3/33	192,390 C2857
2/8/34	256,814 C2857
14/3/36	335,887 C2891
24/1/38	424,062 C2891
18/4/40	508,779 C2891
28/3/42	584,799 C4973
3/3/45	692,848 C4973
6/5/48	787,209 C4930
6/12/50	897,009 C4025
3/7/53	993,669 C4025
28/9/55	1,088,114 C9285
17/3/58	1,183,194 C2985
14/10/60	1,276,202 C4492

Sheds and Works history

16/1/29	Truro
14/4/29	Penzance
23/5/29	Penzance shops **L**
24/9/29	Penzance shops **L**
25/3/30	Swindon Works **L**
	ATC fitted
12/4/30	Old Oak
30/8/30	Westbury
2/9/30	Neath shops **R**
27/9/30	Old Oak
12/8/31	Swindon Works **I**
29/8/31	Chester
14/7/32	Wolverhampton Works **L**
9/3/33	Swindon Works **G**
4/4/33	Old Oak shops **R**
1933	Swindon
19/12/33	Swindon Works **L**
2/8/34	Swindon Works **I**
25/8/34	Westbury
6/4/35	Truro
28/11/35	Truro shops **R**
14/3/36	Swindon Works **G**
10/8/37	Newton Abbot Works **L**
24/1/38	Swindon Works **I**
5/2/38	Penzance
20/8/38	Newton Abbot Works **L**
6/4/39	Penzance shops **R**
10/8/39	Newton Abbot Works **L**
18/4/40	Swindon Works **I**
9/1940	Laira
17/10/40	Newton Abbot Works **R**
12/1940	Penzance
1/1/41	Penzance shops **R**
3/1941	Truro
25/6/41	Newton Abbot Works **L**
18/10/41	Penzance shops **R**
24/1/42	Truro shops **R**
28/3/42	Swindon Works **G**
27/1/43	Newton Abbot Works **L**
10/8/43	Newton Abbot Works **L**
10/1/44	Newton Abbot Works **R**
21/3/44	Newton Abbot Works **R**
23/4/44	Truro shops **R**
3/3/45	Swindon Works **I**
29/11/45	Truro shops **R**
28/10/46	Newton Abbot Works **L**
3/1/47	Truro shops **R**
18/9/47	Laira shops **R**
6/5/48	Swindon Works **G**
15/9/49	Swindon Works **LC**
6/12/50	Swindon Works **HG**
1/10/52	Truro shops **U**
31/10/52	Newton Abbot Works **LC**
3/7/53	Swindon Works **HI**
7/1/54	Truro shops **U**
28/9/55	Swindon Works **HG**
13/7/57	St. Blazey
17/3/58	Swindon Works **HI**
14/10/60	Swindon Works **HG**
3/12/60	Oxley
20/2/62	Oxley shops **U**
29/8/62	Banbury shops **U**

Tenders

From new	1772
29/1/30	1844
19/5/31	1682
7/12/32	1876
9/12/33	1790
12/6/34	1941
6/2/36	1934
6/12/37	1913
6/3/40	2215
17/2/42	1696
12/1/45	2676
5/10/46	2397
18/12/46	1840
4/3/48	2246
15/9/49	2818
31/10/50	2635
18/5/53	2567
28/9/55	2530
17/3/58	2604
9/8/58	4103
4/10/60	4119

Final mileage 1,341,287

Withdrawn 21/9/62, Sold to J. Cashmore, Great Bridge, 17/10/63

4906 BRADFIELD HALL pilots a 2-6-0 on a Paddington-bound train, crossing Clinnick Viaduct a little way east of Bodmin Road on 18 August 1951. A. Lathey, transporttreasury

Now with a Hawksworth 4,000 gallon tender, 4906 comes in to Par with the 9.30am Paddington-Falmouth on 2 September 1958. The through portion to Newquay has already been detached and taken across to the up platform. ColourRail

4907 BROUGHTON HALL

Built in 1928 to Lot no.254 at Swindon Works
To traffic 17/1/29

Mileages and Boilers

From new	4906
10/6/30	71,730 C4906
15/1/32	137,548 C4906
9/8/33	195,612 C4905
12/2/36	305,137 C4915
21/12/37	392,972 C4915
6/2/40	479,616 C2852
19/10/42	583,184 C2852
4/12/44	658,789 C7227
16/5/47	737,970 C2872
21/4/50	785,278 C7210
14/10/51	844,586 C8213
2/4/54	934,048 C8213
24/5/56	1,021,248 C4413
25/6/58	1,103,369 C7236
24/2/61	1,196,363 C7236

Sheds and Works history

17/1/29	Laira
14/4/29	Penzance
1/6/29	Penzance shops **L**
4/10/29	Penzance shops **L**
24/1/30	Newton Abbot shops **L**
10/6/30	Swindon Works **L ATC fitted**
14/10/30	Penzance shops **L**
13/2/31	Newton Abbot Works **R**
14/2/31	Newton Abbot
14/3/31	Penzance
25/6/31	Newton Abbot Works **R**
15/1/32	Swindon Works **I**
13/2/32	Exeter
12/3/32	Penzance
7/7/32	Penzance shops **R**
28/10/32	Newton Abbot Works **R**
13/12/32	Penzance shops **R**
7/3/33	Penzance shops **R**
9/8/33	Swindon Works **G**
5/9/33	Taunton shops **R**
5/3/34	Penzance shops **R**
28/11/34	Swindon Works **L**
26/2/35	Penzance shops **R**
2/6/35	Penzance shops **R**
12/2/36	Swindon Works **G**
4/4/36	Truro
10/7/37	Truro shops **R**
21/12/37	Swindon Works **I**
5/2/38	Penzance
13/7/38	Penzance shops **R**
17/10/38	Penzance shops **R**
16/11/38	Old Oak shops **L**
10/12/38	Old Oak
6/2/40	Swindon Works **G**
10/10/41	Old Oak shops **R**
19/10/42	Swindon Works **I**
31/5/44	Old Oak shops **R**
4/12/44	Swindon Works **G**
27/1/45	Old Oak shops **L**
5/1945	Southall
15/6/46	Old Oak
21/8/46	Old Oak shops **R**
16/9/46	Old Oak shed **R**
16/5/47	Swindon Works **I**
	Converted to oil burning
25/4/47	**Renumbered 3903**
9/4/48	Old Oak shed **R**
31/8/48	Old Oak shops **R**
29/3/50	In store at Swindon
21/4/50	Swindon Works **HC**
	Converted to coal burning
	Renumbered 4907
20/5/50	St. Philips Marsh
8/9/50	Bath Road shops **U**

14/10/51	Swindon Works **HG**
26/1/52	Weymouth
21/2/53	Swindon
13/6/53	Llanelly
5/9/53	Carmarthen
3/10/53	Hereford
5/11/53	Worcester shops **U**
2/2/54	Hereford shops **U**
2/4/54	Swindon Works **HI**
26/3/55	Old Oak
21/5/55	Oxford
5/11/55	Old Oak shops **U**
24/5/56	Swindon Works **HG**
22/11/57	Wolverhampton Works **LC**
13/1/58	Oxford shops **U**
22/3/58	Southall
25/6/58	Swindon Works **HG**
28/11/59	Worcester
24/2/61	Wolverhampton Works **HI**
7/11/61	Wolverhampton Works **LC**
21/4/62	Hereford
28/1/63	Ebbw Jct. Shops **U**
23/4/63	Ebbw Jct. Shops **U**
19/6/63	Oswestry Works **U**

Tenders

From new	1714
3/5/33	2046
12/12/35	1665
11/11/37	2171
18/12/39	2395
25/8/42	2254
9/10/44	2266
5/4/47	2933
2/4/54	2641
8/12/55	2755
24/5/56	2857
13/1/58	2587
23/6/58	2773

Final mileage 1,252,377
Withdrawn 1/8/63, Sold to J. Cashmore 31/12/63

4907 BROUGHTON HALL at Lostwithiel, 22 May 1935. It later ran as an oil burner, numbered 3903. A note in *The Railway Observer* in 1939 recorded that 4907 was allocated to Laira when new in January 1929 (which the engine history confirms) and was subsequently transferred to Penzance about May, 1929. Since that date, until the departure to factory last November, she has only been shedded at Penzance and Truro. As engines from these depots do not normally work beyond Exeter, this particular locomotive must have been one of the 'rarest' of the Hall class on the whole of the system. H.C. Casserley, courtesy R.M. Casserley.

4908 BROOME HALL

Built 1929 to Lot no.254 at Swindon Works
To traffic 18/1/29

Mileages and Boilers

From new	4907
24/4/31	111,426 C4907
31/3/33	189,150 C4907
31/1/35	265,996 C4472
12/6/36	339,871 C4472
19/1/38	431,900 C2927
19/10/39	520,977 C2927
17/6/42	624,527 C2927
17/1/44	690,545 C7245
28/6/46	779,266 C2961
9/8/48	845,171 C4467
27/2/51	941,292 C7236
19/6/53	1,025,504 C7236
17/11/55	1,120,399 C2864
22/10/57	1,216,129 C2864
1/12/60	1,329,248 C2885

Sheds and Works history

18/1/29	Laira
24/7/29	Laira shops **L**
30/12/29	Swindon Works **L ATC fitted**
1/4/30	Newton Abbot Works **L**
11/10/30	Laira shops **L**
24/4/31	Swindon Works **I**
9/5/31	Old Oak
13/2/32	Oxley
5/7/32	Oxford shops **R**
31/3/33	Swindon Works **I**
1933	Didcot
28/7/34	Worcester
22/9/34	Oxley
9/2/35	Westbury
31/3/35	Swindon Works **G**
12/6/36	Swindon Works **I**
27/6/36	Newton Abbot
19/1/38	Swindon Works **G**
15/10/38	Truro
16/11/38	Truro shops **R**
15/2/39	Truro shops **R**
19/10/39	Swindon Works **I**
16/1/40	Newton Abbot Works **R**
7/12/40	Swindon Works **L**
29/5/41	Newton Abbot Works **L**
6/1942	Laira
17/6/42	Swindon Works **I**
15/10/43	Laira shops **L**
17/1/44	Swindon Works **G**
8/11/44	Truro shops **R**
9/3/45	Laira shops **R**
29/5/45	Laira shops **R**
9/8/45	Laira shops **R**
10/10/45	Laira shops **R**
27/3/46	Laira shops **R**
28/6/46	Swindon Works **I**
30/8/46	Newton Abbot Works **R**
10/3/47	Newton Abbot Works **L**
4/7/47	Neath shops **I**
12/7/47	Landore
4/10/47	Llanelly
9/8/48	Swindon Works **G**
10/5/49	Swindon Works **LC**
4/9/49	Landore
20/5/50	St. Philips Marsh
17/6/50	Neyland
22/6/50	Llanelly shops **LC**
9/9/50	Severn Tunnel Jct.
27/2/51	Swindon Works **HG**
19/4/52	Old Oak
4/10/52	Southall
7/11/52	Tyseley shops **U**
4/12/52	Old Oak shops **U**
5/5/53	Southall shops **U**

19/6/53	Swindon Works **HI**
27/2/54	Old Oak
19/6/54	Southall
1/1/55	Penzance
7/2/55	Bath Road shops **U**
15/4/55	Truro shops **U**
17/11/55	Swindon Works **HG**
22/10/57	Swindon Works **HI**
22/11/57	Newton Abbot Works **LC**
15/9/58	To store at Penzance
26/3/60	Reading
1/12/60	Swindon Works **HI**
4/11/61	Oxford
11/8/62	Didcot

Tenders

From new	2173
12/11/29	1764
7/3/31	1840
9/1/33	1925
10/12/34	1512
5/5/36	1913
14/12/37	2256
19/10/39	2248
1/5/42	2242
17/1/44	1831
18/4/44	2738
14/7/45	2688
15/6/46	2349
9/7/46	2253
30/11/47	2258
8/6/48	2095
6/4/49	2917
30/1/51	2562
9/10/54	2590
17/11/55	2781
22/10/57	2910
1/12/60	2927

Final mileage 1,408,430

Withdrawn 22/10/63, Sold to Messrs Coopers Ltd, Swindon 31/12/63

4908 BROOME HALL at Wednesbury. The strange assemblage on the smokebox door was once (at the beginning of the journey at least) one of the makeshift frames that carried the running number of the train. In steam days on the WR it was particularly important for signalmen at junctions to know the number, both to identify the train and ensure it took the correct route. Many sheds ran out of the purpose-made frames, and used this sort of thing which has slipped and lost most of its number. RailOnline

With southbound oil tanks at Oxford, 7 August 1963; it was withdrawn a few months later.

4909 BLAKESLEY HALL

Built in 1929 to Lot no.254 at Swindon Works
To traffic 22/1/29

Mileages and Boilers

From new	4908
13/6/30	57,851 C4908
5/11/31	119,992 C4908
23/12/32	170,780 C4463
2/5/34	240,571 C4481
6/3/36	327,788 C4481
29/1/38	412,089 C4976
9/10/39	492,838 C4976
27/5/42	576,527 C2802
6/3/46	685,113 C7254
31/5/48	758,075 C9220
4/4/50	824,143 C7270
10/6/52	908,337 C4459
26/8/54	997,225 C4021
28/8/56	1,081,986 C4021
14/11/58	1,173,676 C2992
22/6/60	1,243,921 C4909

Sheds and Works history

22/1/29	Laira
13/7/29	Newton Abbot Works **L**
6/11/29	Laira shops **R**
18/12/29	Laira shops **R**
15/2/30	Penzance
10/4/30	Newton Abbot Works **L**
13/6/30	Swindon Works **L**
	ATC fitted
5/7/30	Chester
5/5/31	Chester shops **R**
12/6/31	Tyseley shops **L**
5/11/31	Swindon Works **I**
21/11/31	Stafford Road
19/12/31	Chester
23/12/32	Swindon Works **G**
2/5/34	Swindon Works **G**
30/6/34	Tyseley
6/3/36	Swindon Works **I**
29/1/38	Swindon Works **G**
5/3/38	Chester
9/10/39	Swindon Works **I**
14/10/39	Banbury
27/5/42	Swindon Works **G**
3/12/43	Birkenhead shops **R**
7/1/44	Birkenhead shops **R**
7/5/44	Banbury shops **R**
6/6/45	Exeter shops **R**
6/3/46	Swindon Works **I**
14/11/47	Banbury shops **L**
31/5/48	Swindon Works **G**
23/4/49	Oxley
18/6/49	Neyland
16/7/49	St. Philips Marsh
4/4/50	Swindon Works **HG**
21/4/51	Swindon
23/8/51	Swindon shed **U**
10/6/52	Swindon Works **HI**
29/12/52	Reading shops **U**
8/10/53	Swindon shed **U**
28/11/53	Bath Road
26/8/54	Swindon Works **HG**
24/8/55	Taunton shops **U**
28/1/56	St. Philips Marsh
28/8/56	Swindon Works **HI**
30/11/57	Westbury
14/11/58	Swindon Works **HI**
26/6/60	Swindon Works **HI**
4/11/61	Exeter
24/3/62	Swindon
22/9/62	Gloucester shops **U**

Tenders

From new	1677
3/5/29	1834
29/4/30	1995
23/9/31	1674
3/10/32	1772
2/5/34	1824
20/12/37	1856
6/9/39	2592
4/4/42	2822
10/12/45	2632
2/4/48	2426
22/2/50	2671
7/5/52	2803
25/11/52	2424
13/8/53	2679
21/7/54	2734
28/8/56	2712
14/11/58	2886
22/6/60	2623

Final mileage 1,321,819

Withdrawn 21/9/62, Sold to J. Cashmore Ltd. 16/9/63

With the 'shirt button' roundel which appeared from 1934. W. Hermiston, transporttreasury

A scintillating 4909 BLAKESLEY HALL, with low tender in the days before the roundel – GREAT WESTERN in serif with the badge. Snow Hill is best bet as to location. ColourRail

4910 BLAISDON HALL

Built in 1929 to Lot no.254 at Swindon Works
To traffic 7/2/39

Mileages and Boilers

From new	4909
16/7/31	123,859 C4909
28/7/33	205,167 C4412
11/1/35	280,073 C4412
25/10/35	212,814 C4477
11/8/36	357,749 C4477
9/5/38	441,004 C4477
3/2/40	518,720 C4477
24/11/41	594,523 C2893
25/7/44	691,159 C2893
19/4/47	794,881 C4442
8/12/49	893,464 C4902
6/6/52	984,152 C2843
9/12/54	1,085,927 C4986
25/3/59	1,240,172 C6625
6/7/61	1,306,604 C6625

Sheds and Works history

7/3/29	Laira
30/8/29	Laira shops **L**
31/1/30	Laira shops **L**
4/4/30	Swindon Works **L** ATC fitted
26/11/30	Laira shops **L**
16/7/31	Swindon Works **I**
1/8/31	Banbury
28/7/33	Swindon Works **G**
1933	Penzance
4/6/34	Newton Abbot shops **I**
11/1/35	Swindon Works **I**
9/2/35	Truro
6/4/35	Laira
25/10/35	Swindon Works **G**
17/3/36	Laira shops **R**
11/8/36	Swindon Works **I**
4/12/37	Laira shops **R**
9/5/38	Swindon Works **I**
29/6/39	Newton Abbot shops **L**
3/2/40	Swindon Works **I**
3/1940	Carmarthen
9/4/40	Swindon Works **L**
9/1/41	Carmarthen shops **R**
24/11/41	Swindon Works **G**
2/9/43	Carmarthen shops **L**
25/7/44	Swindon Works **I**
8/9/44	Stafford Road shed **R**
15/1/46	Swindon Works **L**
19/4/47	Swindon Works **G**
19/11/47	Carmarthen shops **R**
8/2/49	Carmarthen shops **LC**
	Tender work only
8/12/49	Swindon Works **HG**
9/2/50	Swindon Work **U**
21/9/51	Carmarthen shops **U**
6/6/52	Swindon Works **HI**
9/12/54	Swindon Works **HG**
6/10/56	Landore
26/2/57	Swindon Works **HI**
12/6/58	Ebbw Jct. shops **U**
12/9/58	Newton Abbot Works **LC**
5/12/58	Newton Abbot Works **U**
25/3/59	Swindon Works **HG**
26/3/60	Banbury
30/6/60	Wolverhampton Works **LC**
16/7/60	Tyseley
8/10/60	Banbury
3/12/60	Didcot
15/3/61	Old Oak shops **LC**
4/5/61	Gloucester shops **U**
6/7/61	Wolverhampton Works **HI**
1/11/62	Wolverhampton Works **LC**

Tenders

From new	1785
22/4/31	2230
25/10/35	2239
25/6/36	1825
23/3/38	2618
6/12/39	2537
26/3/40	2700
4/1/41	2633
5/1944	2795
25/7/44	2750
21/11/45	2394
19/4/47	1560
8/12/48	2885
14/11/49	2540
16/4/52	2591
6/11/54	2924
26/2/57	2700
25/3/59	2543

Final mileage 1,367,749

Withdrawn 2/12/63, Sold to A. King, Norwich 25/2/64

4910 BLAISDON HALL AT Carmarthen shed, 13 May 1956. It might be considered better practice to concentrate engines of (particularly a new) class at individual sheds but instead (typically) the 150 or so Halls in service by 1935 were scattered far and wide, in ones and twos and half dozens. Yet this is to misunderstand the times. Carmarthen had four and Bath Road and Taunton for instance one each, but given that labour was cheap and given, too, the Divisional Factory system in use on the GWR (as well as on other companies) it made perfect sense to spread the new powerful engines around for the better/more remunerative duties. It's hard to tell, but maybe more of them were engaged on goods work than passenger by the mid-1930s; Oxley, Tyseley and St Philips Marsh had a few each so it seems likely they were mixed traffic in the sense of working goods from some sheds and passenger from others, rather than a combination of both at the same shed. Carmarthen had a similar number of Halls even in 1962. A.R. Carpenter, transporttreasury

4910 a few years later, with the second emblem on the tender; in the meantime it has also re-acquired an original chimney, markedly more squat than the narrower one it carries at Carmarthen. A.R. Carpenter, transporttreasury

4911 BOWDEN HALL

Built 1929 to Lot no.254 at Swindon Works
To traffic 16/2/29

Mileages and Boilers

From new	4910
18/6/30	68,762 C4910
11/9/31	127,861 C4910
16/2/33	195,118 C4080
11/12/34	370,098 C4463
7/8/36	347,249 C4463
15/6/38	425,810 C4936
23/5/40	515,713 C4936

Sheds and Works history

16/2/29	Laira
5/8/29	Laira shops **L**
23/12/29	Laira shops **L**
9/4/30	Newton Abbot Works **L**
5/7/30	Chester
18/6/30	Swindon Works **I ATC fitted**
27/2/31	Chester shops **R**
11/9/31	Swindon Works **I**
26/9/31	Oxford
21/1/32	Oxford shops **R**
5/7/32	Old Oak shops **R**
16/2/33	Swindon Works **G**
28/6/33	Swindon Works **L**
1933	Penzance
2/11/33	Swindon Works **L**
2/4/34	Swindon Works **L**
11/12/34	Swindon Works **G**
19/10/35	Truro shops **R**
16/11/35	Truro
7/8/36	Swindon Works **I**
22/8/36	Penzance
15/5/37	Newton Abbot Works **L**
11/1/38	Penzance shops **R**
15/6/38	Swindon Works **G**
23/7/38	Laira
18/2/39	Penzance shops **R**
15/6/39	Truro shops **R**
29/9/39	Truro
21/10/39	Newton Abbot Works **L**
23/5/40	Swindon Works **I**

Tenders

From new	1726
8/5/30	2255
1/7/31	1704
5/12/32	1782
3/10/34	2229
9/6/36	1851
15/6/38	2225
16/4/40	2701

Final mileage 556,193 to 9/3/41

'Damaged by enemy action at Keyham 29 April 1941'

Withdrawn 10/6/41, Cut up 3/1/42

The premature demise of 4911 BOWDEN HALL means pictures are few and far between, but here it is (in a somewhat imperfect image, true) at Bristol Temple Meads, new, in February 1929 in the snow and the first of a batch of ten. By an odd twist the last of this batch, 4920 was not withdrawn until December 1965, the longest-lived of the 4900s. With Class B lamp 4911 is actually running in on a local passenger train. 4911 was always a local engine, hence it was at Keyham, Devonport on 29 April 1941 when it received almost a direct hit during the serious bombing of Plymouth of that time. It was scrapped at Swindon in June as beyond repair. C.A.W. Cawston, courtesy Brian Bailey.

The Germans brought an end to poor 4911 BOWDEN HALL early in the War. The History Card note, that it had been 'Damaged by enemy action at Keyham 29 April 1941', understated the case, for it was withdrawn a few weeks later and recorded 'cut up' on 3/1/42. This, it might be thought, would be done wherever the mortal remains were shifted to after the attack – it surely wouldn't have warranted hauling the carcase off to Swindon in this state. Yet *The Railway Observer* the following year confirmed that it indeed went to Swindon 'and has remained there ever since.' Its nameplates were in store in the event that 'following the G.W. example of replacing modern engines damaged beyond repair a new engine may be built which will carry No.4911.' It had acquired the roundel, we can see. It is said that 4911 had been stopped at the signal box because of the air raid, and the crew survived by sheltering under the steps of the box. ColourRail

4911 BOWDEN HALL at Swindon (it is thought) with low tender – before the War and its violent end at the hands of the enemy. RailPhotoprints

4912 BERRINGTON HALL

Built in 1929 to Lot no.254 at Swindon Works
To traffic 20/2/29

Mileages and Boilers

From new	4911
8/5/30	62,734 C4911
10/12/31	134,646 C4911
21/9/33	206,580 C4918
5/4/35	288,223 C4918
10/2/37	371,755 C2866
1/12/38	457,041 C2866
10/12/40	530,857 C4026
15/3/43	615,883 C4026
23/1/45	680,987 C8261
28/9/46	747,405 C4915
16/2/49	835,385 C2955
5/4/51	926,782 C4011
24/3/53	997,156 C4475
22/9/55	1,082,788 C4019
20/12/57	1,158,523 C7241
13/6/61	1,258,777 C2872

Sheds and Works history

20/2/29	Laira
18/7/29	Laira shops **L**
13/11/29	Laira shops **L**
7/3/30	Newton Abbot Works **L**
8/5/30	Swindon Works **L**
	ATC fitted
12/8/30	Penzance shops **L**
30/8/30	Newton Abbot
14/2/31	Penzance
1/4/31	Newton Abbot Works **L**
11/4/31	Newton Abbot
10/12/31	Swindon Works **I**
12/2/32	Penzance
7/5/32	Exeter
6/7/32	Exeter shops **L**
30/7/32	Penzance
19/11/32	Newton Abbot
17/12/32	Penzance
3/4/33	Penzance shops **R**
21/9/33	Swindon Works **G**
1933	Old Oak
5/4/35	Swindon Works **I**
4/5/35	Reading
10/2/37	Swindon Works **G**
29/5/37	Oxford
16/6/37	Banbury shops **R**
1/12/38	Swindon Works **I**
10/12/38	Stafford Road
12/7/40	Tyseley shops **R**
11/1940	Worcester
10/12/40	Swindon Works **G**
1/1941	Westbury
4/1942	Pontypool Road
15/3/43	Swindon Works **I**
20/6/44	Pontypool Road shops **R**
23/1/45	Swindon Works **G**
28/9/46	Swindon Works **I**
18/2/48	Pontypool Road **L**
	Tender work only
17/9/48	Ebbw Jct. Shops **L**
16/2/49	Swindon Works **HG**
2/12/50	St. Philips Marsh
5/4/51	Swindon Works **HI**
7/6/51	Swindon
24/3/53	Swindon Works **HG**
21/2/54	Bath Road **U**
27/3/54	Stafford Road
15/11/54	Stafford Road shed **U**
4/4/55	Stafford Road shed **U**
3/6/55	Shrewsbury [WR shed] **U**
22/9/55	Swindon Works **HI**
6/3/56	Laira shops **U**
13/6/56	Stafford Road shed **U**

14/8/56	Tyseley shops **U**
15/5/57	Stafford Road shed **U**
18/6/57	Tyseley shops **U**
19/9/57	Oxley shops **U**
20/12/57	Swindon Works **HG**
1/8/58	Banbury shops **U**
29/11/58	Shrewsbury
18/4/59	Oxley
23/7/59	Tyseley shops **U**
29/10/59	Wolverhampton Works **HC**
4/12/59	Tyseley shops **U**
27/5/60	Oxley shops **U**
30/12/60	Tyseley shops **U**
13/6/61	Swindon Works **HI**
28/11/61	Southall shops **U**

Tenders

From new	2227
26/3/30	1775
27/5/32	2262
3/7/33	1960
21/2/35	1911
4/1/37	1945
31/10/38	2240
9/10/40	2393
11/2/43	2418
13/11/44	2609
7/9/46	1513
28/2/46	2663
12/1/49	2836
7/3/51	1514
10/2/53	1459
22/9/55	2652
20/12/57	2607
13/6/61	2440

Final mileage 1,345,017

Withdrawn 24/8/62, Cut up 29/12/62

4912 BERRINGTON HALL at Shrewsbury shed around 1950 in lined green, when it carried a 4,000 gallon tender; no shed plate yet. W. Hermiston, transporttreasury

4912 BERRINGTON HALL at Birmingham Snow Hill, waiting to leave with the 9.50am to Birkenhead, Sunday 13 April 1958. Michael Mensing.

4913 BAGLAN HALL

Built in 1929 to Lot no.254 at Swindon Works
To traffic 21/2/29

Mileage and Boilers

From new	4912
10/4/31	112,476 C4912
7/9/33	211,902 C2877
15/3/35	291,267 C2877
22/8/36	366,810 C4953
26/5/38	451,880 C4953
2/6/40	535,233 C4953
2/4/43	632,547 R9219
3/8/45	713,974 C4445
27/6/47	786,427 C7267
28/6/49	863,437 C4465
23/8/51	945,258 C7256
8/9/53	1,032,465 C7256
2/3/56	1,126,431 C7259
28/5/58	1,215,866 C8256
5/10/60	1,283,231 C4940

Sheds and Works history

21/2/29	Laira
9/9/29	Laira shops **L**
14/1/30	Swindon Works **L** ATC fitted
22/8/30	Laira shops **L**
12/12/30	Laira shops **L**
10/4/31	Swindon Works **L**
9/5/31	Banbury
7/9/33	Swindon Works **G**
30/6/34	Newton Abbot
10/8/34	Newton Abbot Works **L**
25/8/34	Penzance
4/10/34	Penzance shops **R**
15/3/35	Swindon Works **I**
6/4/35	Newton Abbot
22/11/35	Newton Abbot Works **R**
5/3/36	Newton Abbot Works **L**
22/8/36	Swindon Works **G**
19/9/36	Hereford
14/10/37	Worcester shops **L**
26/5/38	Swindon Works **I**
15/8/39	Swindon Works **L**
2/6/40	Swindon Works **I**
21/1/41	Swindon Works **L**
22/9/41	Swindon Works **L**
4/1942	Canton
2/1/43	Canton shops **R**
2/4/43	Swindon Works **G**
4/11/43	Canton shops **R**
11/8/44	Canton shops **L**
20/10/44	Laira shops **R**
3/8/45	Swindon Works **I**
31/10/46	Ebbw Jct. shops **L**
18/12/46	Old Oak shops **R**
27/6/47	Swindon Works **G**
4/7/47	Continued **G**, one day
18/11/48	Westbury shops **R**
28/6/49	Swindon Works **HG**
29/3/50	Canton shops **U**
21/12/50	Bath Road shops **U**
23/8/51	Swindon Works **HG**
8/9/53	Swindon Works **HI**
10/2/55	St. Philips Marsh shops **U**
24/8/55	Gloucester shops **U**
2/3/56	Swindon Works **HG**
26/1/57	Oxley
2/11/57	Shrewsbury
30/11/57	Oxley
26/1/58	Oxley shops **U**
5/3/58	Swindon Works **HG**
28/5/58	Caerphilly Works **HG**
25/11/58	Oxley shops **U**
11/7/59	Laira
3/10/59	Reading
2/11/59	Didcot
26/12/59	Hereford
3/2/60	Hereford **U**
5/10/60	Swindon Works **HI**

Tenders

From new	1838
21/2/31	1926
23/6/33	2262
12/7/34	2563
24/1/35	1825
2/7/36	1858
6/3/37	2220
9/4/38	2124
27/5/39	2251
15/6/39	2266
2/6/40	1795
17/2/43	2406
17/6/45	2738
24/6/47	2531
4/7/47	2386
2/7/51	2853
25/1/55	2812
2/3/56	2703
15/3/58	2439
23/5/59	2397
5/10/60	2644

Final mileage 1,347,386

Withdrawn 21/9/62, Sold to R.S. Hayes Ltd. Bridgend 26/8/63

4913 BAGLAN HALL – respectably clean, it's just the murk from its home shed opposite – passing Canton (coal stage on right) with a down six coach stopping passenger train for Swansea about 1956. D.K. Jones Collection.

Clean enough to catch the low light, 4913 BAGLAN HALL runs an up ten coach express passenger train away from Rumney, Cardiff, on Saturday 17 March 1956. 4913 and its train are on the Up Main between Rumney River Bridge and St. Mellons; it is a Cardiff to Portsmouth or Brighton service, the stock of SR origin, with the first two coaches of Bulleid design. Many are painted in carmine and cream. Presumably the stock on these services alternated with a train of WR coaches, on an out and home basis. The reception sidings on the down side are connected to the Down Relief Line. Towards Cardiff there was a small station at Roath, closed by 1956, and the next station on the Up Line was at Marshfield. Roath Power Station beyond was built in 1902, to provide power for the newly electrified Cardiff Tramways, and was subsequently re-named Cardiff Power Station. It was demolished in 1972. The banks of the River Rumney can be seen in the distance, left-hand side. The far-off signal box, just about visible alongside the Up Main, is Rumney River Bridge Box. One of its duties was to control traffic into the private sidings of the works of Connies and Meadens, which can be seen in the background, right-hand side. It is a completely different landscape today of course! D.K. Jones Collection.

BAGLAN HALL still in South Wales (it had been at Canton since 1942) with a down express at Severn Tunnel Junction, 26 June 1956. D.K. Jones Collection.

4914 CRANMORE HALL

Built in 1929 to Lot no.254 at Swindon Works
To traffic 25/2/29

Mileages and Boilers

From new	4913
12/8/31	122,832 C4913
27/3/33	198,034 C4913
21/12/34	270,865 C4488
4/7/36	347,899 C4488
9/5/38	429,806 C4948
30/5/40	513,063 C4948
1/6/43	602,977 C4948
3/10/44	646,380 C7251
17/6/46	696,591 C7251
23/9/48	761,453 C2950
4/6/51	813,607 C8265
2/4/52	845,565 C8265
14/9/54	935,036 C4061
28/9/56	1,020,532 C4445
23/3/59	1,104,296 C4999
22/6/61	1,188,138 C4994

Sheds and Works history

Date	Location
25/2/29	Laira
25/9/29	Laira shops **L**
27/2/30	Swindon Works **L ATC fitted**
15/3/30	Goodwick
14/2/31	Carmarthen
31/3/31	Landore shops **R**
11/4/31	Goodwick
12/8/31	Swindon Works **I**
15/7/32	Goodwick shops **R**
6/1933	Oxford
27/3/33	Swindon Works **I**
18/10/33	Swindon Works **L**
1933	Reading
8/5/34	Reading shops **R**
21/12/34	Swindon Works **G**
4/7/36	Swindon Works **I**
9/5/38	Swindon Works **G**
30/5/40	Swindon Works **I**
6/1941	Didcot
12/1/42	Didcot shops **R**
8/6/42	Didcot shops **R**
10/1942	Reading
30/1/43	Reading shops **R**
1/6/43	Swindon Works **I**
7/7/43	Reading shops **R**
3/10/44	Swindon Works **L**
17/6/46	Swindon Works **I**
17/8/46	Oxford shops **R**
23/9/48	Swindon Works **G**
2/10/48-25/6/49	Stored at Swindon Works
18/6/49	Bath Road
16/7/49	St. Philips Marsh
5/8/49	Newton Abbot Works **U**
28/4/50-26/7/50	Stored at Swindon Works
12/8/50	Bath Road
4/6/51	Swindon Works **HC**
2/4/52	Swindon Works **HI**
9/9/52	Swindon Works **LC**
22/1/53	Taunton shops **U**
14/9/54	Swindon Works **HG**
27/3/54	St. Philips Marsh
9/10/54	Bath Road
12/4/55	Swindon Works **U**
16/6/56	St. Philips Marsh
28/9/56	Swindon Works **HG**
19/3/58	Reading shops **U**
23/3/59	Swindon Works **HI**
19/4/59	Laira shops **U**
8/12/60	Ebbw Jct. shops **U**
22/6/61	Swindon Works **HG**
20/1/62	Ebbw Jct. shops **LC**
27/12/62	Shrewsbury shops **U**

Tenders

From new	2316
15/1/30	1792
19/12/30	1717
7/1931	2380
12/8/31	2224
5/1/33	1948
25/9/33	2168
5/11/34	2268
19/5/36	1775
28/3/38	2624
30/5/40	2663
1/6/43	2250
15/8/44	2842
16/7/48	2911
26/4/51	2432
4/6/51	2420
9/9/52	2573
10/8/54	2711
13/4/55	2917
28/9/56	2447
22/3/58	2724
24/1/59	2447
2/3/59	2836

Final mileage 1,259,673

Withdrawn 2/12/63, Sold to Birds Ltd. Morriston, 28/2/64

St Philips Marsh's 4914 at Shrewsbury shed in 1960; oil has been leaking (more than usually anyway) from the lubricator valve on the smokebox. D.K. Jones Collection.

4914 CRANMORE HALL at Exeter shed, 20 August 1963. The shed was a thoroughly forlorn place by now, with few if any active engines, dead locos en route to South Wales and oblivion stored by the coal stage and the roof removed because of its unsafe condition. The portion of the building standing behind 4914 still houses the offices, stores, etc. J.L. Stevenson, courtesy Hamish Stevenson.

4915 CONDOVER HALL

Buitl in 1929 to Lot no.254 at Swindon Works
To traffic 1/3/29

Mileages and Boilers

From new	4914
7/8/31	121,485 C4914
17/5/33	191,908 C4904
28/12/34	271,830 C4479
4/7/36	351,465 C4479
11/5/38	427,246 C4479
23/4/40	501,672 C4479
1/7/42	588,394 C2971
6/9/44	672,758 C2971
18/9/46	750,412 C4900
11/2/49	837,523 C7265
23/5/51	925,989 C7229
9/7/53	1,008,018 C9217
21/2/56	1,096,350 C9217
14/5/58	1,178,740 C4475
21/2/61	1,271,058 C8232

Sheds and Works history

1/3/29	Gloucester
1/9/29	Goodwick
1/10/29	Goodwick shops R
29/1/30	Goodwick shops R
4/4/30	Swindon Works L ATC fitted
10/5/30	Old Oak
7/8/31	Swindon Works I
5/10/31	Old Oak shops R
24/10/31	Oxford
11/3/32	Oxford shops R
17/5/33	Swindon Works G
7/1933	Stafford Road
1933	Chester
13/1/34	Oxley
10/2/34	Tyseley
10/3/34	Oxley
28/12/34	Swindon Works G
12/1/35	Canton
4/7/36	Swindon Works I
25/7/36	Landore
18/2/37	Landore shops R
23/11/37	Swindon Works L
11/5/38	Swindon Works I
12/11/38	Carmarthen
24/10/39	Carmarthen shops L
	Tender work only
23/4/40	Swindon Works I
17/9/41	Carmarthen shops L
2/3/42	Carmarthen shops L
1/7/42	Swindon Works G
22/10/43	Carmarthen shops L
13/5/44	Carmarthen shops L
6/9/44	Swindon Works I
24/9/45	Carmarthen shops L
18/9/46	Swindon Works G
8/2/47	Carmarthen shops L
12/6/47	Carmarthen shops R
11/8/48	Canton shops L
	Tender work only
11/2/49	Swindon Works HG
23/5/51	Swindon Works HI
9/7/53	Swindon Works HG
2/10/53	Swindon Works LC
6/11/54	Shrewsbury
21/5/55	Tyseley
16/7/55	Shrewsbury
21/2/56	Swindon Works HI
8/10/57	Shrewsbury shops U
1/1/58	Shrewsbury shops U
14/5/58	Swindon Works HG
15/9/58-6/10/58	Stored at Shrewsbury
1/11/58	Old Oak
21/1/59	Didcot
3/6/60	Old Oak shops U
21/7/60	Taunton shops U
21/2/61	Swindon Works HI
5/12/61	Banbury shops U
27/1/62	Reading
24/9/62	Reading shops U

Tenders

From new	1857
4/2/30	1778
8/5/31	2380
29/1/33	1560
27/5/36	2248
25/10/37	2246
29/3/38	2700
15/3/40	2761
1/7/42	2895
15/7/44	2396
6/9/44	1993
9/8/46	1511
10/1/49	2540
28/1/50	2571
29/5/53	2718
21/2/56	2658
14/5/58	2424
21/2/61	2557
2/1962	2573

Final mileage 1,328,672

Withdrawn 26/2/63, Cut up 18/5/63

4915 CONDOVER HALL in a stirring image, with the 8.10pm Birmingham Snow Hill-Paddington, just east of Hatton station, 18 July 1959. Another case of 'reversed' coupling rods – from hereon the reader will enjoy spotting them himself! Michael Mensing.

Hereford's CONDOVER HALL at Old Oak Common, electrification flashes on firebox only, 20 December 1962. J.L. Stevenson, courtesy Hamish Stevenson.

4916 CRUMLIN HALL

Built in 1929 to Lot no.254 at Swindon Works
To traffic 2/3/29

Mileages and Boilers

From new	4923
17/7/30	63,977 C4923
27/11/31	128,182 C4902
24/1/34	229,245 C2964
22/8/35	307,909 C4941
31/3/37	389,948 C4941
21/2/38	444,650 C2871
1/4/39	491,063 C2871
6/8/41	560,397 C2871
30/9/43	634,286 C4969
18/1/46	711,715 C4969
4/8/48	777,990 C4413
12/4/50	828,277 C7253
8/5/51	870,640 C7253
2/9/53	954,643 C7253
15/2/56	1,033,477 C4032
19/8/58	1,133,269 C4032
8/9/61	1,222,463 C7271

Sheds and works history

2/3/29	Gloucester
12/5/30	Reading
17/7/30	Swindon Works **L**
	ATC fitted
2/8/30	Stafford Road
30/8/30	Chester
27/11/31	Swindon Works **G**
19/12/31	Old Oak
27/8/32	Westbury
22/10/32	Oxley
24/1/34	Swindon Works **G**
10/2/34	Stafford Road
28/7/34	Oxley
15/2/35	Swindon Works **L**
22/8/35	Swindon Works **G**
21/9/35	Stafford Road
31/3/37	Swindon Works **I**
1/5/37	Oxley
21/2/38	Swindon Works **L**
1/4/39	Swindon Works **I**
20/8/40	Damaged in air raid at Newton Abbot
6/8/41	Swindon Works **I**
30/9/43	Swindon Works **G**
18/1/46	Swindon Works **I**
29/4/47	Swindon Works **R**
14/8/47	Swindon Works **L**
18/9/47	Old Oak shops **R**
18/11/47	Bath Road shops **R**
4/8/48	Swindon Works **G**
23/12/48	Oxford shops **R**
18/6/49	Neyland
16/7/49	St. Philips Marsh
19/8/49	Newton Abbot Works **U**
7/10/49	St. Philips Marsh shops **U**
3/2/50	St. Philips Marsh shops **U**
12/4/50	Swindon Works **HC**
8/5/51	Swindon Works **HI**
11/8/51	Swindon
2/9/53	Swindon Works **HI**
31/10/53	Ebbw Jct.
27/9/55	Ebbw Jct. shops **U**
15/2/56	Swindon Works **HG**
15/3/57	Caerphilly Works **LC**
19/8/58	Swindon Works **HI**
7/1/59-13/6/59	Stored at Ebbw Jct.
11/7/59	Carmarthen
26/12/59	Pontypool Road
9/8/60	Pontypool Road shops **U**
18/11/60	Caerphilly Works **LC**
8/9/61	Swindon Works **HG**
14/7/62	Hereford
8/3/63	Ebbw Jct. shops **U**
16/5/63	Hereford shops **U**
30/11/63	Pontypool Road
22/6/64	Swindon

Tenders

From new	1774
20/10/31	2267
21/11/33	2210
25/6/35	1835
15/2/37	1936
13/6/38	2258
25/2/39	2778
30/5/41	2440
22/7/43	2180
20/1/44	2668
14/8/47	2550
10/6/48	1514
1/3/50	2670
9/4/51	2554
8/5/51	2572
1/5/53	2392
2/9/53	2658
15/2/56	2407
19/8/58	2783
7/1961	2614
8/9/61	2829

Mileage at 28/12/63 1,287,830

Withdrawn 10/8/64

4916 CRUMLIN HALL, freshly overhauled, has been traversed out of Swindon 'AE' Shop and is awaiting a move to the turntable area, to be coupled up to a tender. The tender will have been overhauled in 'B' Shop, in the original Factory complex, and moved up to the turntable lines. The 86G plate indicates the period to be December 1959-July 1962, so the occasion would be 4916's Heavy General of September 1961. The Hall at the far side of the traverser is probably awaiting a move into 'AE' Shop to commence its overhaul on the Stripping Gang. See the notes under 'The Record'.

CRUMLIN HALL passing the site of Dinmore station near Hereford, with the 9.30am from Manchester on 9 July 1963.

4917 CROSSWOOD HALL

Built in 1929 to Lot no.254 at Swindon Works
To traffic 11/3/29

Mileages and Boilers

From new	4916
5/4/31	108,408 C4916
7/11/33	209,006 C4906
14/6/35	286,486 C4492
23/3/37	368,074 R2948
11/8/38	442,751 R2948
19/7/40	521,352 R2948
11/9/41	558,340 C2846
27/8/43	622,664 C2846
23/8/44	655,115 C4492
26/4/46	707,266 C8289
19/2/48	775,639 C4029
17/4/50	854,300 C4053
24/1/52	918,140 C4937
27/5/54	1,009,420 C9282
6/6/56	1,114,704 C9282
7/3/58	1,188,427 C6207
14/10/60	1,309,072 C6207
10/11/61	1,346,410 C4933

Sheds and Works history

11/3/29	Old Oak
9/6/29	Bath Road
1/9/29	Goodwick
6/11/29	Swindon Works R
24/11/29	Penzance
18/3/30	Swindon Works L
	ATC fitted
12/4/30	Old Oak
30/8/30	Neath
27/9/30	Old Oak
5/4/31	Swindon Works I
6/6/31	Reading
12/2/32	Oxford
1933	Stafford Road
7/11/33	Swindon Works G
13/1/34	Oxley
28/7/34	Stafford Road
14/6/35	Swindon Works G
29/6/35	Chester
9/6/36	Chester shops R
14/8/36	Stafford Road shed L
23/3/37	Swindon Works G
29/5/37	Stafford Road
11/8/38	Swindon Works I
20/8/38	Tyseley
21/10/39	Wolverhampton Works L
19/7/40	Swindon Works I
5/3/41	Tyseley shops R
11/9/41	Swindon Works L
29/1/42	Tyseley shops R
16/2/43	Tyseley shed R
27/8/43	Swindon Works I
13/9/43	Swindon Works L
	Collision
23/8/44	Swindon Works L
26/1/45	Tyseley shops R
9/1/46	Taunton shops R
26/4/46	Swindon Works G
19/2/48	Swindon Works I
1/9/49	Ebbw Jct. shops U
31/12/49	Southall
22/2/50	Southall shops U
17/4/50	Swindon Works HG
21/4/51	St. Philips Marsh
24/1/52	Swindon Works HI
16/3/53	Bath Road shops U
29/8/53	Landore shops U
3/10/53	Chester
21/11/53	Hereford shops R
28/11/53	Hereford
26/12/53	Exeter
24/4/54	Westbury
27/5/54	Swindon Works HG
6/6/56	Wolverhampton Works HI
6/1/58	Bath Road shops U
7/3/58	Swindon Works HG
14/10/60	Wolverhampton Works HI
10/11/61	Swindon Works HI

Tenders

From new	2100
24/1/30	1940
3/1931	1993
5/5/33	2249
7/11/33	1947
14/6/35	2236
11/2/37	2262
3/6/40	2818
27/8/43	2622
13/9/43	2729
23/8/44	2134
23/2/46	2141
16/4/46	1666
12/7/47	2928
6/3/50	2432
26/4/51	2911
24/1/52	2579
6/9/52	4127
4/10/52	2579
23/11/53	2723
27/5/54	2826
3/2/58	2581
7/3/58	2647
5/11/60	2655
10/11/61	2418

Final mileage 1,376,381

Withdrawn 21/9/62, Sold to John Cashmore, Newport 21/10/63

4917 CROSSWOOD HALL heads a down train a little west of Taunton station in August 1955, shadowed in its own smoke. The view is from 'Forty Steps Bridge' long ago extended to more than twice that, though retaining its traditional name. J. Robertson, transporttreasury

4917 CROSSWOOD HALL at No.3 platform Weymouth station, on an express passenger train for Paddington, 18 June 1959. D.K. Jones Collection.

4918 DARTINGTON HALL

Built in 1929 to lot no.254 at Swindon Works
To traffic 11/3/29

Mileages and Boilers

From new	4924
28/6/30	66,809 C4924
22/12/31	136,482 C4934
10/11/33	229,733 C4934
8/7/35	304,088 C4414
22/1/37	389,572 C4414
15/9/38	461,919 C2876
5/9/40	541,975 C2876
4/1/43	612,255 C2876
19/10/43	633,353 C2979
2/10/45	695,183 C8284
1/7/47	751,009 C8253
17/11/48	793,396 C8253
16/2/50	827,005 C8212
13/8/51	874,034 C2885
12/1/54	965,076 C4930
13/6/56	1,052,216 C7229
10/6/58	1,137,979 C7229
8/8/60	1,219,562 C4065
17/11/61	1,256,491 C6214

Sheds and Works history

11/3/29	Old Oak
24/11/29	Oxley
28/6/30	Swindon Works **L ATC fitted**
5/7/30	Stafford Road
25/10/30	Oxley
19/11/30	Swindon Works **L**
22/12/31	Swindon Works **G**
6/1/32	Oxford
26/8/32	Oxford shops **R**
10/11/33	Swindon Works **I**
11/2/35	Wolverhampton Works **L**
8/7/35	Swindon Works **G**
27/7/35	Tyseley
22/1/37	Swindon Works **I**
15/9/38	Swindon Works **G**
15/10/38	Chester
13/11/39	Chester shops **R**
5/9/40	Swindon Works **I**
10/11/41	Chester shops **R**
10/10/42	Wolverhampton Works **R**
4/1/43	Swindon Works **I**
19/10/43	Swindon Works **L**
2/10/45	Swindon Works **I**
18/2/47	Tyseley shops **R**
1/7/47	Swindon Works **L**
11/6/48	Chester shops **L**
17/11/48	Swindon Works **I**
17/9/49	Oswestry Works **U**
16/2/50	Swindon Works **HC**
28/7/50	Tyseley shops **U**
2/12/50	Banbury
13/8/51	Swindon Works **HI**
9/8/52	Stafford Road
28/8/52	Westbury shops **U**
3/3/53	Tyseley shops **U**
13/6/53	Oxley
12/1/54	Swindon Works **HG**
25/2/55	Oxley shops **U**
25/3/55	Swindon Works **U**
16/7/55	Landore
6/9/55	Llanelly shops **U**
8/10/55	Bath Road
13/6/56	Swindon Works **HG**
19/4/58	St. Philips Marsh
10/6/58	Swindon Works **HI**
12/7/58	Bath Road
21/3/59	Shrewsbury
13/6/59	Stafford Road
8/8/60	Swindon Works **HI**
15/5/61	Worcester shops **U**
17/11/61	Swindon Works **HC**
2/12/61	Canton
24/5/62	Aberdare shops **U**
8/9/62	Cardiff East Dock

Tenders

From new	2210
14/5/30	2166
31/8/33	2246
25/5/35	1783
7/12/36	2250
9/8/38	1834
24/7/40	2757
11/11/42	2180
20/7/43	1952
3/12/45	2319
18/5/46	1863
1/7/47	2711
17/11/48	1666
16/2/50	2741
15/7/50	2773
12/8/50	2586
13/8/51	2530
12/1/54	2814
13/6/56	4010
29/1/58	2367
3/2/58	2568
10/6/58	2628
8/8/60	2660
17/11/62	2631

Final mileage 1,309,911

Withdrawn 24/6/63, Sold to R. S. Hayes, Bridgend, 1/1/64

4918 DARTINGTON HALL at Chester West 28 March 1959; engine shed in background. Hamish Stevenson.

Rolling along at Cholsey on a parcels; it is quite late, about 1961 probably, with electrification flashes up and before its transfer from Stafford Road to Canton. J.Davenport, Initial Photographics.

4919 DONNINGTON HALL

Built in 1929 to Lot no.254 at Swindon Works
To traffic 13/3/29

Mileages and Boilers

From new	4925
21/7/30	66,317 C4925
14/4/32	153,867 C4923
25/1/34	245,959 C4407
8/7/35	321,736 C4407
21/4/37	405,878 C4449
7/1/39	490,288 C4449
30/9/41	572,431 C4035
15/5/45	687,711 C4986
17/12/47	776,462 C7204
9/10/50	865,217 R9289
4/11/50	866,110 R9289
23/9/52	936,592 C4922
9/2/55	1,016,629 C4905
31/10/56	1,079,233 C8277
10/3/59	1,172,272 C8277
3/3/61	1,247,336 C7253

Tenders

From new	1793
3/2/32	2210
31/10/33	1871
25/5/35	2258
13/3/37	2247
28/11/38	2351
7/6/40	2266
7/8/41	2265
20/10/43	2741
9/2/44	2417
15/5/45	1539
18/5/46	2837
17/12/47	2249
18/10/50	2828
14/8/52	2835
25/8/53	2536
1/10/56	2535
31/10/56	2767
4/10/58	4067
10/3/59	2384
3/3/61	2878
25/5/62	2533

Mileage at 28/12/63 1,320,248

Withdrawn 21/10/64

Sheds and Works history

13/3/29	Old Oak
12/5/29	Oxley
4/10/29	Oxley shops **L**
21/7/30	Swindon Works **L ATC fitted**
2/8/30	Canton
14/4/32	Swindon Works **G**
25/1/34	Swindon Works **G**
8/7/35	Swindon Works **I**
27/7/35	Stafford Road
21/9/35	Oxford
21/4/37	Swindon Works **G**
7/1/39	Swindon Works **I**
4/2/39	Banbury
2/1940	Shrewsbury
2/4/40	Shrewsbury shops **R**
7/6/40	Swindon Works **L**
9/1/41	Shrewsbury shops **R**
30/9/41	Swindon Works **G**
20/11/43	Swindon Works **L**
25/3/44	Swindon Works **L**
15/5/45	Swindon Works **I**
18/6/46	Hereford shops **R**
17/8/46	Shrewsbury shops **R**
10/2/47	Shrewsbury shops **R**
17/5/47	Shrewsbury shops **R**
10/10/47	Shrewsbury shops **R**
17/12/47	Swindon Works **I**
30/8/48	Shrewsbury shops **R**
14/1/49	Shrewsbury shops **U**
9/10/50	Swindon Works **HG**
18/10/50-4/11/50	Stored at Swindon Works
2/12/50	Oxley
23/9/52	Swindon Works **HG**
7/11/52	Wolverhampton Works **U**
4/2/54	Tyseley shops **U**
8/4/54	Oxley shops **U**
9/2/55	Swindon Works **HI**
14/7/56	Old Oak
31/10/56	Swindon Works **HG**
27/2/58	Gloucester shops **U**
16/5/58	Old Oak shops **U**
24/9/58	Old Oak shops **LC**
10/3/59	Swindon Works **HI**
3/3/61	Swindon Works **HG**
24/11/61	Old Oak shops **LC**
25/5/62	Swindon Works **HC**
6/10/62	Oxford
9/2/63	Swindon
27/1/64	Southall
5/10/64	Worcester

In a livery of pure 'BR Grey' 4919 stands at Southall shed, its brief home near the end, on 5 July 1964. The framing over the tender footplate coal space was primarily fitted to prevent firemen going back into the tender to pull the coal forward and carried the warning 'flash' – see 4946 on page 20. Peter Groom.

DONNINGTON HALL passing West Ealing with motley stock – a parcels train – on 8 June 1962. The smoke behind the signal box is from 7009 ATHELNEY CASTLE in the milk yard waiting to reverse into the station and then come forward to either the Slow or Fast line via the 'ladder'. B.W.L. Brooksbank, Initial Photographics.

4920 DUMBLETON HALL

Built in 1929 to Lot no.254 at Swindon Works
To traffic 21/3/29

Mileages and Boilers

From new	4922
6/6/30	64,591 C4921
1/12/31	133,153 C4921
22/8/33	213,356 C2820
7/2/35	294,415 C2820
18/9/36	363,370 C4973
15/3/38	447,986 C4973
23/10/39	529,903 C4973
10/9/41	602,940 C7213
8/8/43	677,978 C7213
13/9/45	757,067 C2839
6/5/47	821,396 C8206
22/11/49	902,460 C4431
30/4/52	981,747 C4053
18/3/55	1,080,618 C2813
30/5/57	1,157,238 C6200
8/9/59	1,254,162 C8200
3/4/62	1,345,648 C8243

Sheds and Works history

21/3/29	Old Oak
12/5/29	Carmarthen
6/6/30	Swindon Works **L**
	ATC fitted
5/7/30	Truro
20/10/30	Truro shops **L**
14/3/31	Newton Abbot Works **R**
1/12/31	Swindon Works **I**
29/12/31	Old Oak
16/1/32	Oxley
12/3/32	Old Oak
22/8/33	Swindon Works **G**
1933	Oxford
10/3/34	Old Oak
20/10/34	Oxford
7/2/35	Swindon Works **I**
18/9/36	Swindon Works **G**
1/11/37	Oxford shops **R**
15/3/38	Swindon Works **I**
23/10/39	Swindon Works **I**
11/11/39	Canton
21/3/41	Chester shops **R**
10/9/41	Swindon Works **G**
27/4/42	Swindon Works **L**
8/8/43	Swindon Works **I**
27/6/44	Banbury shops **R**
13/9/45	Swindon Works **G**
6/5/47	Swindon Works **I**
17/5/47	Reading
3/11/47	Swindon Works **L**
15/6/48	Old Oak shops **R**
26/8/48	Swindon Works **R**
24/12/48	Swindon Works **L**
22/11/49	Swindon Works **HG**
6/10/51	Reading shops **U**
30/4/52	Swindon Works **HG**
19/1/53	Reading shops **U**
13/6/53	Taunton
20/7/53	Old Oak shops **U**
16/6/54	Taunton shops **U**
17/10/54	Taunton shops **U**
18/3/55	Swindon Works **HI**
27/4/55	Newton Abbot Works **LC**
25/8/56	Taunton shops **U**
4/1/57	Taunton shops **U**
30/5/57	Swindon Works **HG**
21/3/58	Newton Abbot Works **LC**
27/12/58	Newton Abbot
8/9/59	Swindon Works **HI**
16/4/60	Laira
18/12/61	Laira shops **U**
3/4/62	Swindon Works **HG**
21/2/63	Laira shops **U**
7/5/64	Worcester shops **U**
16/5/64	St. Philips Marsh
13/6/64	Barrow Road
20/11/65	Oxford

Tenders

From new	1865
5/5/30	1726
29/9/31	2349
14/5/33	2127
27/12/34	2255
13/8/36	1932
3/2/38	1947
18/9/39	2247
18/10/39	2255
23/12/39	2542
10/7/41	2615
10/9/41	2266
27/4/42	2749
8/8/43	2611
13/9/45	2535
1/4/47	2557
6/9/47	2682
3/11/47	2727
26/8/48	2862
18/10/49	2799
5/11/49	2537
22/11/49	2754
30/4/52	2631
15/2/55	2423
26/.1/57	2417
30/5/57	2714
8/9/59	2771
16/7/60	2536
9/9/61	4041
3/4/62	2717

Mileage at 28/12/63 1,396,966

Withdrawn 27/11/65, Sold to
Woodham Brothers Barry, Engine preserved

DUMBLETON HALL at Oxley shed; this is the period 1953-1958 when 4920 was a Taunton engine, before it transferred to Newton Abbot. J. Davenport, Initial Photographics.

DUMBLETON HALL with a down milk/van train in Sonning cutting, 29 May 1960. Peter Groom.

4921 EATON HALL
Built in 1929 to Lot no.254 at Swindon Works
To traffic 24/4/49

Mileages and Boilers

From new	4915
29/5/30	65,953 C4915
16/12/31	133,636 C4915
23/8/33	207,478 C4914
2/4/35	287,394 C4914
27/8/36	351,397 C2929
7/6/38	432,540 C2929
22/2/40	511,500 C2929
7/7/42	590,026 C2903
8/6/45	672,820 C2903
28/6/47	740,935 C2997
9/2/49	803,015 C2854
20/4/51	879,711 C4047
10/12/53	974,572 C4047
25/4/56	1,056,418 C2946
12/8/58	1,144,683 C2946
17/10/60	1,206,543 C8205

Sheds and Works history

24/4/29	Old Oak
5/1929	Swindon Works **ATC fitted**
29/5/30	Swindon Works **I**
7/6/30	Stafford Road
5/7/30	Oxley
16/12/31	Swindon Works **I**
1933	Oxford
12/4/33	Old Oak shops **R**
23/8/33	Swindon Works **G**
7/11/33	Tyseley shops **R**
8/3/34	Oxford shops **R**
2/4/35	Swindon Works **I**
27/8/36	Swindon Works **G**
18/12/37	Oxford shops **R**
7/6/38	Swindon Works **I**
30/3/39	Swindon Works **L**
16/5/39	Oxford shops **R**
22/2/40	Swindon Works **I**
25/7/40	Oxford shops **R**
11/1941	Old Oak
6/2/42	Bath Road shops **R**
7/7/42	Swindon Works **G**
7/1942	Oxford
9/9/42	Didcot shops **R**
30/5/44	Swindon Works **L**
10/10/44	Old Oak shops **R**
8/6/45	Swindon Works **I**
31/3/46	Oxford shops **R**
10/8/46	Banbury
24/1/47	Oxford shops **R**
22/2/47	Oxford
12/4/47	Oxford shops **R**
28/6/47	Swindon Works **G**
3/8/48	Oxford shops **L**
9/2/49	Swindon Works **G**
19/4/49	Oxford shops **U**
26/9/49	Old Oak shops **U**
20/4/51	Swindon Works **HG**
4/12/52	Old Oak shops **U**
10/12/53	Swindon Works **HI**
1/10/54	Old Oak shops **U**
5/11/54	Swindon Works **U**
26/8/55	Old Oak shops **U**
25/4/56	Swindon Works **HG**
12/8/58	Swindon Works **HI**
1/10/58	Gloucester shops **U**
3/1/59	Tyseley shops **U**
25/2/59	Gloucester Barnwood shops **U**
15/7/59	Wolverhampton Works **LC**
26/12/59	Old Oak
23/4/60	Reading
17/10/60	Swindon Works **HI**

Tenders

From new	1995
28/4/30	1941
6/10/31	1758
29/3/33	2238
30/4/33	1714
13/2/35	1960
6/6/36	2255
2/4/38	2427
7/6/38	2330
30/3/39	2259
22/2/40	2245
8/11/41	2690
21/5/42	2817
30/5/44	2534
7/4/45	2631
4/7/47	2924
7/1/49	2698
4/11/53	2394
9/10/54	2615
9/10/54	4080
5/11/54	2615
26/3/55	4089
25/4/56	2839
12/8/58	2413
17/10/60	2534
11/1962	2590

Final mileage 1,273,602

Withdrawn 21/9/62, Sold to A. King, Norwich 8/11/63

Lined black 4921 EATON HALL at Oxford, 22 June 1954; 4,000 gallon tender, first emblem. M. Robertson, transporttreasury

4922 ENVILLE HALL

Built in 1929 to Lot no.254 at Swindon Works
To traffic 4/5/29

Mileages and Boilers

From new	4917
30/5/30	62,299 C4917
23/12/31	130,653 C4917
27/4/33	194,261 C4971
19/12/34	231,445 C4971
19/6/36	353,387 C4901
11/2/38	438,285 C4901
8/9/39	514,326 C4901
26/3/42	607,586 C4982
13/5/44	681,836 C4982
17/9/46	760,773 C4480
19/5/49	862,582 C4051
14/11/51	960,218 C4935
8/6/54	1,056,138 C7250
12/10/56	1,145,135 C7250
8/1/59	1,131,988 C2988
1/9/61	1,233,169 C4996

Sheds and Works history

4/5/29	Old Oak
5/1929	Swindon Works **ATC fitted**
31/10/29	Swindon Works **R**
30/5/30	Swindon Works **I**
7/6/30	Oxley
23/12/31	Swindon Works **I**
16/1/32	Oxford
27/4/33	Swindon Works **G**
26/6/33	Swindon Works **L**
19/12/34	Swindon Works **I**
19/6/36	Swindon Works **G**
2/10/37	Tyseley shops **R**
11/2/38	Swindon Works **I**
8/9/39	Swindon Works **I**
14/10/40	Tyseley shops **R**
26/3/42	Swindon Works **G**
25/8/42	Old Oak shops **L**
5/1943	Carmarthen
13/5/44	Swindon Works **I**
29/3/46	Swindon Works **L**
17/9/46	Swindon Works **G**
31/3/48	Oxford shops **R**
14/6/48	Carmarthen shops **L**
19/5/49	Swindon Works **HG**
5/7/51	Carmarthen shops **U**
14/11/51	Swindon Works **HI**
8/6/54	Swindon Works **HG**
3/3/55	Carmarthen shops **U**
31/12/55	St. Philips Marsh
12/10/56	Wolverhampton Works **HI**
13/7/57	Bath Road
12/2/58	Bath Road shops **U**
3/4/58	Newton Abbot Works **LC**
8/1/59	Swindon Works **HG**
26/3/60	St. Philips Marsh
1/7/60	Bath Road shops **LC**
16/11/60	St. Philips Marsh shops **U**
1/9/61	Swindon Works **HI**
25/6/63	St. Philips Marsh shops **U**
29/6/63	Oxford

Tenders

From new	2242
26/4/30	1906
24/1/33	2245
8/11/34	1913
13/5/36	1725
1/1/38	2253
8/9/39	1663
30/7/46	2736
19/5/49	2667
16/10/51	2542
1/11/52	2921
8/6/54	2387
3/11/56	4120
8/1/59	2672
1/9/61	2760

Final mileage 1,287,068

Withdrawn 4/7/63, Sold to John Cashmore, Newport 4/11/63

4922 ENVILLE HALL waits at Llanelly on 7 July 1947. The tender side is bare of badge or lettering, as can often be found in this period. Nine tank travelling gas wagon on the right. H.C. Casserley, courtesy R.M. Casserley.

ENVILLE HALL and, presumably, its driver, at Shrewsbury shed on 8 March 1957. Hawksworth 4,000 gallon tender. S.Rickard/ J&J Collection.

4922 out on the road at an unspecified location, though it is alongside the Kennet and Avon Canal; the reporting number indicates an up summer extra from Plymouth. The period is not known either but it's definitely summer! transporttreasury

4923 EVENLEY HALL
Built in 1929 to Lot no.254 at Swindon Works
To traffic 3/5/29

Sheds and Works history
3/5/29	St. Philips Marsh		
20/12/30	Bath Road		
7/5/32	Swindon		
22/10/32	St. Philips Marsh		
1933	Weymouth		
12/12/36	St. Philips Marsh		
23/7/38	Swindon		
4/2/39	Stafford Road		
29/4/39	Oxley		
5/1940	Shrewsbury		
6/1940	Stafford Road		
1/8/42	Swindon Works **L**		
29/4/44	Swindon Works **L**		
10/11/45	Swindon Works **I**	108,809	
29/12/45	St. Blazey		
2/3/46	Tyseley shops **L**		
23/3/46	Bath Road		
17/5/46	Oxley		
18/10/47	Swindon Works **I**	64,858	
19/6/48	Tyseley shops **L**		
27/8/48	Swindon Works **G**	66,336	325,694
27/11/48	Old Oak		
17/3/51	Swindon Works **G**	71,904	71,904
10/10/53	Swindon Works **HI**	111,901	
16/6/56	Landore		
12/12/58	Swindon Works **HG Boiler no.7233**		
26/3/60	Banbury		
18/6/60	Carmarthen		
13/8/60	Stafford Road		
7/10/61	Oxley		
22/1/62	Swindon Works **HI Boiler no.7243**		

Tenders [where known]
3/1935	2353
1936	2330
6/1937	1911
2/1940	2817
6/1942	2417
6/1947	2028
1949	1657
1953	2628
1956	2420

Withdrawn 5/64

4923 EVENLEY HALL at Bristol Temple Meads; larger, box-like cover to the lubricator feed valve cover on the boiler/smokebox. The period is 1947-48, with BR smokebox door number plate and GW with badge on the 4,000 gallon tender. M. Robertson, transporttreasury

4923 EVENLEY HALL at Platform 12, Birmingham Snow Hill, waiting to leave with an up parcels train on 28 March 1961. Michael Mensing.

4923 EVENLEY HALL at Abergavenny Junction station about 1957 with another of those dodgy reporting number frames; pannier 6433 waits with a local. Stan Brown/D.K. Jones Collection.

4924 EYDON HALL
Built in 1929 to Lot no.254 at Swindon Works
To traffic 4/5/29

Mileages and Boilers

From new	4919
1/7/30	68,362 C4919
28/10/31	132,216 C4919
31/10/33	225,386 C4941
15/3/35	301,511 C2812
11/11/36	381,274 C2812
18/3/38	445,544 C4492
23/1/40	521,221 C4492
9/10/42	615,327 C4492
7/6/44	660,405 C4983
2/2/46	706,945 C4983
19/9/47	758,329 C8291
3/11/49	832,771 C2986
17/12/51	917,691 C4977
9/12/53	1,005,813 C2967
20/3/56	1,089,215 C7272
14/4/58	1,181,854 C4470
13/3/61	1,289,717 C2850

Sheds and Works history

4/5/29	Old Oak
5/1929	Swindon Works **ATC fitted**
1/7/30	Swindon Works **I**
2/8/30	Goodwick
25/4/31	Goodwick shops **R**
28/10/31	Swindon Works **I**
21/11/31	Oxford
19/11/32	Didcot shops **R**
1933	Stafford Road
31/10/33	Swindon Works **G**
10/2/34	Chester
15/3/35	Swindon Works **G**
6/4/35	Tyseley
6/2/36	Oxford shops **R**
11/11/36	Swindon Works **I**
18/3/38	Swindon Works **G**
12/11/38	Leamington Spa
10/12/38	Tyseley
14/10/39	Banbury
11/11/39	Tyseley
23/1/40	Swindon Works **I**
19/12/40	Tyseley shops **R**
7/10/41	Tyseley shops **R**
9/10/42	Tyseley shops **I**
7/6/44	Swindon Works **L**
31/8/45	Westbury shops **R**
2/2/46	Wolverhampton Works **I**
13/7/46	Leamington Spa
10/8/46	Tyseley
9/6/47	Tyseley shops **R**
19/9/47	Swindon Works **G**
17/7/48	Tyseley shops **R**
3/11/49	Swindon Works **HG**
2/6/51	Gloucester shops **U**
7/12/51	Swindon Works **HG**
27/12/52	Oxley
9/12/53	Swindon Works **HG**
21/3/55	Tyseley shops **LC**
16/7/55	Landore
8/10/55	Bath Road
20/3/56	Swindon Works **HI**
4/12/56	Newton Abbot Works **U**
13/7/57	Laira
5/10/57	Truro
2/11/57	Banbury
14/4/58	Swindon Works **HG**
11/7/59	Taunton
21/5/60	Exeter
8/10/60	Taunton
5/11/60	Exeter
13/3/61	Swindon Works **HI**
6/3/62	St. Blazey shops **U**
14/7/62	Shrewsbury
1/10/62	Ebbw Jct. Shops **U**
3/11/62	Swindon

Tenders

From new	2243
20/5/30	2380
7/1931	1717
13/9/31	2250
21/9/33	2249
20/1/35	2244
31/1/38	2738
23/1/40	2430
18/8/42	2886
24/2/44	2403
7/6/44	2260
19/9/47	2593
21/9/49	2783
16/11/51	2644
3/11/53	2411
20/3/56	2401
14/4/58	2878
13/3/61	2613

Final mileage 1,364,143

Withdrawn 3/10/63, Sold to Messrs. Coopers Ltd. Swindon 31/12/63

4924 EYDON HALL taking coal at Shrewsbury shed on 6 August 1960. If the date is correct, 4924 has been an Exeter engine for some weeks, though it still carries its 84C Banbury plate. D. Preston, ColourRail

4924 in the shed yard at Swindon, thoroughly begrimed, 16 May 1962. transporttreasury

4925 EYNSHAM HALL

Built in 1929 to Lot no.254 at Swindon Works
To traffic 11/5/29

Mileages and Boilers

From new	4920
13/5/30	60,182 C4920
8/1/32	134,752 C2951
8/12/33	226,460 C4962
20/6/35	308,437 C4962
6/5/36	356,772 C4954
22/3/37	398,863 C4954
18/11/38	479,060 C4954
29/3/41	599,737 C4954
15/2/44	661,651 C2863
24/11/45	725,838 C2950
20/9/48	807,631 C7254
21/2/51	901,906 C7238
9/1053	1,002,095 C7238
19/9/95	1,077,063 C2922
2/8/57	1,147,546 C7209
17/12/59	1,236,329 C2984

Sheds and Works history

11/5/29	Old Oak
5/1929	Swindon Works **ATC fitted**
13/5/30	Swindon Works **I**
7/6/30	Carmarthen
30/8/30	Carmarthen shops **R**
21/7/31	Carmarthen shops **R**
8/1/32	Swindon Works **G**
12/3/32	Old Oak
9/4/32	Oxford
24/1/33	Swindon Works **L**
8/12/33	Swindon Works **G**
15/2/34	Reading shops **R**
20/6/35	Swindon Works **I**
29/6/35	Bath Road
6/5/36	Swindon Works **I**
25/7/36	St. Philips Marsh
23/3/37	Swindon Works **I**
19/1/38	St. Philips Marsh shops **R**
26/8/38	Ebbw Jct. shops **L**
18/11/38	Swindon Works **I**
10/12/38	Weymouth
29/3/41	Swindon Works **I**
21/2/42	Weymouth shops **R**
3/1942	Swindon
24/12/42	Swindon Works **L**
15/2/44	Swindon Works **G**
24/11/45	Swindon Works **I**
23/5/46	Swindon Works **L**
9/7/47	Didcot shops **R**
17/10/47	Newton Abbot Works **L**
22/6/48	Swindon Works **L**
20/9/48	Swindon Works **G**
14/10/50	Swindon shed **U**
11/12/50	Swindon shed **U**
21/2/51	Swindon Works **HG**
15/3/51	Swindon Works **U**
14/4/51	Swindon Works **U**
11/10/51	Swindon Works **U**
25/4/52	Swindon Works **U**
9/10/53	Swindon Works **HI**
12/7/54	Swindon Works **U**
19/9/55	Swindon Works **HG**
14/3/56	Swindon Works **U**
1/12/56	Old Oak
18/4/57	Old Oak shops **U**
2/8/57	Swindon Works **HG**
23/1/58	Bath Road shops **U**
19/4/58	Southall
22/1/59	Southall shops **U**
17/12/59	Swindon Works **HG**
17/9/60	Old Oak shops **U**
23/3/62	Southall shops **U**

Tenders

From new	1939
1/4/30	1933
11/1930	1677
24/11/31	1457
11/1932	2005
31/1/33	1979
8/12/33	2247
19/2/37	2236
17/10/38	1945
29/3/41	1915
18/12/43	2645
24/11/44	2641
20/3/46	2862
28/6/48	2753
13/10/50	2722
16/1/51	2673
15/4/52	2781
24/8/53	2652
9/8/55	2867
14/9/55	2644
14/3/56	2837
2/8/57	2904
23/2/58	2536
27/12/58	2555
17/12/59	2905

Final mileage 1,323,110

Withdrawn 7/8/62, Cut up 8/9/62

4925 EYNSHAM HALL by the yards at 'Moreton Cutting' (here actually an embankment) near Didcot, 4 July 1953. R.C. Riley, transporttreasury

4926 FAIRLEIGH HALL
Built in 1929 to Lot no.254 at Swindon Works
To traffic 16/5/29

Mileages and Boilers

From new	4921
9/5/30	58,399 C4921
3/9/31	120,297 C4921
28/6/32	160,983 C4920
18/4/34	240,178 C4923
8/5/36	319,834 C4923
10/3/38	395,383 C4925
25/11/39	476,877 C4925
27/6/42	570,057 C4925
2/3/44	614,358 C4974
6/3/46	665,258 C2847
28/6/48	740,353 C4948
22/5/50	794,855 C2939
9/8/51	837,636 C2939
1/7/53	895,624 C7280
22/6/54	930,739 C4906
15/9/55	981,804 C4420
31/12/56	1,033,366 C2984
22/5/59	1,122,526 C8239

Sheds and Works history

16/5/29	Old Oak
5/1929	Swindon Works **ATC fitted**
9/5/30	Swindon Works **I**
7/6/30	Laira
4/11/30	Laira shops **L**
3/9/31	Swindon Works **I**
26/9/31	Newton Abbot
23/1/32	Newton Abbot Works **R**
28/6/32	Swindon Works **G**
30/7/32	Penzance
22/10/32	Laira
19/11/32	Penzance
18/2/33	Penzance shops **R**
12/6/33	Newton Abbot Works **R**
30/9/33	Penzance shops **R**
30/11/33	Penzance shops **R**
18/4/34	Swindon Works **G**
3/5/34	Taunton Shops **R**
9/5/34	Newton Abbot Works **R**
2/6/34	Truro
2/8/34	Laira shops **R**
15/2/35	Newton Abbot Works **L**
21/3/35	Laira shops **R**
18/6/35	Newton Abbot Works **R**
11/10/35	Newton Abbot Works **L**
8/5/36	Swindon Works **I**
30/5/36	Westbury
15/9/37	Swindon Works **L**
10/3/38	Swindon Works **G**
8/4/38	Swindon Works **L**
25/11/39	Swindon Works **I**
3/1940	Bath Road
7/2/41	Bath Road shops **R**
26/6/41	Bath Road shops **R**
17/11/41	Bath Road shops **R**
19/3/42	Bath Road shops **R**
3/1942	St. Philips Marsh
27/6/42	Swindon Works **I**
7/1942	Westbury
22/2/43	Westbury shops **R**
2/3/44	Swindon Works **L**
6/3/46	Swindon Works **G**
12/2/47	Westbury shops **R**
5/6/47	Westbury shops **R**
3/12/47	Westbury shops **R**
23/3/48	Westbury shops **R**
28/6/48	Swindon Works **I**
15/8/49	Westbury shops **U**
22/5/50	Swindon Works **HC**
9/8/51	Swindon Works **HI**
23/8/51	Swindon Works **U**

23/8/51	Swindon Works **U**
	Hot box
29/11/52	Oxley
1/7/53	Swindon Works **HC**
9/4/54	Tyseley shops **U**
22/6/54	Swindon Works **HI**
14/8/54	Stafford Road
29/11/54	Tyseley shops **U**
15/9/55	Swindon Works **HC**
31/12/56	Swindon Works **HG**
2/2/57	Shrewsbury LM shops **U**
22/2/58	Worcester
17/5/58	Pontypool Road
22/5/59	Caerphilly Works **HG**
21/9/59	Ebbw Jct. shops **LC**

Tenders

From new	2244
31/3/30	2224
17/6/31	1952
19/8/37	2374
24/10/39	2325
16/5/42	2689
22/8/43	2635
10/12/45	2789
28/6/48	2562
25/5/50	2599
16/6/51	2386
24/4/53	2414
24/5/54	2555
15/9/55	2561
31/12/56	2762

Final mileage 1,200,131

Withdrawn 25/9/61, Cut up 4/11/61

4926 FAIRLEIGH HALL with the 12 noon Wolverhampton-Paddington via Worcester at Stourbridge Junction on 22 October 1953. P.Bland, transporttreasury

4926, smart in lined green but with original lion and wheel (an unusual combination) at Oxford on 8 June 1957. H.C. Casserley, courtesy R.M. Casserley.

4927 FARNBOROUGH HALL

Built in 1929 to Lot no.254 at Swindon Works
To traffic 21/5/29

Mileages and Boilers

From new	4926
24/6/30	63,131 C4926
4/12/31	141,197 C4926
6/7/32	160,619 C4943
16/10/33	216,007 C4909
29/4/35	299,152 C4909
20/11/36	385,660 C4914
29/4/38	461,267 C4914
23/5/40	544,021 C4914
10/9/42	628,951 C4914
11/11/44	706,830 C7230
22/5/47	794,399 C2839
30/11/49	875,694 C4422
22/10/51	956,665 C8238
23/9/52	984,643 C4956
23/3/54	1,047,719 C4938
5/4/56	1,148,129 C4900
29/4/58	1,241,036 C4900
14/3/61	1,336,093 C4445

Sheds and Works history

21/5/29	Old Oak
6/1929	Swindon Works **ATC fitted**
7/6/30	Laira
24/6/30	Swindon Works **I**
4/12/31	Swindon Works **I**
16/1/32	Reading
6/7/32	Swindon Works **L**
28/4/33	Reading shops **R**
16/10/33	Swindon Works **G**
1933	Canton
29/4/35	Swindon Works **I**
30/11/36	Swindon Works **G**
25/1/38	Canton shops **R**
29/4/38	Swindon Works **I**
26/6/38	Weymouth
23/5/40	Swindon Works **I**
8/2/41	Weymouth shops **R**
19/12/41	Weymouth shops **R**
10/9/42	Swindon Works **I**
11/11/44	Swindon Works **G**
2/1945	St. Philips Marsh
26/10/45	Bath Road shops **L**
22/5/47	Swindon Works **I**
14/6/47	Westbury
26/9/48	Westbury shops **R**
7/9/49	Westbury shops **U**
30/11/49	Swindon Works **HG**
22/10/51	Swindon Works **HG**
23/9/52	Swindon Works **HC**
23/3/54	Swindon Works **HG**
5/4/56	Swindon Works **HG**
6/10/56	Bath Road
13/8/57	Worcester shops **U**
29/4/58	Swindon Works **HI**
2/7/59	Swindon Works **LC**
8/8/59	Severn Tunnel Jct.
18/6/60	Neath
14/3/61	Swindon Works **HG**
19/5/61	Swindon shed **U**
27/1/62	Goodwick
16/6/62	Llanelly

Tenders

From new	2240
12/5/30	2136
15/8/33	2250
13/3/35	2330
12/10/36	2369
16/3/38	2573
17/4/40	2442
25/7/42	2229
18/9/44	2141
23/2/46	2134
22/5/47	2798
27/10/49	2608
24/9/51	2536
30/7/52	2883
17/2/54	2934
26/8/55	2585
5/4/56	2421
19/5/56	2730
27/1/58	2918
2/7/59	2588
14/3/61	2630

Mileage 1,416,636

Withdrawn 23/9/63

Sold to G. Cohen Ltd. Morriston 1/1/64

4927 FARNBOROUGH HALL at the east end of the Reception Shed at Swindon Works after one of a series of repairs in the early 1950s. Smokebox and cylinders painted shiny black after attention, while the boiler looks little different from the day 4927 came in – a 'part paint' job in fact. Tender also painted, but unlined without any emblem, suggesting the period might be quite early on, 1949 perhaps.

4927 FARNBOROUGH HALL in what looks like lined black, at Exeter St David's with the boiler/smokebox/tender in the very reverse condition to the previous view. J. Robertson, transporttreasury

4928 GATACRE HALL

Built in 1929 to lot no.254 at Swindon Works
To traffic 12/6/29

Mileages and Boilers

From new	4927
26/8/30	59,197 C4927
13/1/32	118,747 C4049
27/12/33	204,694 C4049
19/10/34	248,586 C4948
21/4/36	305,719 C4948
14/1/38	393,617 C4970
13/11/39	485,034 C4970
14/5/42	572,454 C4970
14/7/44	641,383 C3002
14/11/46	723,907 C7229
10/9/48	786,098 C7255
8/3/51	873,836 C8287
10/8/53	966,441 C8249
15/12/55	1,057,123 C2925
20/8/58	1,140,983 C4988
4/8/61	1,259,726 C7204

Sheds and Works history

6/1929	Swindon Works **ATC fitted**
12/6/29	Stafford Road
4/8/29	Oxley
15/3/30	Shrewsbury
12/4/30	Oxley
26/8/30	Swindon Works **I**
19/12/30	Swindon Works **L**
13/1/32	Swindon Works **G**
13/2/32	Old Oak
10/2/33	Swindon Works **L**
27/12/33	Swindon Works **I**
13/1/34	Worcester
19/10/34	Swindon Works **L**
21/4/36	Swindon Works **I**
2/5/36	Old Oak
12/10/37	Taunton shops **R**
14/1/38	Swindon Works **G**
12/11/38	Oxford
29/4/39	Old Oak
27/5/39	Oxford
13/11/39	Swindon Works **I**
9/12/39	Chester
17/10/41	Ebbw Jct. shops **L**
14/5/42	Swindon Works **I**
14/7/44	Swindon Works **G**
14/11/46	Swindon Works **I**
10/9/48	Swindon Works **G**
3/1/51	Oxford shops **U**
8/3/51	Swindon Works **HI**
10/8/53	Swindon Works **HG**
9/10/54	Swindon
15/12/55	Swindon Works **HI**
27/6/56	Weymouth shops **U**
1/12/56	Old Oak
26/1/57	Didcot
23/2/57	Taunton
19/6/57	Taunton shops **U**
10/8/57	Laira
28/9/57	Laira shops **U**
5/10/57	Truro
6/11/57	Newton Abbot Works **LC**
12/7/58	Laira
20/8/58	Swindon Works **HG**
31/10/59	Cardiff Canton
19/1/60	Caerphilly Works **LC**
4/8/61	Swindon Works **HI**
16/6/62	Llanelly
9/2/63	Duffryn Yard
14/3/63	Duffryn Yard shops **U**

Tenders

From new	2246
18/6/30	2217
17/11/31	1979
31/12/32	1825
18/10/33	2380
3/3/36	2233
2/5/36	2422
1/12/37	2239
30/3/42	2937
18/5/44	1655
14/11/46	2803
20/7/48	2760
3/2/51	2757
24/6/59	2646
15/12/55	2916
2/11/57	2755
20/8/58	2766
4/8/61	2854

Mileage 1,339,378

Withdrawn 2/12/63

4928 GATACRE HALL in late Great Western days; low tender, with GREAT WESTERN and a badge faintly visible under the grime. The ATC ducting along the running plate is curved around something just above the cylinder. F.H. Stingemore, transporttreasury

Now in BR times with 4,000 gallon tender, in lined black, at Oxford station on 18 September 1954. Vacuum pump lubricator now removed from position by leading splasher. M. Robertson, transporttreasury

4929 GOYTREY HALL

Built in 1929 to Lot no.254 at Swindon Works
To traffic 14/6/29

Mileages and Boilers

From new	4928
26/9/30	67,756 C4928
20/5/31	96,197 R2901
19/10/32	171,048 R2901
19/4/34	240,317 R2901
27/2/36	335,179 C3004
23/12/37	428,122 C3004
12/1/40	516,088 C4989
21/5/42	621,427 C4989
17/5/44	690,607 C4954
7/11/45	743,351 C4076
24/11/47	818,278 C8201
2/12/49	895,953 C2893
27/2/52	986,342 C4020
16/8/54	1,079,582 R6218
28/9/56	1,163,561 R6218
13/3/59	1,242,745 C2844
16/2/62	1,340,728 C2957

Sheds and Works history

6/1929	Swindon Works **ATC fitted**
14/6/29	Stafford Road
29/9/29	Shrewsbury
22/12/29	Cardiff Canton
26/9/30	Swindon Works **H**
25/10/30	Gloucester
20/5/31	Swindon Works **L**
19/10/32	Swindon Works **I**
19/11/32	Weymouth
19/4/34	Swindon Works **I**
5/5/34	Laira
28/8/34	Newton Abbot Works **L**
20/10/34	Penzance
21/5/35	Newton Abbot Works **L**
27/2/36	Swindon Works **G**
7/3/36	Newton Abbot
30/5/36	Truro
19/5/37	Newton Abbot Works **L**
23/12/37	Swindon Works **I**
3/9/38	Swindon Works **L**
20/10/38	Truro shops **R**
3/4/39	Newton Abbot Works **R**
22/5/39	Newton Abbot Works **L**
12/1/40	Swindon Works **G**
29/8/40	Truro shops **R**
14/5/41	Truro shops **R**
13/6/41	Newton Abbot Works **L**
21/5/42	Swindon Works **I**
2/6/43	Truro shops **R**
13/11/43	Newton Abbot Works **L**
17/5/44	Swindon Works **L**
21/9/44	Truro shops **R**
24/6/45	Truro shops **R**
7/11/45	Swindon Works **I**
27/7/46	Truro shops **R**
30/3/47	Truro shops **R**
18/6/47	Newton Abbot Works **L**
4/9/47	Newton Abbot Works **L**
24/11/47	Swindon Works **G**
4/3/49	Newton Abbot Works **LC**
25/5/49	Truro shops **U**
9/9/49	Newton Abbot Works **U**
2/12/49	Swindon Works **HG**
22/4/50	St. Philips Marsh
17/6/50	Neyland
12/8/50	Gloucester
27/2/52	Swindon Works **HI**
24/6/53	Swindon Works **LC**
16/8/54	Swindon Works **HG**
13/1/56	Old Oak shops **U**
28/9/56	Wolverhampton Works **HI**
6/3/58	Wolverhampton Works **LC**
3/6/58	Gloucester shops **LC**
13/3/59	Swindon Works **HG**
6/3/61	Gloucester shops **U**
16/2/62	Swindon Works **HI**
6/3/62	St. Blazey shops **U**
13/11/63	Swindon shed **U**

Tenders

From new	2228
7/8/30	2249
9/4/31	2265
6/3/34	2253
15/1/36	1765
13/11/39	2381
1/12/39	2660
15/4/42	2397
30/1/43	2598
1/9/45	2810
24/11/47	2585
26/1/49	2401
18/6/49	2416
2/12/49	2415
30/1/52	2846
9/5/53	2531
26/6/54	2575
24/7/54	2525
14/12/55	2589
28/12/56	2248
25/4/58	2795
12/3/59	2545
12/8/60	4031
16/2/62	2673

Mileage as at 28/12/63 1,397,264

Withdrawn 3/65

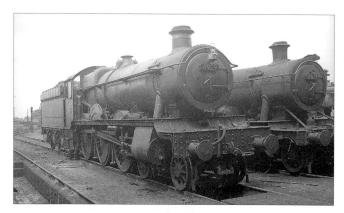

4929 GOYTREY HALL at Gloucester shed, 2-8-0 3817 alongside, in 1952. It had gone there in 1950 and stayed a Gloucester engine right to the end, in 1965. Michael Boakes Collection.

J.L. Stevenson, courtesy Hamish Stevenson.

4929 GOYTREY HALL pilots 6934 BEACHAMWELL HALL up Stoneycombe bank west of Aller Junction on a train for Penzance, 16 July 1955. Les Elsey.

A lovely murky Last Days portrait of a typically filthy Hall; Worcester shed, 12 October 1964. J.L. Stevenson, courtesy Hamish Stevenson.

4930 HAGLEY HALL

Built in 1929 to Lot no.254 at Swindon Works
To traffic 11/6/29

Mileages and Boilers

From new	4929
31/10/30	69,547 C4929
27/4/32	130,091 C4924
3/2/34	209,378 C4954
1/1/36	302,812 C4926
16/9/37	381,940 C4926
11/10/39	461,711 C3001
30/5/42	553,187 C3001
14/8/43	585,062 C4994
14/12/44	627,858 C4994
20/8/45	644,091 C2900
21/11/47	706,414 C4462
13/3/50	791,688 C8204
2/10/52	882,555 C4473
31/3/55	982,230 C2860
18/12/56	1,056,331 C4437
11/9/58	1,138,809 C4437
13/4/61	1,217,568 C8247

Sheds and Works history

6/1929	Swindon Works **ATC**
11/6/29	Stafford Road
27/10/29	Oxley
15/5/30	Oxley shops **L**
31/10/30	Swindon Works **I**
22/11/30	St. Philips Marsh
27/4/32	Swindon Works **G**
15/6/32	Swindon Works **Experimental**
2/7/32	Oxley
26/4/33	Wolverhampton Works **L**
3/2/34	Swindon Works **G**
2/6/34	Stafford Road
9/2/35	Oxley
7/8/35	Weymouth shops **R**
1/1/36	Swindon Works **G**
11/1/36	Chester
21/4/37	Wolverhampton Works **R**
16/9/37	Swindon Works **I**
16/10/37	Oxley
2/9/38	Wolverhampton Works **L**
12/9/39	Wolverhampton Works **R**
11/10/39	Swindon Works **G**
11/11/39	Tyseley
18/10/40	Tyseley shops **R**
12/2/41	Wolverhampton Works **I**
30/5/42	Swindon Works **I**
2/11/42	Tyseley shops **R**
11/1942	Leamington Spa
12/1942	Tyseley
14/8/43	Swindon Works **L**
24/3/44	Oxford shops **R**
14/12/44	Swindon Works **I**
20/8/45	Swindon Works **L**
8/11/46	Old Oak shops **R**
5/3/47	Tyseley shops **R**
21/11/47	Swindon Works **G**
11/8/48	Wolverhampton Works **L**
27/11/48	St. Philips Marsh
25/12/48	Weymouth
2/8/49	Swindon Works **LC**
13/3/50	Swindon Works **HG**
3/6/51	Weymouth shops **U**
14/11/51	Newton Abbot Works **LC**
23/2/52	Bath Road
14/6/52	St. Philips Marsh
2/10/52	Swindon Works **HG**
23/2/53	St. Philips Marsh shops **U**
3/10/53	Westbury
31/3/55	Swindon Works **HI**
22/12/55	Bath Road shops **LC**
24/1/56	Taunton shops **U**
18/12/56	Swindon Works **HG**
8/10/57	Westbury shops **U**
17/5/58	Taunton
11/9/58	Wolverhampton Works **HI**
22/5/59	Wolverhampton Works **HC**
31/10/59	Canton
6/3/60	Canton shops **U**
21/5/60	Exeter
8/10/60	Taunton
5/11/60	Exeter
13/4/61	Swindon Works **HG**
31/10/61	Taunton shops **U**
14/7/62	Old Oak
6/10/62	Swindon

Tenders

From new	2247
8/1930	2021
27/8/30	2361
5/3/32	1773
21/5/32	2384
15/6/32	1773
25/11/33	2251
20/7/35	2436
9/12/35	2251
23/7/37	2257
14/9/39	2141
30/5/42	2851
28/4/43	2702
3/10/44	2412
20/8/45	2318
21/11/47	2706
2/8/49	1509
12/3/50	2930
3/9/52	2706
28/2/55	2711
18/12/56	2617
13/4/61	2407

Mileage 1,295,236

**Withdrawn 2/12/63, Sold to Woodham
Brothers, Barry 30/4/64
Engine preserved**

4930 HAGLEY HALL waits to leave Paddington; the date is not known but the 83B plate means it is one of the two short periods 4930 was at Taunton, from May 1958-May 1960 or for a month or two later in 1960. P. Moffat, ColourRail

4930 when it was a Westbury loco, coming into St Fagans from the east on 4 May 1956. D.K. Jones Collection.

4931 HANBURY HALL

Built in 1929 to Lot no.254 at Swindon Works
To traffic 10/6/29

Mileages and Boilers

From new	4930
12/9/30	68,355 C4930
10/12/31	120,452 R2919
4/12/33	212,324 R2919
14/8/35	289,071 R4988
27/5/37	375,351 C4956
7/2/39	447,835 C4956
1/5/41	529,587 C4956
16/11/43	614,538 C7234
7/6/46	697,404 C4960
23/9/47	734,950 C2866
7/12/49	806,877 C2910
29/5/51	865,323 C8277
3/3/54	962,952 C8277
8/8/56	1,050,404 C6202
26/9/58	1,151,995 C6202
11/7/60	1,222,699 C4066

Sheds and Works history

6/1929	Swindon Works **ATC fitted**
10/6/29	Stafford Road
27/10/29	Chester
12/9/30	Swindon Works **I**
27/9/30	Oxley
10/12/31	Swindon Works **G**
13/2/32	Stafford Road
14/10/32	Swindon Works **R**
1933	Banbury
4/12/33	Swindon Works **I**
7/4/35	St. Philips Marsh
14/8/35	Swindon Works **G**
24/8/35	Banbury
27/6/36	Leamington Spa
14/11/36	Stafford Road
6/2/37	Oxley
27/5/37	Swindon Works **G**
26/6/37	Weymouth
16/10/37	Reading
7/2/39	Swindon Works **I**
13/11/40	Reading shops **R**
1/5/41	Swindon Works **I**
15/8/42	Swindon Works **L**
26/9/42	Reading shops **R**
24/3/43	Reading shops **R**
16/11/43	Swindon Works **G**
6/7/44	Reading shops **R**
24/10/44	Reading shops **R**
29/9/45	Reading shops **R**
7/6/46	Swindon Works **I**
13/2/47	Reading shops **R**
16/5/47	Old Oak shops **R**
23/9/47	Swindon Works **L**
10/4/48	Swindon Works **R**
2/7/48	Bath Road shops **R**
4/8/48	Old Oak shed **R**
7/12/49	Swindon Works **HG**
27/1/51	Southall
29/5/51	Swindon Works **HG**
2/5/52	Swindon Works **LC**
4/10/52	Southall shed **U**
3/3/54	Swindon Works **HI**
9/12/55	Taunton shops **U**
1/1/55	Penzance
8/8/56	Swindon Works **HG**
26/9/58	Swindon Works **HI**
31/10/59	Canton
11/7/60	Swindon Works **HG**
19/12/60	St. Philips Marsh shops **U**

Tenders

From new	2248
20/9/32	1914
7/1933	2341
23/9/33	1834
4/12/33	2374
3/8/35	1933
27/5/37	1871
7/2/39	2423
9/3/41	2417
29/6/42	2700
17/9/43	2588
7/6/46	2593
10/8/47	2404
3/12/49	2626
7/12/49	2393
30/12/53	2691
8/8/56	4103
9/8/58	2604
26/10/58	2633
8/1959	2881
11/7/60	2974

Mileage 1,300,002

Withdrawn 13/7/62, Sold to R S Hayes Ltd Bridgend 1/10/62

With Hawksworth tender and later style lubricator valve cover, at Penzance shed 2 June 1957. ColourRail

And a few weeks later, in more or less the same spot, on 22 July 1957. This time the engine in the background is Grange 6826 rather than mogul 6397. J. Davenport, Initial Photographics.

4932 HATHERTON HALL

Built in 1929 to Lot no.254 at Swindon Works
To traffic 13/6/29

Mileages and Boilers

From new	4931
16/10/30	63,781 C4931
22/4/32	136,991 C4945
6/2/34	211,491 C4421
25/11/35	295,867 C4421
6/2/37	347,290 C4957
14/10/37	374,348 C4957
28/9/39	473,053 C4957
22/12/41	562,909 C7200
17/3/45	667,136 C7200
1/11/46	739,464 C4949
26/11/48	811,717 C4098
26/1/51	885,976 C4911
10/2/53	971,489 C4418
18/2/55	1,047,505 C4418
28/5/57	1,134,850 C7260
19/2/59	1,207,083 C7260
20/11/61	1,300,103 C4999

Sheds and Works history

6/1929	Swindon Works **ATC**
13/6/29	Stafford Road
27/10/29	Tyseley
24/11/29	Oxley
15/2/30	Shrewsbury
8/3/30	Wolverhampton Works **R**
15/3/30	Oxley
16/10/30	Swindon Works **I**
25/10/30	Weymouth
22/4/32	Swindon Works **G**
7/5/32	St. Philips Marsh
30/7/32	Westbury
6/2/34	Swindon Works **G**
17/11/34	Swindon
25/5/35	Hereford shops **R**
25/11/35	Swindon Works **I**
14/12/35	Westbury
11/5/36	Swindon Works **L**
1/7/36	Oxford shops **R**
6/2/37	Swindon Works **L**
14/10/37	Swindon Works **I**
13/11/37	Laira
23/2/39	Newton Abbot Works **L**
28/9/39	Swindon Works **I**
11/11/39	Truro shops **R**
19/3/41	Laira shops **R**
5/1941	Pontypool Road
20/6/41	Pontypool Road shops **R**
22/12/41	Swindon Works **G**
22/4/42	Swindon Works **R**
22/7/43	Swindon Works **R**
7/1/44	Pontypool Road shops **R**
17/3/45	Swindon Works **I**
1/11/46	Swindon Works **G**
12/9/47	Worcester shed **R**
26/11/48	Swindon Works **G**
4/11/50	Bath Road shops **U**
2/12/50	St Philips Marsh
26/1/51	Swindon Works **HI**
27/1/51	Exeter
1/11/52	Taunton
10/2/53	Swindon Works **HG**
5/7/54	Taunton shops **U**
18/2/55	Newton Abbot Works **HI**
14/3/56	St. Blazey shops **U**
25/9/56	Taunton shops **U**
28/5/57	Swindon Works **HG**
19/2/59	Swindon Works **HI**
12/1/60	Newton Abbot Works **LC**
20/11/61	Swindon Works **HG**
9/10/62	Taunton shops **U**
5/10/64	Neath
7/11/64	Severn Tunnel Jct.

Tenders

From new	2021
8/1930	2247
4/9/30	2377
22/2/32	1763
30/11/33	2141
15/10/35	2267
28/9/39	2797
1/11/41	2748
25/6/63	2414
8/3/45	2734
4/11/46	2817
21/10/48	2167
9/9/50	2556
21/12/50	2821
6/1/53	2596
28/5/57	2805
19/2/59	2759
20/11/61	2893

Mileage at 28/12/63 1,359,393

Withdrawn 11/64

A lined black 4932 HATHERTON HALL at Old Oak Common, 12 August 1956. W. Hermiston, transporttreasury

HATHERTON HALL at Kingskerwell station, date unknown; the plate 83B Taunton reveals little, for 4932 was there all through the 1950s and a 4,000 gallon Collett tender seems to have accompanied her throughout. Only through the second emblem is it possible to declare it post-1956. J. Davenport, Initial Photographics.

4933 HIMLEY HALL

Built in 1929 to Lot no.254 at Swindon Works
To traffic 20/6/29

Sheds and Works history

20/6/29	Bath Road		
27/10/29	St. Philips Marsh		
20/12/30	Bath Road		
12/3/32	Weymouth		
1933	Penzance		
21/9/35	Oxford		
26/6/37	Gloucester		
24/7/37	Worcester		
16/10/37	Gloucester		
5/1942	Pontypool Road		
9/1/43	Wolverhampton Works **I**	123,532	
18/3/44	Newton Abbot Works **L**		
24/3/45	Swindon Works **L**		
14/9/46	Swindon Works **G**	115,629	411,023
5/10/46	Carmarthen		
4/12/48	Pontypool Road **L**		
11/6/49	Swindon Works **HG**	93,744	93,744
18/6/49	Pontypool Road		
20/1/51	Swindon Works **HC**		
22/12/51	Swindon Works **HI**	87,952	
29/12/51	Westbury		
9/8/52	Oxford		
10/4/54	Swindon Works **HG**	82,219	170,171
8/10/55	Didcot		
5/10/57	Worcester		
25/1/58	Leamington Spa		
6/9/58	Westbury		
14/12/58	Swindon Works **HG**		
15/2/59	Swindon Works **U**		
17/11/62	Taunton		
6/7/63	Tyseley		
5/10/63	Shrewsbury		

Withdrawn 8/64

Some works info available is from the GWR 'Repair History' card, early 1940s to 1954.
Mileage figures =
First column: 'Miles run since previous repair'
Second column: 'Miles run since last "general"'

4933 HIMLEY HALL at Old Oak Common, 15 March 1959. J.A.C. Kirke, transporttreasury

4933 HIMLEY HALL passing Kidderminster (the station is lost in the background) with the 4.55pm for Worcester, 28 February 1964. Behind the tender is one of the distinctive six-wheel Palethorpes vans conveying (classically) sausages from the firm's factory near Tipton. Palethorpes had ordinary box vans and bogie vehicles but these six-wheelers were the ones most closely associated with the firm; there were only six, built in 1936 by the LMS and GWR at Wolverton and Swindon respectively. They were insulated and kept cool by air circulated from ice bunkers in the roof. They were readily recognisable in their maroon/ brown livery with the company name very prominent and a large picture of a pack of sausages emblazoned on the panels at one end. By 1964 the sausage maker had moved much of its output to lorries and the traffic ceased altogether in 1965, perhaps the last commercial vehicles to run in passenger trains. ColourRail

Entering Westbury station from the west, with a South Coast-South Wales train, 16 April 1963. Hamish Stevenson.

4934 HINDLIP HALL

Built in 1929 to Lot no.254 at Swindon Works
To traffic 20/6/29

Mileages and Boilers

from new	4938
30/9/30	63,470 C4938
18/4/32	129,081 C4930
18/2/34	209,447 C4930
1/8/35	285,855 C4930
23/6/36	328,323 R7204
26/7/37	375,754 R7204
24/10/39	460,232 C4986
19/6/42	551,038 C4986
17/1/45	631,722 C7257
10/12/46	691,693 C2830
16/9/48	754,372 C7245
5/1/50	803,282 C4919
1/2/52	875,532 C2930
8/10/54	966,616 C2829
14/12/56	1,054,047 C2829
18/8/59	1,133,450 C2838

Sheds and Works history

20/6/29	Bath Road
7/1929	Swindon Works **ATC**
27/10/29	St. Philips Marsh
30/9/32	Swindon Works **I**
18/4/32	Swindon Works **G**
22/10/32	Neath
1933	Llanelly
18/2/34	Swindon Works **I**
10/3/34	Oxley
7/12/34	Swindon Works **L**
1/8/35	Swindon Works **I**
24/8/35	Stafford Road
19/2/36	Wolverhampton Works **L**
23/6/36	Swindon Works **L**
26/7/37	Swindon Works **I**
24/8/37	Tyseley
29/9/37	Tyseley shops **R**
5/8/38	Tyseley shops **R**
24/10/39	Swindon Works **G**
12/4/40	Stafford Road shops **L**
13/11/41	Tyseley shops **R**
19/6/42	Swindon Works **I**
15/12/42	Tyseley shops **R**
24/3/43	Tyseley shops **R**
11/3/44	Tyseley shed **L**
17/1/45	Swindon Works **G**
3/8/45	Hereford shops **R**
10/8/46	Leamington Spa
5/10/46	Tyseley
10/12/46	Swindon Works **I**
6/9/47	Leamington Spa
16/9/48	Swindon Works **L**
21/11/48	St. Philips Marsh
5/1/50	Swindon Works **HG**
2/8/50	Old Oak shops **U**
25/5/51	Taunton shops **U**
24/7/51	Shrewsbury shops **U**
5/11/51	Taunton shops **U**
1/2/52	Swindon Works **HI**
1/5/52	Swindon Works **U**
12/7/52	Weymouth
1/11/52	Swindon
21/3/53	Oxley
16/5/53	Tyseley
3/10/53	Gloucester
6/4/54	Gloucester shops **LC**
22/5/54	Canton
26/6/54	Newport Ebbw Jct. **LC**
8/10/54	Swindon Works **HG**
6/6/56	Ebbw Jct shops **U**
24/9/56	Canton **U**
14/12/56	Wolverhampton Works **HI**
11/1/58	Canton **LC**

22/2/58	Southall
25/7/58	Southall shops **U**
18/8/59	Swindon Works **HG**
15/12/59	Oxley shops **U**
16/7/60	Newton Abbot
17/2/61	Ebbw Jct shops **LC**
22/4/61	Swindon
17/6/61	Newton Abbot
17/10/61	Ebbw Jct shops **U**
14/7/62	Taunton

Tenders

From new	2351
13/8/30	2247
4/3/32	1944
18/11/33	2252
2/6/35	1509
25/5/36	2210
11/6/37	1655
21/9/39	1649
12/5/42	2803
3/1/44	2825
27/11/44	2426
10/12/46	2797
16/9/48	2390
5/1/50	2444
1/1/52	2911
31/3/52	2783
7/9/54	2888
18/8/59	2919

Mileage 1,213,555

Withdrawn 21/9/62, Sold to John Cashmore Newport 21/10/63

Canton's 4934 HINDLIP HALL at Old Oak Common in 1954, shinily perfect in lined black from its recent overhaul. It was at Canton from May 1954 to February 1958. Michael Boakes Collection.

A HINDLIP HALL of very different appearance after a while in the clutches of Southall; 4934 has found its way to Dawlish about 1959. ColourRail

4935 KETLEY HALL

Built in 1929 to Lot no.254 at Swindon Works
To traffic 28/6/29

Mileages and Boilers

From new	4934
9/9/30	63,594 4934
13/10/31	108,987 C2972
1/2/33	173,794 C3008
3/8/34	250,641 C4920
21/3/36	331,230 C4085
4/4/38	419,004 C4085
14/3/40	498,457 C4085
17/11/42	600,442 C7214
20/11/46	758,494 C8263
8/2/49	841,530 C4935
16/10/51	949,050 C4438
20/11/53	1,023,089 C2988
24/5/56	1,113,023 C6201
4/9/58	1,197,532 C6201
16/3/61	1,290,675 C7278

5/10/42	2820
5/1/45	2806
20/11/46	2646
30/12/48	2836
15/2/49	2657
17/9/51	2796
15/10/53	4073
24/5/56	2654
4/9/58	4046
15/4/59	2431
16/3/61	2819

Mileage 1,358,688

Withdrawn 22/3/63, Sold to J Cashmore 14/11/63

Sheds and Works history

28/6/29	Chester
9/9/30	Swindon Works **I**
25/10/30	Oxley
13/10/31	Swindon Works **G**
21/11/31	Chester
1/2/33	Swindon Works **G**
8/11/33	Swindon Works **L**
3/8/34	Swindon Works **G**
30/8/34	Worcester shops **R**
22/9/34	Stafford Road
21/9/35	Oxley
21/3/36	Swindon Works **G**
4/4/36	Old Oak
6/5/36	Banbury shops **R**
23/6/37	Swindon Works **L**
14/8/37	Swindon Works **L**
4/4/38	Swindon Works **I**
4/10/38	Ebbw Jct shops **R**
11/11/38	Old Oak shops **R**
14/3/40	Swindon Works **I**
5/5/42	Old Oak shops **I**
17/11/42	Swindon Works **G**
28/2/44	Swindon Works **R**
11/9/46	Laira shops **R**
20/11/46	Swindon Works **I**
16/12/47	Old Oak shops **R**
19/11/48	Old Oak shops **L**
8/2/49	Swindon Works **HG**
13/8/49	Didcot
21/3/51	Didcot shops **U**
16/10/51	Swindon Works **HI**
25/3/53	Didcot shops **U**
20/11/53	Swindon Works **HG**
24/5/56	Swindon Works **HG**
13/7/57	Carmarthen
6/9/57	Carmarthen shops **U**
26/4/58	Carmarthen shops **U**
4/9/58	Swindon Works **HI**
15/4/59	Swindon Works **LC**
16/3/61	Swindon Works **HG**
7/10/61	Goodwick
4/11/61	Canton
24/2/62	Gloucester
14/7/62	Didcot

Tenders

From new	2249
14/7/30	2378
23/5/34	1884
10/2/36	2381
9/4/36	2635
26/4/37	2231
22/2/38	2414
11/3/40	2679

4935 KETLEY HALL in lined green with the as-usual fairly anonymous GWR roundel, at Old Oak Common, 26 March 1937. B.K.B. Green Collection, Initial Photographics.

4935 KETLEY HALL at Bournemouth shed, August 1954. Hawksworth tender with first emblem.

4936 KINLET HALL

Built in 1929 to Lot no.254 at Swindon Works
To traffic 29/6/29

Mileages and Boilers

From new	4935
4/9/30	64,026 C4935
14/9/31	109,171 C3001
7/9/33	192,829 C3001
17/4/35	269,736 C4937
11/11/36	357,371 C4937
30/7/38	438,351 C4437
30/3/40	576,141 C4437
11/12/42	600,406 C4437
23/5/46	695,944 C2989
30/3/49	802,592 C7629
28/6/51	893,928 C7201
4/9/53	978,830 C7201
19/8/55	1,052,328 C2989
1912/57	1,153,553 C2989
27/9/60	1,260,484 C8284

Sheds and Works history

29/6/29	Chester
7/1929	Swindon Works **ATC fitted**
4/9/30	Swindon Works **I**
14/9/31	Swindon Works **G**
26/9/31	Stafford Road
24/10/31	Shrewsbury
21/11/31	Oxley
12/3/32	Chester
4/6/32	Oxley
27/8/32	Neath
26/9/32	Neath shops **R**
22/10/32	Oxley
7/9/33	Swindon Works **I**
1933	Oxford
30/12/33	Oxford shops **R**
5/5/34	Banbury
17/4/35	Swindon Works **G**
5/5/35	Old Oak
2/6/35	Oxford
11/11/36	Swindon Works **I**
30/7/38	Swindon Works **G**
20/8/38	Old Oak
30/3/40	Wolverhampton Works **I**
28/4/40	Truro
7/6/40	Swindon Works **L**
24/10/40	Bath Road shops **R**
15/4/41	Truro shops **R**
28/5/41	Newton Abbot Works **L**
15/8/41	Truro shops **R**
17/10/41	Newton Abbot shops **R**
2/1/42	Truro shops **R**
11/3/42	Laira shops **R**
15/4/42	Newton Abbot Works **L**
4/6/42	Truro shops **R**
11/12/42	Swindon Works **I**
23/3/43	Newton Abbot Works **L**
14/7/43	Newton Abbot Works **L**
22/10/43	Truro shops **R**
19/3/44	Truro shops **R**
5/2/45	Newton Abbot shed **L**
15/6/45	Newton Abbot Works **L**
31/8/45	Newton Abbot Works **L**
7/12/45	Truro shops **R**
23/5/46	Swindon Works **G**
2/2/47	Truro shops **R**
18/6/47	Newton Abbot Works **L**
13/8/47	Newton Abbot Works **L**
6/4/48	Newton Abbot Works **R**
13/7/48	Newton Abbot Works **L**
14/1/49	Swindon Works **LC**
	Tender work only
30/3/49	Swindon Works **HG**
25/4/50	Newton Abbot Works **U**
23/10/50	Truro shops **U**
5/1/51	Truro shops **U**
28/6/51	Swindon Works **HG**
30/7/51	Swindon Works **U**
29/8/52	Swindon Works **LC**
20/4/53	Newton Abbot Works **U**
4/9/53	Caerphilly Works **HI**
6/11/54	Laira
14/12/54	Laira shops **U**
2/2/55	Laira shops **U**
6/3/55	Laira shops **U**
1/4/55	Laira shops **U**
19/8/55	Swindon Works **HG**
4/1/57	Laira shops **U**
25/2/57	Laira shops **U**
19/12/57	Swindon Works **HI**
28/3/58	Newton Abbot shops **LC**
7/10/58	Newton Abbot
27/9/60	Swindon Works **HG**
8/9/62	Cardiff East Dock
18/10/62	Cardiff East Dock shops **U**
29/8/63	Cardiff East Dock shops **U**

Tenders

From new	2369
4/9/30	2242
14/9/31	2341
26/9/32	1914
7/9/33	1725
17/4/35	1787
11/11/36	2234
30/7/38	2668
7/6/40	2735
11/12/42	2574
5/2/45	2714
23/5/46	1518
27/11/48	2549
30/3/49	2843
28/6/51	2678
29/8/52	2701
19/8/55	2850
19/12/57	2417
27/9/60	2756

Mileage at 28/12/63 1,339,061

Withdrawn 15/1/64, sold to Woodham Bros.
24/3/64, engine preserved

4936 KINLET HALL on a train, location and period unrecorded but note the waiting servicemen. In the 1950s and into the 1960s, throughout the summer reservists across the country went on compulsory camps and military exercises to keep up their basic skills, learnt on national service, while cadets attended annual camp. Judging from the train it has arrived to pick up a contingent returning home, and the soldiers by the engine are regulars who have been the instructors for the duration and are waiting to see off the latest batch. The venue is almost certainly Cornwall, while the rather neglected Hall was a regular at either Penzance or Truro over 1951-54. The stock being Gresley it was probably Yorkshire or North East in origin; no windows are open, so it is probably empty stock taking on passengers. The engine has Class A lamps and Special No. Also the engine appears to be raising steam, rather than at the end of a trip. 4936 was always an 83 Area engine post-war and sometimes the only Hall at Truro shed. When at Truro back in 1954 (this is believed to be the period of the photograph) it had the distinction of being the only second Hall to be repaired at Caerphilly Works. It is in the BR lined black livery under the grime. In preservation days this loco was rescued from Barry and went to Llangollen to be overhauled to BR main line standards. The initial chassis inspection revealed that the frame horn blocks were fitted with manganese steel liners, not GWR practice but to be found on BR Standard locomotives. Later research showed that the liners had been fitted as part of an experiment, the only Hall so fitted, at Swindon in 1955. Interestingly it is the active main line preserved Hall at time of writing (September 2015). transporttreasury

4937 LANELAY HALL

Built in 1929 to Lot no.254 at Swindon Works
To traffic 29/6/29

Mileages and Boilers

From new	4936
8/4/32	141,946 C4932
9/1/34	231,170 C4932
9/12/35	315,099 C4906
27/7/37	395,375 C4906
27/4/39	474,425 C4906
27/3/41	556,957 C4900
3/9/43	655,435 C4900
16/4/46	746,566 C8204
20/5/48	813,873 C8289
25/3/53	990,536 C7217
14/10/55	1,077,754 C7217
15/11/57	1,157,825 C2804
19/10/60	1,243,348 C4046

Sheds and Works history

29/6/29	Stafford Road
9/1929	Swindon Works **ATC fitted**
24/11/29	Canton
13/8/30	Swindon Works **I**
8/4/32	Swindon Works **G**
1933	Truro
9/1/34	Swindon Works **I**
13/1/34	Penzance
28/7/34	Truro
2/10/34	Newton Abbot shed **L**
20/10/34	Penzance
27/6/35	Newton Abbot shed **L**
27/7/35	Newton Abbot
9/12/35	Swindon Works **G**
12/12/36	Swindon Works **L**
20/4/37	Swindon Works **L**
27/7/37	Swindon Works **I**
29/5/37	Penzance
24/8/37	Worcester
27/4/39	Swindon Works **I**
27/5/39	Laira
27/3/41	Swindon Works **G**
8/12/42	Laira shops **R**
3/9/43	Swindon Works **I**
24/11/44	Swindon Works **R**
14/12/44	Laira shops **R**
27/4/45	Laira shops **R**
20/9/45	Laira shops **R**
23/10/45	Laira shops **R**
25/11/45	Laira shops **R**
16/4/46	Swindon Works **I**
9/1/47	Laira shops **R**
30/5/47	Laira shops **R**
20/10/47	Neyland shops **R**
1/11/47	Neyland
18/12/47	Newton Abbot Works **R**
20/5/48	Swindon Works **G**
30/10/48	Landore
19/3/49	Carmarthen shops **U**
23/4/49	Carmarthen
4/5/50	Wolverhampton Works **HI**
12/12/51	Newton Abbot Works **LC**
25/3/53	Swindon Works **HG**
3/6/54	Carmarthen shops **LC**
6/11/54	Shrewsbury
16/7/55	Landore
14/10/55	Swindon Works **HI**
15/9/57	Landore shops **U**
15/11/57	Swindon Works **HG**
30/9/58	Carmarthen shops **U**
15/9/58-23/3/59	Stored at Landore
6/4/59-11/5/59	To store at Llanelly
13/6/59	Carmarthen
28/11/59	Pontypool Road
19/10/60	Swindon Works **HG**
14/8/61	Pontypool Road shops **U**

Tenders

From new	2319
23/6/30	2060
8/2/32	2030
10/10/33	2267
23/10/35	1904
11/3/39	2137
23/3/41	2802
19/7/43	2412
24/11/44	3779
18/2/46	2638
18/2/53	2604
21/4/54	2651
14/10/55	2414
18/11/59	2680
19/10/60	2726

Mileage 1,306,064

Withdrawn 21/9/62, Sold to R S Hayes ltd Bridgend 26/8/63

A nicely lit 4937 LANELAY HALL at Torquay in 1935, with 'intermediate' tender. ColourRail

4937 LANELAY HALL at Shrewsbury shed, 8 February 1960. It is spectacularly dirty of course and while this might be thought a sign of the times there never was, in truth, a tradition of ever-reliably shiny Halls; rather the opposite in fact. It's worth recalling Mr. J.P. Bardsley's appeal to the Railway Executive way back at the beginning of the 1950s: *...if an engine is worthy of a name keep that engine clean. If 'Halls' and 'Granges' were less drab and dirty and the name had not to be deciphered we might take more interest in them.* Little did he (or anyone else) suspect how desirable and sought-after these plates would become! D.K. Jones Collection

4938 LIDDINGTON HALL

Built in 1929 to lot no.254 at Swindon Works
To traffic 6/7/29

Mileage and Boilers

From new	4937
8/8/30	58,439 C4937
7/1/32	126,129 C2821
22/9/33	211,911 C2821
22/11/35	295,820 C4972
8/10/37	383,663 C4972
11/9/39	473,857 C4972
15/12/41	556,003 C4949
23/5/44	636,305 C4949
26/6/46	711,242 C7234
11/6/48	790,113 C4052
29/12/50	892,578 C9201
5/6/53	983,538 C8282
18/5/55	1,070,351 C4477
24/1/58	1,167,132 C8289
13/7/60	1,250,942 C8289

Sheds and Works histories

Date	Location		Date	Value
6/7/29	Bath Road			
7/1929	Swindon Works **ATC**			
24/11/29	Weymouth		24/8/37	1906
8/8/30	Swindon Works **LI**		10/12/38	2677
30/8/30	Bath Road		13/2/41	1739
2/9/31	Bath Road shops **R**		25/3/42	1858
7/1/32	Swindon Works **G**		12/4/44	2929
30/7/32	Newton Abbot		24/11/45	2411
27/8/32	Laira		24/6/46	2869
20/4/33	Newton Abbot Works **L**		11/6/48	2916
1933	Reading		27/11/50	2899
22/9/33	Swindon Works **I**		6/12/51	2419
23/9/34	Reading shops **R**		16/5/53	2666
17/10/34	Oxford shops **R**		21/4/55	2660
22/11/35	Swindon Works **G**		24/1/58	2637
14/12/35	Old Oak			
1/4/37	Old Oak shops **R**		**Mileage 1,287,128**	
11/6/37	Old Oak shops **R**			
8/10/37	Swindon Works **I**		**Withdrawn 26/11/62, Cut up 23/3/63**	
8/7/38	Oxford shops **R**			
11/9/39	Swindon Works **I**			
5/3/41	Old Oak shops **R**			
10/9/41	Old Oak shops **R**			
15/12/41	Swindon Works **G**			
1/1942	Oxford			
12/8/42	Oxford shops **R**			
9/6/43	Old Oak shops **L**			
23/5/44	Swindon Works **I**			
9/8/45	Old Oak shops **R**			
26/11/45	Swindon Works **L**			
26/6/46	Swindon Works **G**			
11/6/48	Swindon Works **I**			
12/10/49	Old Oak shops **U**			
29/12/50	Swindon Works **HG**			
17/12/51	Old Oak shops **LC**			
5/6/53	Swindon Works **HG**			
18/5/55	Swindon Works **HI**			
24/9/56	Tyseley shops **U**			
15/5/57	Reading shops **U**			
24/1/58	Swindon Works **HG**			
19/2/59	Newton Abbot Works **LC**			
26/12/59	Stafford Road			
13/7/60	Wolverhampton Works **HI**			
3/12/60	Tyseley shops **U**			
3/5/61	Wolverhampton Works **LC**			
9/9/61	Llanelly			
31/8/62	Wolverhampton Works **U**			

Tenders

From new	2250
25/6/30	2245
16/11/31	2217
19/7/33	2232
3/5/37	2534

4938 LIDDINGTON HALL at Oxford about 1955. M. Robertson, transporttreasury

4938 LIDDINGTON HALL at Cholsey with an up train from Oxford, 18 August 1953. A.W. Cawston, courtesy Brian Bailey.

4939 LITTLETON HALL

Built in 1929 to Lot no.254 at Swindon Works
To traffic 18/7/29

Mileage and Boilers

From new	4938
24/9/30	53,933 C4938
19/11/31	105,027 C4938
19/10/32	136,772 C4921
30/5/34	220,375 C4921
29/2/36	304,137 C2963
9/12/37	390,977 C2963
2/4/40	470,442 C2963
29/12/41	526,890 C4984
25/5/43	567,891 C4984
13/10/44	612,247 C7265
4/10/46	677,016 C4039
23/3/48	726,699 C4473
26/10/49	780,112 C4921
27/7/51	841,579 C2854
23/4/53	912,272 C2854
22/11/55	998,824 C9287
6/2/58	1,078,545 C9287
13/12/60	1,161,498 C9291

Sheds and Works Histories

18/7/29	Truro
8/1929	Swindon Works **ATC**
25/10/29	Truro shops **U**
24/1/30	Newton Abbot Works **R**
11/3/30	Truro shops **L**
24/9/30	Swindon Works **I**
25/10/30	Penzance
25/2/31	Newton Abbot Works **R**
14/3/31	Newton Abbot
11/4/31	Penzance
19/11/31	Swindon Works **I**
19/12/31	Oxley
19/10/32	Swindon Works **G**
19/11/32	Landore
8/7/33	Goodwick shops **R**
1933	Carmarthen
30/5/34	Swindon Works **I**
20/10/34	Old Oak
9/3/35	St. Philips Marsh
27/4/35	St Philips Marsh shops **R**
29/2/36	Swindon Works **G**
7/3/36	Weymouth
4/3/36	St. Philips Marsh
9/12/37	Swindon Works **I**
17/5/39	Swindon Works **L**
15/7/39	Oxford shops **R**
16/1/40	Wolverhampton Works **R**
2/4/40	Swindon Works **I**
29/12/41	Swindon Works **L**
25/5/43	Swindon Works **I**
13/10/44	Swindon Works **L**
2/8/45	Tyseley shops **R**
4/10/46	Swindon Works **G**
23/3/48	Swindon Works **L**
25/12/48	Reading
26/10/49	Swindon Works **HG**
27/7/51	Swindon Works **HG**
23/4/53	Caerphilly Works **HI**
13/4/54	Bath Road shops **U**
20/9/54	Old Oak shops **U**
19/6/54	Old Oak
6/11/54	Reading
22/11/55	Swindon Works **HG**
29/12/56	Didcot
27/10/57	Didcot shops **U**
6/2/58	Swindon Works **HI**
7/7/59	Didcot shops **U**
13/12/60	Swindon Works **HG**

Tenders

From new	2251
18/8/30	2250
16/9/31	1941
26/1/33	2351
10/4/34	1874
31/12/35	1782
23/10/37	2245
19/2/40	2675
19/4/41	2798
16/4/43	2793
15/10/44	2878
24/8/46	2779
23/1/48	2665
19/9/49	2579
16/6/51	2403
27/7/51	2825
22/11/55	2893
16/6/56	2895
26/4/57	2442
4/2/58	2828
13/12/60	2622
2/4/63	2582

Mileage 1,228,917

Withdrawn 11/2/62, Cut up at Wolverhampton Works 1/6/63

4939 LITTLETON HALL coupled to 7906 FRON HALL at Henley on Thames, 6 July 1962. 4939 had worked into the terminus with the first evening train from Paddington, 7906 following with another. Now they wait in the loop to depart light for Reading shed and servicing. The higher level of the Modified Hall's steam pipe is evident. P. Moffat, ColourRail

4939 not long out of Swindon, in green with second emblem on 16 February 1958. K. Fairey, ColourRail

4940 LUDFORD HALL

Built in 1929 at Lot no.254 at Swindon Works
To Traffic 20/7/39

Mileages and Boilers

26/7/30	59,928 C4939
15/12/31	127,472 C4083
23/10/33	206,423 C4083
7/3/35	267,996 C4967
26/2/37	355,935 C4446
2/3/39	444,149 C4446
14/3/41	520,281 C4034
27/6/43	602,815 C4034
19/9/45	701,404 C2981
25/6/48	813,490 C2936
15/3/50	884,119 C4469
13/2/52	961,981 C9288
13/5/54	1,054,199 C8212
30/4/56	1,133,687 C2967
10/7/58	1,230,851 C7254

Sheds and Works history

20/7/29	Taunton
8/1929	Swindon Works **ATC**
18/11/29	Taunton shops **L**
27/12/29	Laira
6/3/30	Laira shops **L**
26/7/30	Swindon Works **I**
2/8/30	Stafford Road
30/8/30	Chester
15/12/31	Swindon Works **G**
21/4/32	Weymouth shops **L**
25/11/32	St. Philips Marsh shops **R**
23/10/33	Swindon Works **I**
1933	Penzance
9/8/34	Swindon Works **L**
15/12/34	Penzance shops **R**
7/3/35	Swindon Works **G**
9/10/35	Penzance shops **R**
4/2/36	Penzance shops **R**
15/5/36	Newton Abbot Works **L**
26/2/37	Swindon Works **G**
28/10/37	Penzance shops **R**
3/6/38	Newton Abbot Works **L**
23/7/38	Newton Abbot
2/3/39	Swindon Works **I**
2/1940	Penzance
18/4/40	Newton Abbot Works **L**
12/7/40	Newton Abbot Works **L**
14/3/41	Swindon Works **G**
16/12/41	Penzance shops **R**
18/7/42	Newton Abbot Works **L**
17/2/43	Penzance shops **R**
27/6/43	Swindon Works **I**
9/1943	St. Blazey
20/4/44	St. Blazey shops **R**
27/10/44	Newton Abbot Works **L**
7/3/45	Truro shops **R**
19/9/45	Swindon Works **G**
20/2/47	St. Blazey shops **R**
13/6/47	Newton Abbot Works **L**
25/6/48	Swindon Works **I**
15/3/50	Swindon Works **HG**
13/2/52	Swindon Works **HI**
23/3/52	Penzance
12/7/52	St.Blazey
9/8/52	Penzance
20/8/52	Newton Abbot Works **LC**
1/11/52	St.Blazey
2/9/53	Newton Abbot Works **LC**
3/10/53	Taunton
13/5/54	Swindon Works **HG**
26/11/54	Taunton shops **U**
13/10/55	Newton Abbot Works **U**
30/4/56	Swindon Works **HI**
10/7/58	Swindon Works **HG**
7/4/59	Newton Abbot Works **LC**
10/9/59	Newton Abbot Works **U**

Tenders

From new	2030
17/6/30	2246
13/10/31	2245
9/11/32	2427
27/7/33	2166
23/7/34	1825
23/1/35	2249
13/1/37	1713
27/1/39	2221
30/12/40	2658
27/8/43	2535
19/9/45	2408
25/6/48	2789
9/2/50	2709
2/1/52	2713
8/4/54	2587
30/6/56	2415
12/7/58	4010

Mileage 1,284,530

Withdrawn 9/11/59, Cut up 30/1/60

Above. 4940 LUDFORD HALL in lined black, at Exeter St David's on 1 August 1954. After SAINT MARTIN, 4940 was the second Hall to be withdrawn, at the end of 1959. J. Robertson, transporttreasury

Left. 4940, long a Taunton engine, alongside the coal stage at St Philips Marsh. It glitters in newly applied lined green, with second emblem, probably not long after its Heavy General in the summer of 1958. ColourRail

4941 LLANGEDWYN HALL
Built in 1929 to Lot no.254 at Swindon Works
To traffic 25/7/29

Mileages and Boilers

From new	4940
27/11/30	67,472 C4940
7/1/32	115,924 C4940
25/7/33	164,135 C4978
17/4/35	252,156 C4978
13/6/36	308,359 C2917
27/2/37	340,052 C2917
26/11/38	420,392 C2917
7/11/40	504,384 C2917
4/5/43	584,822 C2988
22/2/46	673,703 C2988
21/4/48	746,945 C4908
27/6/50	825,150 C9221
29/9/52	910,294 C9257
4/1/55	993,868 C4935
4/6/57	1,068,766 C4935
26/5/60	1,170,294 C9209

Sheds and Works history

8/1929	Swindon Works **ATC fitted**
25/7/29	Newton Abbot
27/10/29	Exeter
4/12/29	Exeter shops **L**
15/2/30	Penzance
12/3/30	Penzance shops **L**
2/7/30	Penzance shops **L**
27/11/30	Swindon Works **I**
20/12/30	Bath Road
7/1/32	Swindon Works **I**
13/2/32	Laira
25/7/33	Swindon Works **G**
1933	St. Philips Marsh
13/1/34	Westbury
27/4/34	Tyseley shops **R**
20/12/34	Westbury shops **R**
17/4/35	Swindon Works **I**
4/5/35	St. Philips Marsh
13/6/36	Swindon Works **L**
27/2/37	Swindon Works **I**
6/3/37	Swindon
28/3/38	Swindon Works **L**
26/11/38	Swindon Works **I**
10/12/38	St. Philips Marsh
5/2/40	St. Philips Marsh shops **R**
7/11/40	Swindon Works **I**
3/4/41	Westbury shops **R**
10/4/42	Westbury shops **R**
5/1942	Ebbw Jct
4/5/43	Swindon Works **G**
6/10/44	Tyseley shops 'No repair'
16/8/45	Ebbw Jct shops **R**
6/10/45	Canton
22/2/46	Wolverhampton Works **I**
20/4/46	Ebbw Jct
27/5/47	Swindon Works **L**
21/4/48	Swindon Works **G**
17/5/49	Swindon Works **LC**
2/8/49	Ebbw Jct shops **U**
9/9/49	Wolverhampton Works **LC**
27/6/50	Swindon Works **HG**
19/4/52	Old Oak
29/9/52	Swindon Works **HI**
16/6/53	Old Oak shops **U**
5/9/53	Severn Tunnel Jct
14/8/54	Llanelly
4/1/55	Swindon Works **HG**
14/7/55	Ebbw Jct shops **LC**
10/11/55	Swindon Works **LC**
4/6/57	Swindon Works **HI**
19/4/58	Reading
30/4/59	Reading shops **U**
26/5/60	Swindon Works **HG**
7/10/61	Westbury
27/2/62	Ebbw Jct shops **LC**
12/7/62	Wolverhampton Works **LC**

Tenders

From new	2006
5/10/30	2226
11/11/31	1775
11/2/35	2180
21/9/35	2241
19/1/37	2049
19/2/38	2249
15/10/38	1758
2/10/40	2419
12/3/43	2798
27/5/47	2758
22/2/48	2654
19/4/49	2863
26/3/51	2539
29/9/52	4098
2/12/54	2803
10/11/55	2622
4/12/56	2884
4/6/57	2599
26/9/60	2852

Mileage 1,242,665

Withdrawn 22/10/62, Sold to John Cashmore Newport 21/10/63

4941 LLANGEDWYN HALL, with Hawksworth tender, takes a freight through Totnes station in September 1954. D.K. Jones Collection.

4941 LLANGEDWYN HALL passing through Eastleigh station. J. Davenport, Initial Photographics.

4942 MAINDY HALL

Built in 1929 to Lot no.254 at Swindon Works
To traffic 29/6/29

Mileages and Boilers

From new	4941
6/10/30	68,136 C4941
22/2/32	134,427 C4941
7/9/33	209,174 C4467
3/6/35	288,996 C4467
16/1/37	369,444 C4467
1/11/38	450,150 C4942
4/11/40	530,038 C4942
22/6/43	614,882 C4943
24/5/45	688,611 C4035
5/7/47	751,124 C4434
17/1/50	851,179 C4984
26/3/52	931,050 C4986
14/4/54	1,010,157 C2811
25/5/56	1,099,509 C2811
2/12/58	1,174,794 C4996
16/6/61	1,259,332 C4995

Sheds and Works history

1/8/29	Newton Abbot
8/1929	Swindon Works **ATC fitted**
27/10/29	Exeter
24/11/29	Newton Abbot
12/3/30	Swindon Works **L**
6/10/30	Swindon Works **I**
25/10/30	Goodwick
28/9/31	Goodwick shops **R**
22/2/32	Swindon Works **I**
9/4/32	Landore
2/7/32	Goodwick
27/9/32	Goodwick shops **R**
7/9/33	Swindon Works **G**
1933	Llanelly
5/9/34	Llanelly shops **R**
3/6/35	Swindon Works **I**
29/6/35	Carmarthen
16/1/37	Swindon Works **I**
6/2/37	Weymouth
30/9/37	Yeovil shops **R**
1/12/37	Weymouth shops **R**
1/11/38	Swindon Works **G**
12/11/38	Westbury
29/4/39	Swindon
27/5/39	Westbury
24/7/39	Westbury shops **R**
4/11/40	Swindon Works **I**
26/11/41	St. Philips Marsh shops **R**
22/6/42	Newton Abbot Works **L**
22/6/43	Swindon Works **G**
24/5/45	Swindon Works **I**
31/10/45	Taunton shops **R**
23/2/46	Tyseley shops **R**
20/4/46	Bath Road
23/8/46	Newton Abbot Works **L**
5/7/47	Swindon Works **G**
10/8/48	Newton Abbot Works **R**
17/1/50	Swindon Works **HG**
10/8/51	Bath Road shops **U**
7/9/51	Bath Road shops **U**
26/3/52	Swindon Works **HI**
23/9/53	Bath Road shops **U**
14/4/54	Swindon Works **HG**
16/7/55	Exeter
20/7/55	Exeter shops **U**
8/10/55	Banbury
1/9/55	Exeter shops **U**
25/5/56	Wolverhampton Works **HI**
5/3/57	Wolverhampton Works **LC**
2/12/58	Swindon Works **HG**
18/6/60	Exeter
3/12/60	St. Philips Marsh
16/6/61	Swindon Works **HG**

11/8/62	Canton
8/9/62	Cardiff East Dock
10/6/63	Worcester shops **U**
22/6/64	Bristol Barrow Road

Tenders

From new	2141
7/8/31	2127
7/9/33	2254
16/1/37	2263
15/2/40	2711
4/4/40	2250
22/6/43	2797
24/5/45	2868
5/7/47	2834
17/1/50	2539
14/4/54	2845
11/6/56	4054
2/12/58	2902
16/6/61	2824

Mileage 1,331,714

Withdrawn 28/12/63, Sold to Woodham Bros., Barry. Engine preserved, being rebuilt as Saint 2999 LADY OF LEGEND at Didcot Railway Centre.

4942 MAINDY HALL at the east end of the (then) almost new Reception Shed at Swindon on 4 July 1947, seven months before Nationalisation. The tender is carrying the last version of the GW badge; vacuum pump lubricator still in original position in front of leading splasher. Although the tender is lined out the loco appears to be painted in unlined green – no doubt a temporary pairing, something not unusual in the works yard. H.C. Casserley, courtesy R.M. Casserley.

In clean lined green 4942 puts a local 3F tank somewhat in the shade at Mold Junction, 20 August 1961. RailOnline

4943 MARRINGTON HALL

Built in 1929 to Lot no.254 at Swindon Works
To traffic 24/7/29

Mileages and Boilers

From new	4942
12/11/30	63,660 C4942
3/10/32	138,764 C4942
19/3/34	205,864 C4955
31/2/36	300,729 C4907
26/11/37	396,946 R7245
7/10/39	480,661 R7245
22/4/42	572,090 R7245
6/12/43	623,677 C4962
24/5/45	671,131 C4962
10/6/47	744,398 C8207
30/8/49	831,247 C4931
16/1/52	922,416 C2856
19/11/53	995,980 C2856
8/5/56	1,086,880 C4961
24/9/58	1,179,936 C9217
6/10/61	1,280,125 C8220

Sheds and Works history

Date	Location
24/7/29	Old Oak
31/7/29	Swindon Works **ATC**
15/9/30	Old Oak shops **R**
12/11/30	Swindon Works **I**
22/11/30	St. Philips Marsh
17/1/31	Westbury
21/11/31	St. Philips Marsh
3/10/32	Swindon Works **I**
22/10/32	Tyseley
19/3/34	Swindon Works **G**
7/4/34	Oxley
28/7/34	Stafford Road
12/1/35	Oxley
31/2/36	Swindon Works **G**
7/3/36	Newton Abbot
7/12/36	Newton Abbot Works **L**
8/6/37	Newton Abbot Works **L**
26/11/37	Swindon Works **G**
11/12/37	Truro
16/6/38	Truro shops **R**
23/7/38	Laira
15/10/38	Penzance
18/11/38	Newton Abbot Works **L**
20/6/39	Penzance shops **R**
7/10/39	Swindon Works **I**
11/11/39	Old Oak
27/5/40	Old Oak shops **L**
20/10/40	Swindon Works **L**
22/4/42	Swindon Works **I**
6/11/42	Old Oak shops **R**
16/2/43	Old Oak shops **R**
1/6/43	Old Oak shops **L**
6/12/43	Swindon Works **L**
4/3/44	Swindon Works **R**
17/8/44	Old Oak shops **L**
24/5/45	Swindon Works **I**
23/7/46	Old Oak shops **L**
25/1/47	Old Oak shops **L**
10/6/47	Swindon Works **L**
1/11/47	Southall
29/11/47	Old Oak
30/8/49	Swindon Works **HG**
5/11/49	Reading
1/11/50	Newton Abbot Works **U**
27/1/51	Oxley
16/1/52	Swindon Works **HG**
4/10/52	Stafford Road
1/11/52	Oxley
18/4/53	Reading
11/7/53	Old Oak
19/11/53	Swindon Works **HI**
7/1/55	Swindon Works **LC**
5/4/55	Old Oak shops **U**
8/5/56	Swindon Works **HG**
6/10/56	Reading
23/2/57	Tyseley
31/8/57	Worcester shops **U**
7/1/58	Oxford shops **U**
22/2/58	Hereford
17/5/58	Pontypool Road
24/9/58	Swindon Works **HG**
9/8/60	Gloucester shops **U**
5/12/60	Pontypool Road shops **U**
20/3/61	Ebbw Jct shops **U**
13/4/61	Pontypool Road shops **U**
6/10/61	Swindon Works **HG**

Tenders

From new	1946
19/9/30	2256
12/1/34	1459
21/9/35	2341
10/11/36	2056
11/10/37	1782
23/7/38	2546
8/9/39	2604
7/10/39	2614
14/9/40	2600
2/3/42	1459
18/8/43	2538
6/4/45	2819
31/5/46	2570
14/8/46	2723
2/5/47	2934
21/7/49	2925
3/12/51	2398
11/7/53	2532
3/10/53	2406
19/11/53	2405
4/12/54	2443
9/1/55	2545
13/4/56	2401
5/5/56	2897
14/4/58	2234
6/11/61	2779

Mileage 1,353,901

Withdrawn 16/12/63, Sold to Birds Ltd Morriston 28/2/64

Black liveried 4943 MARRINGTON HALL at Taunton shed, date unrecorded. J. Davenport, Initial Photographics.

And at Swindon shed in more or less the same period by the look of it. J. Davenport, Initial Photographics.

4944 MIDDLETON HALL

Built in 1929 to Lot no.254 at Swindon Works
To traffic 1/8/29

Mileages and Boilers

From new	4945
19/9/30	68,325 C4945
1/2/32	138,176 R2923
12/12/33	215,150 R2923
26/6/35	292,338 R2923
22/4/37	379,800 C2898
12/11/38	461,190 C2898
22/10/40	537,139 C4917
19/3/43	615,328 C4917
6/7/44	650,868 C2970
26/4/46	708,990 C2970
21/11/47	758,289 C2990
19/4/50	832,102 C9220
25/2/52	899,580 C2943
26/8/53	955,429 C2873
21/1/55	998,992 C4427
26/2/57	1,077,223 C4427
17/2/60	1,191,512 C7249

Sheds and Works history

1/8/29	Old Oak
8/1929	Swindon Works **ATC**
19/9/30	Swindon Works **I**
1/2/32	Swindon Works **G**
13/2/32	Oxford
25/8/32	Oxford shops **R**
1/12/32	Old Oak shops **R**
18/6/33	Worcester shops **R**
12/12/33	Swindon Works **I**
13/1/34	Old Oak
7/3/35	Old Oak shops **R**
26/6/35	Swindon Works **I**
27/7/35	Oxley
22/4/37	Swindon Works **G**
13/11/37	Stafford Road
12/11/38	Swindon Works **I**
14/10/39	Oxley
22/10/40	Swindon Works **G**
11/1940	Stafford Road
12/4/41	Swindon Works **I**
5/7/41	Wolverhampton Works **L**
8/7/42	Stafford Road shed **R**
19/3/43	Swindon Works **I**
17/9/43	Stourbridge shops **R**
6/7/44	Swindon Works **L**
11/5/45	Old Oak shops **R**
26/4/46	Wolverhampton Works **I**
13/12/46	Old Oak shops **R**
17/5/47	Oxley
21/11/47	Swindon Works **G**
5/3/48	Swindon Works **R**
31/3/49	Tyseley shops **U**
5/11/49	Southall
19/4/50	Swindon Works **HG**
11/5/51	Southall shops **U**
16/8/51	Old Oak shops **U**
8/10/51	Southall shops **U**
25/2/52	Swindon Works **HI**
26/8/53	Swindon Works **HC**
12/2/54	Worcester shops **U**
5/5/54	Ebbw Jct shops **U**
21/1/55	Swindon Works **HG**
7/3/56	Southall shops **U**
3/10/56	Southall shops **U**
26/2/57	Swindon Works **HI**
28/12/57	Laira
18/7/58	Newton Abbot Works **LC**
15/9/58-16/10/58	Stored at Laira
1/11/58	Exeter
17/2/60	Swindon Works **HG**
25/1/61	Swindon Works **HC**
31/10/61	Newport Ebbw Jct **LC**
11/5/62	Wolverhampton Works **LC**
14/7/62	Shrewsbury
11/8/62	Southall

Tenders

From new	2259
27/9/33	2173
25/4/35	1947
5/3/37	1795
6/10/38	1838
19/9/40	2749
24/2/41	2551
4/11/39	2706
10/2/43	2630
28/8/44	2239
18/11/47	2659
6/3/48	2263
13/3/50	2877
25/1/52	2415
2/7/53	2757
8/12/54	2388
26/2/57	2624
12/2/60	2860
25/1/61	2600
30/12/61	2646
9/3/62	2583
16/6/62	2560

Mileage 1,257,046

Withdrawn 21/9/62, Sold to A King Norwich 8/11/63

4944 MIDDLETON HALL climbing Hatton bank with a down class 'H' freight. Michael Boakes Collection.

4944 MIDDLETON HALL, now a Southall engine, at home on 4 November 1962; electrification flashes and the almost-obligatory painted smokebox door straps. Peter Groom.

4945 MILLIGAN HALL
Built in 1929 to Lot no.254 at Swindon Works
To traffic 19/8/29

Mileages and boilers

From new	4944		
17/3/31	70,464 C4944	12/11/34	1515
5/5/32	117,116 C4944	27/5/36	2229
14/6/33	158,316 C4959	2/6/37	2261
21/1/35	232,424 C4959	27/3/39	1934
7/7/36	309,494 R7202	28/4/39	1965
28/1/38	392,764 R7202	7/2/40	2261
7/2/40	486,800 R7202	27/3/40	2536
28/8/41	536,969 C2819	26/11/42	2404
30/12/42	589,904 C2819	30/12/42	2623
5/11/45	680,445 C4994	20/8/45	2796
24/9/47	751,021 C8292	6/7/45	2434
23/12/49	831,237 C8292	24/9/47	2641
20/6/52	921,830 C4905	18/11/49	1560
21/12/54	1,030,292 C4071	7/9/51	2395
4/2/57	1,117,000 C4071	20/6/52	2791
21/9/59	1,218,436 C2923	27/5/54	2625
		20/11/54	4098
		21/9/59	2884

Mileage 1,318,962

Withdrawn 3/11/61, Cut up 24/2/62

Sheds and Works history

19/8/29	Reading
8/1929	Swindon Works **ATC fitted**
22/12/29	Oxley
15/2/30	Shrewsbury
12/4/30	Oxley
11/4/31	Tyseley
19/5/31	Oxley
17/3/31	Swindon Works **I**
4/6/32	St. Philips Marsh
12/1/35	Weymouth
19/2/35	St. Philips Marsh
5/5/32	Swindon Works **I**
14/6/33	Swindon Works **G**
16/7/434	St. Philips Marsh shops **R**
21/1/35	Swindon Works **I**
25/9/35	St. Philips Marsh **R**
7/7/36	Swindon Works **G**
25/7/36	Bath Road
26/5/37	Bath Road shops **R**
28/1/38	Swindon Works **I**
2/4/38	Swindon
28/4/39	Swindon Works **L**
7/2/40	Swindon Works **I**
27/3/40	Swindon Works **I** [continuation of previous visit]
28/8/41	Swindon Works **L**
30/12/42	Swindon Works **L**
12/6/44	Newton Abbot Works **L**
5/11/45	Swindon Works **G**
4/12/45	Swindon Works **G** [continuation of previous visit]
14/3/47	Swindon shed **R**
24/9/47	Swindon Works **I**
23/12/49	Swindon Works **HG**
20/6/52	Swindon Works **HG**
12/1/53	Swindon Works **U**
16/5/53	Oxford
11/7/53	Old Oak
24/7/53	Old Oak shops **U**
3/10/53	Didcot
26/4/54	Old Oak shops **U**
31/12/54	Swindon Works **HG**
16/6/56	Westbury
4/2/57	Wolverhampton Works **HI**
18/9/58	Westbury shops **U**
21/9/59	Swindon Works **HG**
5/11/60	Old Oak
25/3/61	Southall
13/5/61	Hereford shops **U**

Tenders

From new	2147
17/8/31	2375
7/5/32	2260
4/6/33	2234

4945 rattles along near Pewsey, 14 September 1956.; Hawksworth tender. D.K. Jones Collection.

4945 with a train at Shrewsbury, snaking past the giant signal box. transporttreasury

4946 MOSELEY HALL

Built in 1929 to Lot no.254 at Swindon Works
To traffic 20/8/29

Mileages and Boilers

From new	4950
27/9/30	58,523 C4950
4/4/32	119,699 C4939
23/2/34	206,187 C4939
23/8/35	284,355 R4989
30/12/36	365,162 R4989
29/12/38	445,678 C4471
27/3/41	535,034 C4471
3/2/43	616,170 C2929
7/7/45	696,613 C2929
19/1/48	784,423 C4433
11/10/50	894,463 C4913
6/11/52	980,167 C7234
19/1/55	1,063,084 C7240
14/5/57	1,153,809 C7240
24/11/59	1,240,751 C4076

Sheds and works history

8/1929	Swindon Works **ATC**
20/8/29	Bristol Bath Road
27/9/30	Swindon Works **HI**
25/10/30	St. Philips Marsh
20/2/31	Swindon Works **R**
4/4/32	Swindon Works **G**
18/11/32	St. Philips Marsh shops **R**
22/3/33	St. Philips Marsh shops **R**
21/9/33	St. Philips Marsh shops **R**
23/2/34	Swindon Works **I**
10/3/34	Laira
19/10/34	Laira shops **R**
9/2/35	Truro
6/4/35	Laira
23/8/35	Swindon Works **G**
30/12/36	Swindon Works **I**
9/1/37	Penzance
4/5/37	Penzance shops **R**
15/7/37	Penzance shops **R**
4/11/37	Penzance shops **R**
2/2/38	Penzance shops **R**
5/7/38	Penzance shops **R**
29/12/38	Swindon Works **G**
29/4/39	Truro
9/8/39	Truro shops **R**
13/4/40	Newton Abbot Works **L**
27/3/41	Swindon Works **I**
4/1941	Penzance
5/1941	Truro
22/7/41	Truro shops **R**
30/10/41	Swindon Works **R**
12/1941	St. Blazey
11/4/42	Newton Abbot Works **L**
3/2/43	Swindon Works **G**
8/1943	Penzance
7/10/43	Penzance shops **R**
14/6/44	Newton Abbot Works **L**
29/3/45	Penzance shops **R**
7/7/45	Swindon Works **I**
6/11/45	Penzance shops **R**
18/7/46	Newton Abbot Works **L**
16/12/46	Newton Abbot Works **L**
28/2/47	Penzance shops **L**
28/4/47	Penzance shops **R**
23/5/47	Newton Abbot Works **L**
19/1/48	Swindon Works **G**
7/4/49	Penzance shops **U**
19/10/49	Newton Abbot Works **LC**
11/10/50	Swindon Works **HG**
5/6/51	Penzance shops **U**
6/11/52	Swindon Works **HI**
11/7/53	Canton
16/12/53	Canton shops **U**
19/1/55	Swindon Works **HG**
14/9/55	Weymouth shops **U**
20/11/56	Llanelly shops **U**
14/5/57	Caerphilly Works **HI**
2/7/57	Landore shops **U**
18/3/58	Ebbw Jct shops **U**
25/7/58	Caerphilly Works **LC**
18/9/58	Worcester shops **U**
19/9/58-6/10/58	To store at Canton
24/11/59	Swindon Works **HG**
30/1/60	Taunton
23/4/60	Shrewsbury
4/2/61	Shrewsbury shops **U**
8/9/61	Wolverhampton Works **LC**
16/2/62	Wolverhampton Works **HC**
12/12/62	Shrewsbury shops **U**
11/1/63	Shrewsbury shops **U**

Tenders

From new	2112
12/8/30	2252
29/12/33	1915
26/6/35	1675
18/11/36	2240
9/11/38	2249
23/1/41	2409
2/2/42	2582
11/7/45	2671
15/6/46	2899
14/6/47	2671
14/1/48	2565
21/5/49	2582
28/1/50	2732
6/10/52	2812
21/5/55	2784
19/7/55	2830
24/11/59	2894

Mileage 1,328,947

Withdrawn 24/6/63, Sold to G Cohen Ltd Morriston 1/1/64

4946 MOSELEY HALL draws the attention of the assorted mac and beret-sporting *cognoscenti* as it speeds past Swindon in the 1950s. ColourRail

With very little to identify period or location, 4946 MOSELEY HALL nevertheless makes a magnificent sight on a freight of tanks, opens and vans; it's lined green with the second emblem but the shed plate is missing.

4947 NANHORAN HALL
Built in 1929 to Lot no.254 at Swindon Works
To traffic 20/8/29

Mileages and Boilers

From new	4946
19/11/30	64,487 C4946
25/7/32	148,739 C4946
18/8/33	198,945 C4995
30/1/35	273,639 C4471
25/7/36	351,534 C4471
12/5/38	432,097 C4481
25/6/40	525,391 C4481
10/10/42	612,529 C4404
26/11/45	714,717 C4954
22/1/48	791,935 C2864
27/9/50	902,881 C2906
18/2/53	990,075 C4435
23/8/55	1,092,119 C2924
21/11/57	1,184,646 C4051
23/3/60	1,281,020 C6203

Sheds and Works history

20/8/29	Gloucester
19/11/30	Swindon Works I
22/11/30	Old Oak
12/3/32	Oxford
20/7/32	Stafford Road
25/7/32	Swindon Works I
19/11/32	Chester
1933	Weymouth
18/8/33	Swindon Works G
20/4/34	Swindon Works L
30/1/35	Swindon Works G
9/2/35	Laira
23/9/35	Penzance shops R
25/7/36	Swindon Works I
22/8/36	Truro
6/5/37	Truro shops L
8/2/38	Truro shops R
12/5/38	Swindon Works G
21/1/39	Truro shops R
21/4/39	Truro shops R
29/4/39	Penzance
15/11/39	Newton Abbot Works L
25/6/40	Swindon Works I
18/3/41	Penzance shops R
9/4/41	Penzance shops R
27/8/41	Newton Abbot Works R
15/1/42	Penzance shops R
9/1942	Truro
10/10/42	Swindon Works G
8/5/43	Truro shops R
10/9/43	Newton Abbot Works L
7/1944	Newton Abbot
22/7/44	Newton Abbot Works L
9/1944	Penzance
3/10/44	Penzance shops R
29/11/44	Penzance shops R
28/2/45	Penzance shops R
31/5/45	Penzance shops R
26/11/45	Swindon Works I
16/7/46	Penzance shops R
3/9/46	Penzance shops R
31/3/47	Penzance shops R
6/8/47	Newton Abbot Works L
22/1/48	Swindon Works G
21/9/48	Newton Abbot Works L Tender work only
16/5/49	Newton Abbot Works LC
13/8/49	Newton Abbot
5/11/49	Penzance
25/3/50	Newton Abbot
20/5/50	Penzance
27/9/50	Swindon Works HG
24/10/50-4/11/50	To store at Swindon shed and return to traffic
2/12/50	St. Philips Marsh
27/1/52	Penzance

4/2/52	Penzance shops U
14/6/52	St Philips Marsh
26/6/52	Newton Abbot Works LC
18/2/53	Swindon Works HG
19/10/54	St Philips Marsh shops U
23/8/55	Swindon Works HI
24/5/56	Didcot shops U
19/5/56	Bath Road
21/11/57	Swindon Works HG
3/10/59	St. Philips Marsh
23/3/60	Swindon Works HI
27/2/61	Shrewsbury shops U
1/8/61	Caerphilly Works LC
7/10/61	Swindon
2/12/61	Goodwick
27/1/62	St. Philips Marsh
7/3/62	Didcot shops U

Tenders

From new	2247
20/5/32	2254
28/5/33	2238
10/4/34	1539
3/12/34	2168
12/6/36	2035
31/3/38	2599
30/10/39	2574
23/5/40	2698
30/12/41	2219
19/8/42	2885
20/11/45	2774
22/1/48	2447
21/6/49	2536
31/12/49	2569
22/9/50	2605
14/6/52	2604
10/11/52	2789
18/4/53	2850
23/8/55	2902
26/11/59	2689
27/3/60	2877

Mileage 1,352,851

Withdrawn 21/9/62, Sold to Messrs John Cashmore Ltd Newport 23/8/63

4947 NANHORAN HALL heads a down goods near Scorrier, on 5 April 1952. A. Lathey, transporttreasury

4947 NANHORAN HALL keeps company with 2-6-0 7317; the shed is thought to be Westbury. ColourRail

4948 NORTHWICK HALL

Built in 1929 to Lot no.254 at Swindon Works
To traffic 28/8/29

Mileages and Boilers

From new	4947
10/12/30	65,707 C4947
16/9/32	140,478 C4947
8/3/34	206,676 C2927
31/7/35	283,119 C2927
6/4/37	365,059 C4909
21/10/38	446,754 C4909
22/6/40	510,927 C4909
14/1/43	594,416 R8278
9/3/45	664,967 C8210
14/5/47	740,827 C4072
18/5/50	828,599 C4029
31/3/52	880,208 C4961
30/9/53	937,480 C4961
13/1/56	1,037,847 C7215
31/1/58	1,132,102 C8232
24/11/60	1,231,275 C2823

Sheds and Works history

8/1929	Swindon Works **ATC**
28/8/29	Bath Road
11/7/30	Bath Road shops **R**
10/12/30	Swindon Works **I**
20/12/30	Old Oak
14/3/31	Stafford Road
24/10/31	Oxley
28/11/31	Oxley shops **R**
27/3/32	Oxley shops **R**
16/9/32	Swindon Works **I**
24/9/32	Canton
8/3/34	Swindon Works **G**
10/3/34	Swindon
31/7/35	Swindon Works **I**
18/5/36	Swindon Works **L**
6/4/37	Swindon Works **G**
21/10/38	Swindon Works **I**
7/1/39	St Philips Marsh
22/6/40	Swindon Works **I**
20/3/41	Tondu shops **R**
10/6/41	Reading shops **R**
7/8/41	St Philips Marsh shops **R**
21/10/41	St Philips Marsh shops **R**
14/1/42	St. Philips Marsh shops **R**
14/1/43	Swindon Works **G**
26/6/44	Gloucester shops **R**
20/10/44	St Philips Marsh shops **R**
9/3/45	Swindon Works **I**
18/7/46	Bristol Bath Road shops **R**
25/4/47	**Renumbered 3902 [oil fired]**
14/5/47	Swindon Works **G**
1/7/47	Canton shops **R**
5/8/47	Severn Tunnel Jct shops **R**
1/11/47	Newton Abbot
29/11/47	Laira
3/3/48	Laira shops **R**
20/3/48	Old Oak
12/7/48	**Renumbered 4948 [coal fired]**
15/9/48	Swindon Works **L**
2/5/49	Laira shops **U**
16/12/49	Laira shops **U**
18/5/50	Swindon Works **HG**
17/6/50	St. Philips Marsh
3/8/50	Newton Abbot Works **U**
7/10/50	Reading
15/11/50	Old Oak shops **U**
21/3/52	Swindon Works **HC**
27/12/52	Exeter
30/9/53	Swindon Works **HI**
20/9/54	Exeter shops **U**
4/2/55	Newton Abbot Works **LC**
13/1/56	Swindon Works **HG**
31/1/58	Swindon Works **HG**
1/3/58	Exeter shops **U**
20/5/59	Newton Abbot Works **U**
24/11/60	Swindon Works **HI**
7/10/61	Swindon
23/1/62	Swindon Works **LC**

Tenders

From new	2256
15/10/30	2374
9/1931	1980
28/12/33	2256
4/6/35	2210
18/5/36	1822
20/2/37	2014
27/10/38	2329
17/4/40	2262
14/11/42	2623
14/11/43	2390
20/5/44	2777
9/3/45	2767
16/7/49	2558
21/4/50	2548
16/6/50	2840
2/3/51	2554
31/3/52	2534
30/9/53	2386
13/1/56	2558
31/3/58	2542
23/1/62	2601

Mileage 1,293,341

Withdrawn 21/9/62, Sold to J Cashmore Ltd 16/9/63

NORTHWICK HALL, once an oil burner, heading west from Exeter St David's, 6 August 1955. J. Robertson, transporttreasury

4948, an Exeter engine for almost all of the 1950s, at St David's at some point during that period. The sliding roof ventilator from its oil burning days can just be seen but the cabside hand rail has returned to its original (higher) position. J. Davenport, Initial Photographics.

4949 PACKWOOD HALL

Built in 1929 to Lot no.254 at Swindon Works
To traffic 9/9/29

Mileages and Boilers

From new	4948
2/3/31	67,049 C4948
8/12/31	105,757 C2978
30/11/33	204,923 C2978
12/12/34	253,218 C4968
6/7/35	278,796 C4968
2/6/37	356,423 C4968
29/10/38	417,656 C4952
23/11/40	501,316 C4952
28/1/43	586,221 C4938
12/10/46	697,513 C8231
20/5/49	792,856 C4032
12/12/50	865,614 C4914
20/8/52	934,476 C4429
5/1/55	1,032,938 C4937
27/2/57	1,123,084 C4932
2/4/59	1,205,701 C2947
8/1/62	1,306,978 C4474
15/8/63	1,347,712 C2904

Sheds and Works history

5/9/29	Swindon Works **ATC**
9/9/29	Stafford Road
24/11/29	Oxley
17/1/30	Swindon Works **L**
2/3/31	Swindon Works **I**
14/3/31	Oxford
8/12/31	Swindon Works **G**
19/12/31	Old Oak
3/8/32	Oxford shops **R**
30/11/33	Swindon Works **I**
12/12/34	Swindon Works **G**
9/2/35	Oxford
6/7/35	Swindon Works **I**
27/7/35	Westbury
28/11/35	Westbury shops **R**
18/3/36	Swindon Works **L**
25/7/36	Westbury shops **R**
2/6/37	Swindon Works **I**
26/6/37	Bath Road
5/2/38	Bath Road shops **R**
27/4/38	Swindon Works **L**
29/10/38	Swindon Works **G**
12/11/38	Carmarthen
4/1940	Newton Abbot
14/4/40	Swindon Works **L**
5/1940	Carmarthen
23/11/40	Swindon Works **I**
3/1941	Taunton
25/3/42	Swindon Works **L**
6/1943	Penzance
28/1/43	Swindon Works **G**
4/11/43	Penzance shops **R**
16/8/44	Newton Abbot Works **L**
6/6/45	Penzance shops **R**
16/7/45	Newton Abbot Works **L**
3/10/45	Newton Abbot Works **L**
24/5/46	Penzance shops **R**
12/10/46	Swindon Works **I**
29/6/47	Penzance shops **R**
3/8/47	Penzance shops **R**
30/1/48	Newton Abbot Works **L**
13/5/48	Newton Abbot Works **L**
	Tender work only
15/7/48	Newton Abbot Works **L**
5/10/48	Newton Abbot Works **L**
20/5/49	Swindon Works **HG**
17/6/50	Taunton
12/8/50	Gloucester
12/12/50	Swindon Works **HG**
17/9/51	Taunton shops **U**
16/11/51	Taunton shops **U**
20/8/52	Swindon Works **HI**
9/7/54	Taunton shops **U**
5/1/55	Swindon Works **HG**
17/6/56	Taunton shops **U**
12/12/56	Taunton shops **U**
27/2/57	Swindon Works **HI**
22/3/58	St. Philips Marsh
20/6/58	St. Philips Marsh shops **U**
1/11/58	Bath Road
29/11/58	St. Philips Marsh
2/4/59	Swindon Works **HG**
12/8/60	Bath Road shops **LC**
8/1/62	Swindon Works **HI**
14/7/62	Westbury
18/9/62	Taunton shops **U**
6/10/62	Reading
3/11/62	St. Philips Marsh
15/8/63	Wolverhampton Works **HC**
22/6/64	Barrow Road

Tenders

From new	2257
21/1/31	1758
12/10/31	2246
11/9/33	2258
16/5/35	1871
19/4/37	2215
9/3/40	2437
9/10/40	2767
9/2/41	2661
26/12/42	2639
28/1/43	2409
6/7/44	2794
24/1/45	2574
28/8/46	2720
15/5/48	2448
10/7/48	2388
31/10/50	2693
15/7/52	2701
22/8/52	2758
30/11/54	2795
27/2/57	2768
2/4/59	2833
3/1/62	2908

Mileage 1,355,415 as at 28/12/63

Withdrawn 1/9/64

An elegant broadside of 4949 PACKWOOD HALL, against the austere bulk of Temple Meads Loco Yard box , 8 August 1954. J. Robertson, transporttreasury

PACKWOOD HALL at Bournemouth Central station, leaving for Weymouth; the date is not given but it is during the period of 4949's allocation to 82B St Philip's Marsh which came to an end when it transferred (on closure) to Barrow Road, from where residual Bristol steam duties were conducted. Typically of the period, a number plate has disappeared. J. Davenport, Initial Photographics.

4950 PATSHULL HALL

Built in 1929 to Lot no.254 at Swindon Works
To traffic 10/9/29

Mileages and Boilers

Date	Mileage/Boiler
From new	4949
10/1/31	62,376 C4949
2/9/32	145,050 C4933
28/3/34	226,381 C4933
5/6/36	325,764 C7200
31/1/38	410,001 C7200
30/5/40	495,555 C2997
6/10/42	521,854 C2997
21/8/44	629,547 C4037
11/1/47	700,667 C8001
25/8/49	796,014 C4464
10/1/52	882,579 C4480
23/2/54	966,439 C4989
27/4/56	1,061,581 C4989
25/11/58	1,168,088 C8212
13/7/61	1,244,792 C4927

Sheds and works history

8/1929	Swindon Works **ATC**
10/9/29	Stafford Road
24/11/29	Oxley
10/1/31	Swindon Works **I**
14/2/31	Canton
2/9/32	Swindon Works **G**
28/3/34	Swindon Works **I**
7/4/34	Truro
6/3/35	Newton Abbot Works **L**
9/3/35	Newton Abbot
6/4/35	Truro
12/7/35	Newton Abbot Works **L**
16/11/35	Newton Abbot
14/12/35	Truro
5/6/36	Swindon Works **G**
27/6/36	Stafford Road
31/1/38	Swindon Works **I**
10/5/39	Swindon Works **L**
27/5/39	Chester
24/6/39	Oxley
17/8/39	Ebbw Jct shops **R**
30/5/40	Swindon Works **G**
17/5/41	Wolverhampton Works **L**
1/9/41	Swindon Works **L**
6/10/42	Swindon Works **L**
2/2/43	Swindon Works **L**
29/10/43	Swindon Works **L**
21/8/44	Swindon Works **L**
19/9/44	Old Oak shops **R**
26/2/45	Bath Road shops **R**
30/5/45	Oxley shops **R**
15/9/45	Tyseley shops **L**
9/4/46	Reading shops **R**
11/1/47	Swindon Works **I**
1/11/47	Stafford Road
20/4/48	Laira shops **R**
26/6/48	Stafford Road shed **L**
19/8/48	Stafford Road shed **R**
4/1/49	Wolverhampton Works **LC**
25/8/49	Swindon Works **HG**
4/11/50	Oxley
9/2/51	Stafford Road shed **U**
10/1/52	Swindon Works **HI**
18/4/53	Reading
16/5/53	Laira
17/5/53	Laira shops **U**
4/11/53	Laira shops **U**
23/2/54	Swindon Works **HG**
5/11/54	Laira shops **U**
20/8/55	Banbury shops **U**
27/4/56	Newton Abbot Works **HI**
7/8/57	Laira shops **U**
5/10/57	Penzance
1/11/57	Newton Abbot Works **LC**
25/3/58	Penzance shops **U**
25/11/58	Swindon Works **HG**
2/3/59-13/6/59	Stored at Penzance
11/7/59	Laira
7/9/60	Laira shops **U**
8/10/60	Didcot
13/7/61	Swindon Works **HI**
27/7/63	Swindon
27/1/64	Didcot

Tenders

Date	Tender
From new	2258
5/11/30	2260
11/7/32	1649
16/1/34	2259
25/2/34	2225
26/6/35	2228
24/4/36	1926
6/12/37	1765
13/4/40	2410
5/8/41	2849
13/8/42	2823
19/8/43	2622
25/5/44	2818
6/6/45	2587
12/3/46	2647
30/12/46	2658
30/11/48	2624
6/12/51	2643
18/1/54	4039
20/3/56	2610
25/9/57	2691
25/11/58	2618
14/7/61	2738

Mileage as at 28/12/63 1,310,762

Withdrawn 6/5/64, Sold to Central Wagons Co Wigan 22/6/64

4950 PATSHULL HALL, not long out of shops in lined green, at Reading shed, 11 September 1961. Peter Groom.

4950 at Old Oak Common, 21 December 1962. It had gone to Didcot a year or two before and was withdrawn from there in 1964, one of a growing bunch of derelict Halls gathered there and at Oxford before transport to South Wales. H.C. Casserley, courtesy R.M. Casserley.

4951 PENDEFORD HALL

Built in 1929 to Lot no.254 at Swindon Works
To traffic 27/7/29

Mileages and Boilers

From new	4943
16/10/30	68,857 C4943
16/6/32	146,971 C4948
6/4/34	222,417 C4925
26/3/36	323,419 C4925
21/9/37	406,088 R2953
26/5/39	496,494 R2953
5/6/41	587,470 R2953
19/5/43	662,642 C4942
12/2/46	747,127 C4063
28/1/48	823,059 C4415
23/9/49	882,935 C7259
10/9/52	967,077 C2827
24/2/55	1,051,383 C8209
6/8/58	1,170,517 C9221
21/4/61	1,261,351 C8274

Sheds and Works history

27/7/29	Old Oak
8/1929	Swindon Works **ATC**
16/10/30	Swindon Works **I**
21/3/32	Old Oak shops **R**
16/6/32	Swindon Works **G**
2/7/32	Penzance
29/6/33	Penzance shops **R**
1/11/33	Newton Abbot Works **R**
6/4/34	Swindon Works **G**
5/5/34	Laira
31/8/34	Newton Abbot Works **L**
21/1/35	Newton Abbot Works **L**
5/6/35	Newton Abbot Works **L**
9/7/35	Newton Abbot Works **L**
27/7/35	Penzance
4/4/36	Laira
26/3/36	Swindon Works **I**
21/9/37	Swindon Works **G**
24/11/38	Laira shops **R**
26/5/39	Swindon Works **I**
3/1940	Truro
5/6/40	Newton Abbot Works **L**
7/1940	Laira
5/6/41	Swindon Works **I**
13/10/41	Laira shops **R**
27/2/42	Gloucester shops **R**
29/4/42	Newton Abbot Works **L**
8/1/43	Newton Abbot Works **L**
15/4/43	Truro shops **R**
19/5/43	Swindon Works **G**
18/1/45	Swindon Works **R**
29/5/45	Laira shops **R**
20/10/45	Laira shops **R**
12/2/46	Swindon Works **I**
2/7/46	Laira shops **R**
24/3/47	Newton Abbot Works **L**
19/4/47	Old Oak
28/1/48	Swindon Works **G**
28/4/48	Old Oak shops **L**
7/7/48	Didcot shops **R**
3/12/48	Bath Road shops **R**
13/8/49	Reading
23/9/49	Swindon Works **HG**
5/11/49-6/7/50	Stored at Swindon
12/8/50	Bath Road
4/11/50	Swindon
10/9/52	Swindon Works **HI**
31/10/53	Ebbw Jct
24/2/55	Swindon Works **HG**
7/12/56	Caerphilly Works **HC**
23/2/57	Oxley
23/3/57	Reading
6/8/58	Swindon Works **HG**
1/8/59	Reading shops **U**

26/2/60	Newton Abbot Works **LC**
21/4/61	Swindon Works **HG**
6/10/62	Oxford
14/11/62	Wolverhampton Works **LC**
9/2/63	Swindon
18/4/63	Westbury shops **U**
13/5/63	Swindon Works **U**
2/8/63	Worcester shops **U**
25/1/64	Oxford

Tenders

From new	2252
3/9/30	2375
29/12/30	2534
27/4/32	2263
21/2/34	1663
13/2/36	1865
11/8/37	2251
19/4/39	2611
2/4/42	2688
20/6/43	2669
10/12/45	2672
22/2/47	2621
25/11/48	2546
13/8/49	1766
31/7/52	2603
26/1/55	2714
13/9/56	2607
6/8/58	1750
21/4/61	2642

Mileage 1,334,534 at 28/12/63

Withdrawn 25/6/64

As a Swindon loco, at Westbury shed on 16 April 1963. Hamish Stevenson.

4951 comes into Frome with a down train on 13 September 1958. R. Broughton, ColourRail

PENDEFORD HALL on a freight near St Fagans, it is thought, 4 May 1956. S.Rickard/J&J Collection.

4952 PEPLOW HALL

Built in 1929 to lot no.254 at Swindon Works
To traffic 8/8/29

Mileages and Boilers

From new	4951
2/12/30	68,939 C4959
6/9/32	148,001 C4936
11/5/34	217,457 C4945
3/1/36	302,587 C4945
15/1/37	359,226 C2959
30/11/37	399,773 C2959
30/10/39	481,372 C2959
20/8/43	593,805 C2958
17/5/46	690,643 C2957
5/8/48	775,156 C2874
2/2/51	860,719 C2874
1/9/53	944,812 C4911
28/3/56	1,045,600 C4911
22/8/58	1,132,560 C9206
22/11/60	1,207,485 C8228

Sheds and Works history

8/1929	Swindon Works **ATC**
8/8/29	Old Oak
2/12/30	Swindon Works **I**
20/12/30	Oxley
6/9/32	Swindon Works **G**
24/9/32	Leamington Spa
1933	Tyseley
6/1/34	Tyseley shops **R**
11/5/34	Swindon Works **G**
2/6/34	Chester
3/1/36	Swindon Works **I**
8/2/36	Hereford
15/1/37	Swindon Works **L**
30/11/37	Swindon Works **I**
10/10/38	Swindon Works **L**
15/10/38	Worcester
12/11/38	Hereford
30/10/39	Swindon Works **I**
2/6/41	Hereford shops **R**
1/11/41	Worcester shops **L**
9/12/41	Shrewsbury shops **L**
	Tender Work Only
26/2/42	Hereford shops **R**
4/1942	Canton
8/12/42	Canton shops **L**
20/8/43	Swindon Works **G**
22/2/44	Canton shops **R**
13/3/44	Canton shops **R**
1/2/45	Wolverhampton Works **L**
15/11/45	Wolverhampton Works **L**
17/5/46	Swindon Works **I**
3/12/46	Ebbw Jct shops **R**
16/1/47	Ebbw Jct shops **R**
16/6/47	Canton shops **L**
12/2/48	Canton shops **L**
	Tender Work only
5/8/48	Swindon Works **G**
11/9/48	Hereford shops **R**
25/10/48	Stourbridge shops **R**
5/1/49	Llanelly shops **U**
16/9/49	Bath Road shops **U**
24/2/50	Canton shops **U**
2/2/51	Wolverhampton Works **HI**
23/2/52	St. Blazey
23/3/52	Canton
19/4/52	Severn Tunnel Jct
24/6/52	Didcot shops **U**
19/9/52	Laira shops **U**
1/9/53	Swindon Works **HG**
14/8/54	Llanelly
8/10/55	Hereford
28/3/56	Swindon Works **HI**
18/5/57	Worcester
13/7/57	Caerphilly Works **LC**
22/8/58	Swindon Works **HG**
9/3/59	Worcester shops **LC**
16/5/59	Canton
2/7/59	Worcester shops **U**
18/5/60	Didcot shops **U**
22/11/60	Swindon Works **HG**
19/9/61	Cathays **U**
23/7/62	Hereford shops **U**
2/10/62	Shrewsbury shops **U**

Tenders

From new	2254
22/10/30	2258
13/6/62	2259
6/1/34	2242
9/11/35	1795
2/12/36	1861
26/9/39	2255
24/5/43	2391
24/8/43	2562
18/3/46	2926
25/1/47	2558
4/6/48	2802
14/6/52	2262
18/4/53	2435
1/9/53	2597
31/3/56	2533
22/8/58	4065
9/3/59	2540
21/5/60	2801
22/11/60	2851

Mileage 1,270,461

Withdrawn 21/9/62, Sold to R S Hayes Ltd Bridgend 26/8/63

4952 PEPLOW HALL fitted with an experimental lubricator – under that distinctive cover. It was removed about 1936.

4952 PEPLOW HALL newly garbed in lined black at Swindon, outside the Iron Foundry, fresh off 'AE' Shop, 25 April 1954. Whatever criticisms were levelled at this livery, it surely made for a fine picture – when clean. transporttreasury

4953 PITCHFORD HALL

Built in 1929 to Lot no.254 at Swindon works
To traffic 8/8/29

Mileages and Boilers

Date	Mileage/Boiler
From new	4952
6/12/30	65,535 C4952
14/9/32	136,132 C4952
13/3/34	212,824 C2969
3/12/35	299,237 C2969
12/10/37	391,994 R2988
26/10/39	485,565 R2988
24/10/41	563,552 R2988
28/11/42	599,164 C4976
8/7/44	653,736 C4976
14/12/46	736,124 C4423
2/2/49	827,301 C7206
8/6/51	827,301 C7206
28/10/53	1,024,375 C7206
8/3/56	1,122,861 C4966
10/7/58	1,204,719 C4966
17/1/61	1,284,393 C9285

Sheds and Works history

8/1929	Swindon Works **ATC fitted**
8/8/29	Old Oak
20/5/30	Swindon Works **L**
5/7/30	Weymouth
6/12/30	Swindon Works **I**
20/12/30	Old Oak
7/4/30	Taunton
17/1/31	Westbury
14/9/32	Swindon Works **I**
24/9/32	Weymouth
1933	Bath Road
9/8/33	Weymouth shops **R**
13/3/34	Swindon Works **G**
24/1/35	Newton Abbot Works **L**
9/2/35	Penzance
4/5/35	Truro
3/12/35	Swindon Works **I**
10/3/37	Newton Abbot Works **L**
12/10/37	Swindon Works **G**
8/9/38	Newton Abbot Works **L**
21/2/39	Truro shops **R**
4/7/39	Truro shops **R**
26/10/39	Swindon Works **I**
31/1/40	Truro shops R
30/1/41	Newton Abbot Works **L**
5/1941	Pontypool Road
24/10/41	Swindon Works **I**
28/11/42	Swindon Works **L**
23/10/43	Pontypool Road shops **R**
3/3/44	Oxford shops **R**
8/7/44	Swindon Works **I**
4/10/45	Canton shops **L**
22/6/46	Taunton shops **R**
10/8/46	Canton
14/12/46	Swindon Works **G**
11/8/48	Canton shops **R**
2/2/49	Swindon Works **HG**
16/6/50	Canton **U**
8/6/51	Swindon Works **HG**
19/6/51	Swindon Works **U**
2/5/52	Swindon Works **U**
23/5/53	Canton shops **U**
28/10/53	Swindon Works **HI**
8/3/56	Swindon Works **HG**
21/4/56	Swindon
10/7/58	Wolverhampton Works **HI**
5/9/58	Southall shops **U**
27/4/59	Swindon Works **HC**
16/7/60	St. Philips Marsh
13/9/60	St Philips Marsh shops **U**
17/1/61	Swindon Works **HG**
10/8/61	Wolverhampton Works **LC**
11/8/62	Canton
8/9/62	Cardiff East Dock

Tenders

Date	Tender
From new	2255
1/5/30	1934
29/10/30	2239
31/1/34	1582
17/10/35	2243
4/9/37	1649
26/9/39	1952
11/8/41	2159
23/10/42	2795
13/5/44	2521
3/8/45	2567
14/10/46	2619
2/2/49	2703
26/3/52	2897
21/9/53	2420
8/3/56	2722
22/9/58	2767
27/6/59	2532
13/1/61	2702

Mileage 1,344,464

Withdrawn 2/5/63, sold to Woodham Bros. Barry 9/10/63. Engine preserved

A filthy 4953 PITCHFORD HALL at Shrewsbury shed in 1960. There is the faintest hint of lining and a second emblem on the tender, on the original print at least. transporttreasury

An up train comes past the Middle box at Severn Tunnel Junction behind 4953 PITCHFORD HALL on 24 June 1956. S.Rickard/J&J Collection.

PITCHFORD HALL at Cardiff East Dock late on, with scant improvement in the cleaning stakes. J. Davenport, Initial Photographics.

4954 PLAISH HALL

Built in 1929 to Lot no.254 at Swindon Works
To traffic 12/9/29

Mileages and Boilers
Only Engine record Cards available

Sheds and Works history

12/9/29	Stafford Road			
27/10/29	Oxley			
27/8/32	Stafford Road			
1933	Oxley			
10/3/34	Newton Abbot			
8/2/36	Laira			
30/5/36	Taunton			
4/2/39	Newton Abbot			
1/4/39	Taunton			
7/6/41	Swindon Works **I**			
27/3/43	Newton Abbot Works **L**	107,392	289,804	
26/8/44	Swindon Works **G**			
15/6/46	Newton Abbot Works **L**			
7/9/46	Taunton shops **L**			
16/11/46	Newton Abbot Works **L**			
5/7/47	Swindon Works **R**	85,571		
22/10/49	Swindon Works **HG**	78,199	163,770	
27/1/51	Laira			
24/2/51	Exeter			
15/3/52	Swindon Works **HG**	91,226	91,226	
11/7/53	Newton Abbot			
31/8/53	Newton Abbot Works **U**			
24/4/54	Didcot			
10/7/54	Wolverhampton Works **HI**	91,634		
28/8/54	Didcot **LC**			
8/9/56	Oxford			
5/12/56	Swindon Works **HG**			
11/2/59	Swindon Works **HI**			
26/12/59	Stafford Road			
8/3/61	Swindon Works **HG**			
7/10/61	Tyseley			
19/9/63	Wolverhampton Works **HC**			
8/8/64	Oxley			

Withdrawn 11/64

Some works info available is from the GWR 'Repair History' card, early 1940s to 1954.
Mileage figures =
First column: 'Miles run since previous repair'
Second column: 'Miles run since last "general"'

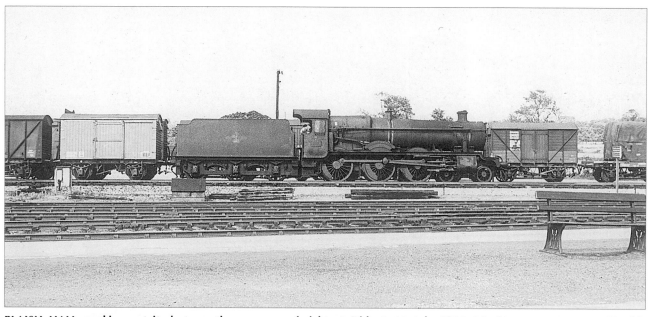

PLAISH HALL working out its last months, on an up freight at Didcot, 14 July 1964. J.L. Stevenson, courtesy Hamish Stevenson.

4954 PLAISH HALL backs out of Paddington departure side in 1954; the large number 18 means it has been serving on the empty stock work. D.K. Jones Collection.

4954 PLAISH HALL resplendent in lined green at Swindon, presumably on the occasion of its February 1959 Heavy Intermediate. ColourRail

4955 PLASPOWER HALL

Built in 1929 to Lot no.254 at Swindon Works
To traffic 3/9/29

Mileages and Boilers

From new	4954
12/12/30	61,560 C4954
18/10/32	142,112 C4954
10/10/33	183,294 C2811
18/4/35	264,474 C2811
24/4/37	345,926 C4436
15/2/39	422,706 C4436
5/3/41	502,213 C4980
21/4/43	579,643 C4980
26/2/45	638,944 C4440
31/1/47	714,618 C4032
27/4/49	797,264 C4423
28/5/51	876,433 C2923
4/7/52	919,645 C7248
16/2/54	969,474 C4448
5/6/56	1,057,109 C8212
14/8/58	1,144,347 C4907
27/4/61	1,250,672 C4475

Tenders

From new	2134
12/12/30	1777
18/7/32	2264
20/7/36	2137
14/3/37	1948
24/4/37	2423
15/2/39	2712
14/1/41	2590
16/3/43	2740
1/1/40	2700
26/2/45	2680
1/5/48	1515
28/3/49	2406
12/6/52	2847
13/1/54	2709
5/6/56	2755
2/11/57	2916
27/4/61	1748

Mileage 1,320,257

Withdrawn 21/10/63, Sold to G Cohen Morriston 1/1/64

Sheds and Works history

8/1929	Swindon Works **ATC**
3/9/29	Bristol Bath Road
24/11/29	St. Philips Marsh
12/12/30	Swindon Works **I**
20/12/30	Old Oak
21/1/31	Swindon Works **L**
14/2/31	Canton
18/10/32	Swindon Works **I**
22/10/32	Swindon
1933	Old Oak
1933	Oxford
10/10/33	Swindon Works **G**
24/11/34	Oxford shops **R**
18/4/35	Swindon Works **I**
29/11/35	Swindon Works **L**
14/8/36	Swindon Works **L**
24/4/37	Swindon Works **G**
29/5/37	Weymouth
16/10/37	Oxley
15/2/39	Swindon Works **G**
5/3/41	Swindon Works **G**
21/4/43	Swindon Works **I**
5/6/44	Oxford shops
26/2/45	Swindon Works **G**
5/7/46	Stafford Road shed **R**
31/1/47	Swindon Works **I**
15/5/48	Oxley shops **R**
23/9/48	Oxley shops **L**
	Tender work only
27/4/49	Swindon Works **HG**
28/5/51	Swindon Works **HI**
4/7/52	Swindon Works **HC**
25/6/53	Wolverhampton Works **U**
22/8/53	St Philips Marsh shops **U**
16/2/54	Swindon Works **HG**
21/3/55	Wolverhampton Works **LC**
16/7/55	Exeter
5/6/56	Swindon Works **HI**
5/10/57	Newton Abbot
31/3/58	Newton Abbot Works **U**
14/8/58	Swindon Works **HG**
28/11/59	Taunton
27/4/61	Swindon Works **HI**
9/2/63	Pontypool Road
29/3/63	Swindon shed **U**

4955 PLASPOWER HALL at Exeter St David's, in lined black, 3 August 1954. J. Robertson, transporttreasury

4955 PLASPOWER HALL at Banbury, 24 May 1962. K. Fairey, ColourRail

4956 PLOWDEN HALL

Built in 1929 to Lot no.254 at Swindon Works
To traffic 11/9/29

Mileages and Boilers

From new	4955
14/3/31	67,650 C4955
11/5/32	119,451 C4955
22/12/33	191,704 C4915
8/11/35	281,141 C4419
31/7/37	361,682 C4419
11/5/39	436,498 C4460
8/8/41	522,517 C4460
28/10/43	595,086 C4460
2/3/46	672,591 C4052
4/3/48	762,408 C2921
25/7/50	859,741 C4974
13/11/50	862,638 [to traffic]
26/9/52	935,004 C8262
19/4/55	1,030,946 C2962
30/8/57	1,131,627 C8201
10/8/61	1,287,821 C2869

Sheds and Works history

11/9/29	Old Oak
27/9/29	Swindon Works **ATC**
24/11/29	Worcester
25/4/30	Worcester shops **L**
30/10/30	Worcester shops **L**
14/3/31	Swindon Works **I**
11/4/31	Old Oak
9/5/31	Swindon
11/5/32	Swindon Works **I**
4/6/32	Old Oak
16/9/32	Tyseley shops **R**
1933	Bath Road
22/12/33	Swindon Works **G**
13/1/34	St Philips Marsh
25/7/34	St Philips Marsh shops **R**
28/3/35	St Philips Marsh shops **R**
8/11/35	Swindon Works **G**
31/7/37	Swindon Works **I**
22/6/38	St Philips Marsh shops **R**
11/5/39	Swindon Works **G**
27/5/39	Swindon
8/8/41	Swindon Works **I**
28/10/43	Swindon Works **I**
16/8/44	Swindon Works **R**
24/9/44	St Blazey shops **R**
2/3/46	Swindon Works **G**
29/8/46	Laira shops **R**
21/10/47	Swindon shed **L**
4/3/48	Swindon Works **I**
25/5/49	Bath Road shops **U**
25/7/50	Swindon Works **HG**
23/8/50	To store at Swindon shed
13/11/50	Returned to traffic
2/12/50	Southall
26/9/52	Swindon Works **HG**
31/3/54	Southall shops **U**
16/9/54	Southall shops **U**
19/4/55	Swindon Works **HI**
19/5/56	Westbury
6/10/56	Bath Road
30/8/57	Swindon Works **HG**
21/2/59	Canton
5/4/61	Canton shops **U**
10/8/61	Swindon Works **HG**
24/2/62	Gloucester
14/7/62	Southall
6/10/62	Westbury
1/3/63	Caerphilly Works **LC**
18/4/63	Westbury shops **U**

Tenders

From new	1758
21/4/30	1738
28/1/31	1851
18/2/32	2247
16/10/33	2368
18/9/35	2351
31/3/37	2629
15/6/37	2210
21/3/39	2644
4/6/41	2768
31/7/43	2533
28/10/43	2640
4/3/48	2811
14/6/50	2552
27/8/52	2930
11/3/55	2556
30/8/57	2563
14/7/59	2825
28/3/59	2923
10/8/61	2672

Mileage 1,343,127

Withdrawn 4/7/63

4956 PLOWDEN HALL runs through Wantage Road on 13 June 1939. H.C. Casserley, courtesy R.M. Casserley.

In lined black, 4956 PLOWDEN HALL waits for signals beside Westbourne Park station, on the way to Old Oak shed from Paddington on 12 February 1955. There is no emblem on the tender. Peter Groom.

4957 POSTLIP HALL

Built in 1929 to Lot no.254 at Swindon Works
To traffic12/9/29

Mileages and Boilers

From new	4956
22/1/31	62,299 C4956
23/9/32	137,181 C4931
18/4/34	213,589 C4931
9/1/36	300,920 C2964
21/2/38	384,621 C2964
28/3/40	469,878 C4932
31/10/42	569,976 C4932
29/7/44	629,393 C7260
23/9/47	745,255 C4422
15/11/49	833,365 C4473
16/4/52	919,373 C4984
16/8/54	1,008,686 R6219
14/12/56	1,099,587 R6219
22/1/59	1,178,844 C2925

Sheds and Works history

9/1929	Swindon Works **ATC**
12/9/29	Oxley
2/10/29	Old Oak shops **R**
14/4/30	Oxley shops **L**
22/1/31	Swindon Works **I**
29/10/31	Old Oak shops **R**
30/11/31	Oxford shops **R**
19/12/31	Worcester
16/1/32	Oxford
23/9/32	Swindon Works **G**
18/8/33	Oxford shops R
18/4/34	Swindon Works **I**
5/5/34	Laira
24/9/34	Newton Abbot Works **L**
17/7/35	Newton Abbot Works **L**
9/1/36	Swindon Works **G**
1/12/36	Newton Abbot Works **L**
20/4/37	Penzance shops **R**
10/12/37	Newton Abbot Works **L**
21/2/38	Swindon Works **I**
17/9/38	Penzance shops **R**
26/1/39	Newton Abbot Works **R**
29/4/39	Truro
15/5/39	Truro shops **R**
26/10/39	Newton Abbot Works **L**
28/3/40	Swindon Works **G**
26/2/41	Truro shops **R**
18/4/41	Laira shops **R**
28/4/42	Canton shops **R**
6/1942	Canton

31/10/42	Wolverhampton Works **I**
29/7/44	Swindon Works **G**
10/1944	Neyland
19/4/45	Carmarthen shops **R**
29/1/46	Swindon Works **L**
28/5/46	Carmarthen shops **L**
8/2/47	Carmarthen shops **L**
23/9/47	Swindon Works **I**
30/10/48	Landore
4/5/49	Landore shops **U**
15/11/49	Swindon Works **HG**
22/4/50	St. Philips Marsh
17/6/50	Neyland
13/10/51	Llanelly shops **U**
16/4/52	Swindon Works **HI**
17/10/53	Llanelly shops **U**
31/10/53	Ebbw Jct
16/8/54	Swindon Works **HG**
14/12/56	Swindon Works **HI**
25/1/58	Oxley
18/6/58	Oxley shops **U**
22/1/59	Swindon Works **HG**
27/2/60	Taunton
26/3/60	Shrewsbury
21/5/60	Westbury
10/6/60	Ebbw Jct shops **U**
12/12/60	Old Oak shops **U**

Tenders

From new	2259
4/12/30	2861
5/2/34	2265
29/11/35	1788
5/1/38	2284
22/1/40	2750
19/5/44	2863
24/11/45	2023
23/9/47	2691
4/5/49	2758
16/4/52	2626
26/6/54	2604
14/12/56	2694
22/1/59	2676

Mileage 1,288,249

Withdrawn 30/3/62, Cut up 16/6/62

4957 POSTLIP HALL, still in lined black with first emblem, at Shrewsbury shed in 1958. D.K. Jones Collection.

4957 POSTLIP HALL makes a fine show at Ely Main Line west of Cardiff, 23 May 1955. S.Rickard/J&J Collection.

4957 at snowy Gerrards Cross on 5 January 1962, with a train of what looks like concrete pipe sections. POSTLIP HALL is unusual in that the lubricating oil pipe to the valve on the smokebox, which normally runs under the boiler cladding, is on the outside. This wouldn't be a replacement or modification; the one underneath must have failed (blocked probably) and this substitute will suffice till the one underneath can be dealt with. C. Leigh-Jones, ColourRail

4958 PRIORY HALL

Built in 1929 to Lot no.254 at Swindon Works
To traffic 25/9/29

Mileages and Boilers

From new	4957
19/1/31	67,309 C4957
3/1/33	146,666 C4957
26/1/34	194,838 C4919
7/8/35	274,953 C4429
7/7/37	354,028 C4429
9/6/39	431,411 C4095
8/7/41	509,283 C4095
12/11/43	597,911 C8209
14/4/46	678,564 C4490
22/2/49	781,382 C8263
19/2/51	859,085 C4419
29/10/53	963,222 C4419
13/4/56	1,051,043 C2828
28/3/58	1,134,534 C2990
23/5/61	1,243,900 C7268

Sheds and Works history

9/1929	Swindon Works **ATC fitted**
25/9/29	Oxley
14/11/29	Swindon Works **L**
24/11/29	Canton
19/1/31	Swindon Works **I**
14/2/31	Penzance
11/5/31	Penzance shops **R**
29/8/31	Exeter
19/12/31	Penzance
18/3/32	Newton Abbot shed **R**
3/1/33	Swindon Works **I**
1933	Oxford
26/1/34	Swindon Works **G**
10/2/34	Weymouth
16/8/34	Old Oak shops **R**
7/8/35	Swindon Works **G**
24/8/35	Penzance
12/2/36	Penzance shops **R**
19/6/36	Newton Abbot Works **L**
7/7/37	Swindon Works **L**
24/7/37	Worcester
13/10/38	Swindon Works **L**
12/11/38	Landore
9/6/39	Swindon Works **G**
24/6/39	Westbury
11/11/39	Canton
14/5/41	Reading shops **R**
8/7/41	Swindon Works **I**
2/1942	Laira
10/2/42	Laira shops **R**
18/9/42	Laira shops **R**
2/12/42	Laira shops **R**
12/11/43	Swindon Works **G**
12/4/44	Laira shops **R**
30/1/45	Swindon Works **L**
22/3/45	Laira shops **R**
9/4/45	Laira shops **R**
9/8/45	Laira shops **R**
19/1/46	Laira shops **R**
14/4/46	Swindon Works **I**
26/11/46	Laira shops **R**
24/1/47	Newton Abbot Works **L**
22/2/47	Old Oak
22/2/47	Old Oak shops **L** *[same date]*
10/10/47	Swindon Works **L**
1/11/48	Old Oak shops **R**
22/2/49	Swindon Works **HG**
13/4/49	Old Oak shops **U**
24/8/49	Old Oak shops **U**
5/10/49	Swindon Works **LC**
19/2/51	Swindon Works **HG**
24/2/51	Swindon
13/6/53	St. Philips Marsh
29/10/53	Swindon Works **HI**
22/5/54	Bath Road
6/11/54	St. Philips Marsh
21/5/55	Bath Road
15/6/55	St Philips Marsh shops **U**
18/6/55	St Philips Marsh
29/11/55	St Philips Marsh shops **U**
13/4/56	Swindon Works **HG**
16/6/56	Bath Road
11/4/57	Bath Road shops **LC**
13/7/57	Carmarthen
28/3/58	Swindon Works **HI**
15/9/58-6/10/58	Stored at Carmarthen shed
28/11/59	Pontypool Road
9/2/60	Tyseley shops **U**
23/5/61	Swindon Works **HG**
29/1/62	Pontypool Road shops **U**
4/10/62	Caerphilly Works **LC**
24/1/63	Wolverhampton Works **U**
26/8/63	Pontypool Road shops **U**
21/4/64	Ebbw Jct shops **U**
22/6/64	Gloucester

Tenders

From new	2260
2/12/30	2259
18/3/32	2422
23/9/32	2141
8/11/33	1518
11/6/35	2228
19/6/36	2225
19/5/37	2252
26/4/39	2419
24/4/41	2403
16/5/41	2652
2/9/43	1459
28/3/44	2409
18/7/44	2665
6/2/46	1509
10/10/47	2412
26/1/49	2735
2/9/49	2827
19/1/51	2581
20/2/52	2861
11/9/53	2732
25/5/55	2556
26/2/56	2581
13/4/56	4075
28/3/58	2709

Mileage 1,316,540 at 28/12/63

Withdrawn 21/10/64

Shrewsbury once more, and lined black 4958 PRIORY HALL brings in a train from the south past the iconic Severn Bridge Junction box; Shrewsbury Abbey rises up beyond the train. D.K. Jones Collection.

The strange case of the Hall and the Great Central ROD tender behind 4958 at Gloucester shed, 26 September 1964. Sadly it was an embrace of death however, a convenient mating for the final scrapyard journey only. J.L. Stevenson, courtesy Hamish Stevenson.

4959 PURLEY HALL

Built in 1929 to Lot no.254 at Swindon Works
To traffic 14/11/29

Mileages and Boilers

From new	4958
19/2/31	65,797 C4958
22/9/32	141,753 C4900
27/4/34	209,742 C4900
14/2/36	291,517 C2843
1/1/38	381,188 C2843
7/2/40	460,447 C4423
17/10/42	552,339 C4423
13/7/44	591,647 C2930
26/9/46	664,912 C2971
2/9/48	733,538 C2999
16/3/51	844,163 C7254
20/8/53	939,499 C9218
2/12/55	1,011,278 C4954
23/4/57	1,075,321 C7221
5/6/59	1,154,472 C4957
13/4/62	1,231,853 C4036

Sheds and Works history

9/1929	Swindon Works **ATC**
29/10/29	Swindon Works **R**
14/11/29	Westbury
15/10/30	Swindon Works **R**
	Tender work
14/2/31	Laira
19/2/31	Swindon Works **I**
3/3/32	Newton Abbot Works **R**
22/9/32	Swindon Works **G**
22/10/32	Truro
5/5/33	Truro shops R
25/5/33	Newton Abbot Works **R**
7/11/33	Newton Abbot Works **R**
27/4/34	Swindon Works **I**
5/5/34	St Philips Marsh
19/9/35	St Philips Marsh shops **R**
14/2/36	Swindon Works **G**
29/6/37	St Philips Marsh shops **R**
1/1/38	Swindon Works **I**
5/2/38	Tyseley
7/2/40	Swindon Works **G**
3/1942	Leamington Spa
5/1942	Tyseley
17/10/42	Swindon Works **I**
1/1/43	Tyseley shops **R**
2/1943	Leamington Spa
5/1943	Tyseley
1/11/43	Swindon Works **L**
13/7/44	Swindon Works **L**
8/1/45	Tyseley shops **R**
26/9/46	Swindon Works **G**
1/10/47	Aberdare shops **R**
3/1/48	Tyseley shops **L**
2/9/48	Swindon Works **I**
30/9/48	Tyseley shops **R**
31/3/50	Tyseley shops **U**
16/3/51	Swindon Works **HI**
1/11/52	Oxley
15/6/53	Reading shops **U**
20/8/53	Swindon Works **HG**
25/1/55	Croes Newydd shops **U**
21/5/55	Bath Road
2/12/55	Swindon Works **HG**
1/12/56	Swindon
23/4/57	Swindon Works **HI**
28/12/57	Bath Road
1/7/58	Ebbw Jct shops **U**
4/10/58	Didcot
5/6/59	Swindon Works **HG**
4/9/59	Wolverhampton Works **LC**
17/11/59	Old Oak **U**
16/3/60	Swindon Works **LC**
7/2/61	Didcot shops **U**
13/4/62	Swindon Works **HG**
6/3/63	Old Oak shops **U**

Tenders

From new	2381
6/1/31	2147
14/7/32	1941
13/3/34	1758
1/1/36	2253
11/6/37	2629
1/3/37	2351
23/11/37	2443
13/12/39	2258
2/8/42	2756
28/6/43	2867
31/3/44	2268
6/8/46	2684
26/9/46	2927
18/7/48	2601
1/7/53	2427
2/12/53	2813
5/6/59	2589
8/8/59	2424
4/9/59	2573
16/3/60	2731
7/2/61	2803
13/4/62	2669

Mileage 1,278,546 as at 28/12/63

Withdrawn 12/64

A lined black PURLEY HALL undergoing attention at Shrewsbury shed. ColourRail

4959 PURLEY HALL heads another (Modified – the steam pipe is markedly higher) Hall out of Plymouth North Road (mail coach behind) on Saturday 15 September 1956. It's an interesting photograph and the photographer, 'local lad' Peter Kerslake has kindly provided some considerable detail. At top, running horizontally, is Gordon Terrace and below it, sloping down, a now gated off and much-abused footpath which used to lead to Mutley station. The rough ground at right foreground and on the far side of the Halls are the remains of Mutley station platforms. This long-lost station was in use before the days of North Road when Millbay, further down towards Millbay Docks, was Plymouth's main station. At top right are engines in the sidings waiting to back down to North Road to relieve locos working up from Cornwall; among them is Britannia 70016 ARIEL, which will take over a relief to Paddington running just behind PURLEY HALL's train. This is the 12 noon 'North Mail' from Penzance, the 3.45pm from Plymouth for Crewe and beyond, a 'West to North' running via the Severn Tunnel and Shrewsbury. There must have been a severe shortage of locos at Laira this day, for the train was almost invariably entrusted to Kings and Castles before the Britannias came to appear on it regularly; a Hall as train engine was highly unusual. The Travelling Post Office will come off at Temple Meads and return the next day while the train engine was rostered for a Bristol-Paddington train after a quick 'once-over' at Bath Road shed. The Foreman there might well take 'avoiding action' when he sees what the engine is! Normally the pilot would assist over the South Devon banks only to Newton Abbot but with a mere Modified Hall on the train itself, the pair might work all the way through to Bristol – especially likely as 4959 is a Bath Road engine, after all. Peter Kerslake, RailOnline

4960 PYLE HALL

Built in 1929 to Lot no.254 at Swindon Works
To traffic 14/11/29

Mileages and Boilers

From new	4959
29/1/31	65,576 C4959
20/12/32	153,940 C4097
4/7/34	230,802 C4097
5/5/36	312,666 C4900
1/1/38	397,064 C4900
25/1/40	477,981 C4987
6/7/42	568,550 C2891
17/7/44	640,335 C2891
12/1/46	687,474 C7268
20/3/47	731,576 C7208
15/12/48	794,289 C8237
28/7/50	852,405 C4054
17/10/50	857,631 C4054
19/3/52	908,775 C2947
23/7/53	957,300 C8907
26/5/54	1,046,427 C8907
28/3/58	1,131,214 C8203
27/7/60	1,209,383 C8273

Sheds and Works history

9/1929	Swindon Works **ATC**
26/10/29	Swindon Works **R**
14/11/29	Westbury
29/1/31	Swindon Works **I**
14/2/31	Laira
9/5/31	Taunton
20/12/32	Swindon Works **G**
1933	Oxford
25/8/33	Reading shops **R**
13/10/33	Swindon Works **L**
4/7/34	Swindon Works **I**
27/7/34	Stafford Road shed **L**
28/7/34	Shrewsbury
30/8/34	Wolverhampton Works **R**
20/10/34	Stafford Road
21/1/35	Oxley
5/5/36	Swindon Works **G**
1/1/38	Swindon Works **I**
5/2/38	Oxley
12/8/38	Swindon Works **L**
25/1/40	Swindon Works **G**
3/1940	Stafford Road shed
4/1940	Oxley
6/7/42	Swindon Works **G**
17/7/44	Swindon Works **I**
13/1/45	Tyseley shops **R**
14/8/45	Swindon Works **L**
12/1/46	Swindon Works **L**
20/3/47	Swindon Works **G**
19/4/47	Stafford Road
10/4/48	Tyseley shops **R**
18/10/48	Banbury shops **R**
15/12/48	Swindon Works **I**

28/7/50	Swindon Works **HG**
19/9/50-17/10/50	Stored at Swindon Works
2/12/50	Banbury
10/10/51	Banbury shops **U**
19/3/52	Swindon Works **HC**
9/8/52	Stafford Road
4/10/52	Oxley
1/11/52	Reading
23/7/53	Swindon Works **HG**
19/1/56	Swindon Works **HI**
23/7/57	Old Oak shops **U**
28/3/58	Swindon Works **HG**
21/2/59	Exeter
3/10/59	St Philips Marsh
4/4/60	Bath Road shops **U**
27/7/60	Swindon Works **HI**
4/8/61	Caerphilly Works **LC**
5/12/61	St Philips Marsh shops **U**

Tenders

From new	2261
30/12/30	2381
15/5/34	2592
24/3/36	2171
12/11/37	2577
25/1/40	2745
23/5/42	2668
30/5/44	2180
17/7/44	2390
17/6/45	2557
12/1/46	2391
10/2/47	2885
24/3/48	2839
8/6/50	2755
11/2/52	2531
30/5/53	2878
19/1/56	2402
28/3/58	2425
27/7/60	2897

Mileage 1,282,859

Withdrawn 21/9/62, Sold to Messrs John Cashmore Ltd Newport 23/8/63

4960 PYLE HALL starts away westwards from Salisbury station platform 3 with a train for the Bristol line, 7 November 1960. J.A.C. Kirke, transporttreasury

PYLE HALL outside the LNW shed at Shrewsbury in August 1962; GW shed in background with its Shrewsbury & Hereford Railway turret, complete with loco weather vane. This side view shows the difference, for instance that results when the coupling rods are 'reversed' – coupling between them in 4960's case is to the *rear* of the crank pin. For the explanation to this odd-sounding statement, see note under 4946 in the introduction. D.K. Jones Collection.

4960 PYLE HALL at Bristol St Philips Marsh shed, 4 October 1962. Michael Boakes Collection.

4961 PYRLAND HALL

Built in 1929 to Lot no.254 at Swindon Works
To traffic 17/11/29

Mileages and Boilers

From new	4969
7/11/30	42,005 C4969
10/12/31	101,872 C4969
30/12/32	145,707 C4972
14/5/34	220,098 C4972
31/5/35	276,736 C4907
8/11/35	298,861 C4485
17/4/37	367,079 C4485
26/11/38	450,153 C4463
14/9/40	525,875 C4463
7/2/43	620,587 C4463
11/4/45	702,111 C2993
16/8/47	793,723 C8274
28/7/49	864,660 C4437
31/8/51	951,893 C8212
30/12/53	1,039,065 C4927
26/1/56	1,122,528 C4927
29/10/58	1,219,386 C2874
6/11/61	1,324,636 C7205

Sheds and Works history

17/11/29	Goodwick
11/1929	Swindon Works **ATC**
21/2/30	Goodwick shops **R**
19/9/30	Danygraig shops **R**
7/11/30	Swindon Works **I**
22/11/30	Oxley
20/12/30	Stafford Road
10/12/31	Swindon Works **I**
2/9/32	Wolverhampton Works **R**
30/12/32	Swindon Works **G**
1933	Newton Abbot
23/2/34	Newton Abbot Works **L**
14/5/34	Swindon Works **I**
2/6/34	Old Oak
31/5/35	Swindon Works **G**
8/11/35	Swindon Works **L**
16/11/35	Oxford
11/1/36	Old Oak
17/4/37	Swindon Works **I**
26/11/38	Swindon Works **G**
24/5/40	Swindon Works **L**
14/9/40	Swindon Works **I**
5/11/40	Swindon Works **R**
25/10/41	Old Oak shops **R**
12/1941	Laira
7/2/43	Swindon Works **I**
19/9/43	Laira shops **R**
10/7/44	Lairs shops **R**
19/8/44	Newton Abbot Works **L**
27/12/44	Laira shops **R**
11/4/45	Swindon Works **G**
14/6/46	Newton Abbot Works **L**
2/2/47	Laira shops **R**
22/3/47	Old Oak
16/8/47	Swindon Works **I**
21/1/49	Bath Road shops **U**
9/2/49	Old Oak shops **U**
28/7/49	Swindon Works **HG**
31/8/51	Swindon Works **HI**
8/9/51	St Philips Marsh
6/10/51	Bath Road
4/10/52	Bath Road shops **U**
22/5/53	Bath Road shops **U**
30/12/53	Swindon Works **HG**
16/7/55	Gloucester
13/8/55	Reading
26/1/56	Swindon Works **HI**
29/10/58	Swindon Works **HG**
8/7/59	Oxley shops **U**
21/5/60	Westbury
5/4/61	Gloucester Barnwood shops **U**
6/11/61	Swindon Works **HI**
13/9/62	Wolverhampton Works **LC**

Tenders

From new	2447
20/9/30	1852
12/1930	2415
18/8/32	2588
15/10/32	2534
14/5/34	2587
31/5/35	2145
5/3/37	2544
22/10/38	2593
20/7/40	2664
7/2/43	2649
10/7/44	2643
11/4/45	2256
14/6/46	2604
16/8/47	2722
28/7/49	2395
26/7/51	2599
30/11/53	2887
26/1/56	2565
29/6/58	2691
6/11/61	2677

Mileage 1,350,042

Withdrawn 5/11/62 Cut up 23/2/63

4961 PYRLAND HALL at Leamington Spa with a Chester service, 16 August 1958. R. Wilson, transporttreasury

4962 RAGLEY HALL

Built in 1929 to Lot no.254 at Swindon Works
To traffic 23/11/29

Mileages and Boilers

From new	4961
27/2/31	63,805 C4961
6/6/33	153,519 C4961
8/6/34	205,952 C4966
21/1/36	290,659 C4966
1/11/37	385,072 R2990
3/6/39	465,002 R2990
26/8/41	548,807 R2990
1/11/43	640,278 R2990
29/10/45	714,526 C8204
6/10/47	785,641 C4994
6/10/49	855,710 C8274
10/3/52	940,772 C2934
12/10/54	1,031,069 C2934
1/2/57	1,116,343 C2953
17/9/59	1,257,662 C2953
31/1/62	1,337,284 C8226

Sheds and Works history

11/1929	Swindon Works **ATC**
23/11/29	Canton
27/2/31	Swindon Works **I**
14/3/31	Reading
6/6/33	Swindon Works **I**
1933	St Philips Marsh
16/2/34	Bath Road shops **R**
8/6/34	Swindon Works **G**
30/6/34	Old Oak
12/2/35	Old Oak shops **R**
21/1/36	Swindon Works **I**
1/11/37	Swindon Works **G**
3/6/39	Swindon Works **I**
24/6/39	Worcester
14/10/39	Gloucester
11/11/39	Canton
26/8/41	Swindon Works **I**
1/1942	Laira
20/4/42	Laira shops **R**
2/2/43	Laira shops **R**
1/11/43	Swindon Works **I**
10/2/45	Truro shops **R**
2/5/45	Laira shops **R**
29/10/45	Swindon Works **G**
11/12/45	Laira shops **R**
1/10/46	Laira shops **R**
7/1/47	Laira shops **R**
22/2/47	Old Oak
15/7/47	Old Oak shops **R**
6/10/47	Swindon Works **I**
17/4/48	Reading
6/10/49	Swindon Works **HG**
4/9/50	Reading shops **U**
10/3/52	Swindon Works **HG**
11/7/53	Old Oak
5/9/53	Reading
4/5/54	Old Oak shops **U**
12/10/54	Swindon Works **HI**
5/5/56	Reading shops **U**
1/2/57	Swindon Works **HG**
17/9/59	Swindon Works **HI**
18/6/60	Carmarthen
1/12/60	Carmarthen shops **U**
9/6/61	Carmarthen shops **U**
31/1/62	Swindon Works **HG**
19/5/62	Goodwick
29/9/63	Old Oak
19/12/63	Old Oak shops **U**
22/6/64	Didcot
10/7/65	Oxford

Tenders

From new	2445
12/1/31	2536
12/2/33	2598
27/4/34	2543
11/11/35	2260
27/9/37	2611
25/4/39	2605
24/6/41	2857
14/1/43	2678
1/11/43	2545
29/10/45	2407
23/8/47	2394
6/10/47	1509
27/5/49	2827
6/10/49	2931
5/4/54	2665
11/9/54	2925
12/10/54	2768
1/2/57	2919
17/9/59	2391
31/1/62	2837

Mileage 1,405,224 at 28/12/63

Withdrawn 10/1965

4962 RAGLEY HALL late on, at Banbury on 3 October 1964. K. Fairey, ColourRail

4962 in its dotage, *sans* nameplate at Oxford, last resting place of sundry Halls, on 6 July 1965. It was withdrawn two or three months later. J.L. Stevenson, courtesy Hamish Stevenson.

4963 RIGNALL HALL

Built in 1929 to Lot no.254 at Swindon Works
To traffic 28/11/29

Mileages and Boilers

From new	4962
2/3/31	72,107 C4962
14/9/33	164,653 C4944
4/6/35	247,818 C4944
16/3/36	292,026 C4420
6/3/37	333,064 C4420
6/12/38	412,887 C4420
3/12/40	493,340 C4420
17/12/42	563,563 C4421
27/2/46	653,078 C4942
24/5/48	727,557 C8215
11/10/50	806,203 C2918
10/3/53	898,087 R6210
11/5/55	990,354 R6210
16/7/57	1,063,019 C6206
5/10/59	1,144,547 C6218

ColourRail

Sheds and Works history

11/1929	Swindon Works **ATC fitted**
28/11/29	Carmarthen
2/3/31	Swindon Works **I**
14/3/31	Old Oak
6/6/31	Reading
27/4/32	Reading shops **R**
1933	Reading
14/9/33	Swindon Works **G**
4/6/35	Swindon Works **I**
29/6/35	Weymouth
16/3/36	Swindon Works **L**
6/3/37	Swindon Works **I**
1/5/37	St Philips Marsh
10/1/38	St Philips Marsh shops **R**
4/5/38	St Philips Marsh shops **R**
6/12/38	Swindon Works **I**
24/10/39	St Philips Marsh shops **R**
3/12/40	Swindon Works **I**
15/7/41	St Philips Marsh shops **R**
26/11/41	St Philips Marsh shops **R**
17/12/42	Swindon Works **G**
16/2/43	Gloucester shops **R**
11/7/44	Swindon Works **L**
29/12/44	Swindon Works **L**
23/4/45	St Philips Marsh **R**
1/7/45	Bath Road shops **R**
27/2/46	Swindon Works **I**
20/4/46	Westbury
11/12/46	Westbury shops **R**
24/5/48	Swindon Works **G**
28/4/49	Bath Road shops **U**
11/10/50	Swindon Works **HG**
23/10/50-4/11/50 to store at Swindon shed	
2/12/50	Canton
15/4/52	Taunton shops **U**
16/9/52	Ebbw Jct shops **U**
10/3/53	Swindon Works **HG**
16/12/53	Laira
9/10/54	Oxley
14/12/54	Tyseley shops **U**
11/5/55	Wolverhampton Works **HI**
16/6/56	Carmarthen
6/10/56	Oxley
23/3/57	Oxley shops **U**
16/7/57	Swindon Works **HG**
6/6/58	Tyseley shops **U**
14/1/59	Oxley shops **U**
5/10/59	Swindon Works **HG**
5/9/60	Worcester shops **U**
6/3/61	Tyseley shops **U**
20/5/61	Westbury
4/11/61	Worcester
31/1/62	Worcester shops **U**

Tenders

From new	2446
11/4/32	2456
4/6/33	2423
14/9/33	2635
12/4/35	2262
27/1/37	2530
6/12/38	2563
14/10/40	2777
20/5/44	2390
5/5/44	2671
19/10/44	2709
10/12/45	2822
19/3/48	2448
16/10/48	2664
28/4/49	2687
23/10/50	2894
10/3/53	2384
7/1957	2559
5/10/59	2640

Mileage 1,230,706

Withdrawal 5/6/62, Cut up 8/9/62

4963 RIGNALL HALL by the turntable at Swindon Works, 12 September 1959; this would be the occasion of its Heavy General that year, with an official release date of 5/10/59. D.K. Jones Collection.

RIGNALL HALL with goods; date/location unknown but the extremes of grime and larger lubrication valve cover (perhaps fitted at the HG pictured previously) indicate the early 1960s – 4963 was in fact withdrawn relatively early, in June 1962. Percy Moseley, transporttreasury

4964 RODWELL HALL

Built in 1929 to Lot no.254 at Swindon Works
To traffic 30/11/29

Mileages and Boilers

From new	4963
30/3/31	64,648 C4963
12/10/32	137,561 C4963
25/5/34	207,970 C4942
6/3/36	292,732 C4942
11/12/37	371,951 R7249
21/10/39	457,232 R7249
28/1/42	534,584 R7249
8/12/43	578,870 C4467
10/1/45	611,144 C4467
7/5/48	695,716 C2959
9/11/49	750,146 C3001
18/1/52	831,962 C2986
29/6/54	919,534 C4932
29/10/56	1,016,439 C4061
30/7/58	1,088,367 C4049
5/12/60	1,162,407 C2804

Sheds and Works history

11/1929	Swindon Works **ATC**
30/11/29	Goodwick
30/3/31	Swindon Works **I**
11/4/31	Old Oak
12/10/32	Swindon Works **I**
22/10/32	Westbury
22/2/34	Westbury shops **R**
25/5/34	Swindon Works **G**
30/6/34	St Philips Marsh
20/3/35	St Philips Marsh shops **R**
6/3/36	Swindon Works **I**
10/6/37	Swindon Works **L**
11/12/37	Swindon Works **G**
5/2/38	Bath Road
4/2/39	Stafford Road
3/3/39	Banbury
21/10/39	Wolverhampton Works **I**
11/11/39	Oxley
10/7/40	Tyseley shops **R**
10/4/41	Wolverhampton Works **L**
21/9/41	Bath Road shops **R**
28/1/42	Swindon Works **I**
27/6/42	Wolverhampton Works **L**
8/12/43	Swindon Works **L**
4/7/44	Swindon Works **L**
10/1/45	Swindon Works **I**
25/1/46	Wolverhampton Works **L**
21/8/46	Swindon Works **L**
24/10/46	Banbury shops **R**
9/8/47	Stafford Road
6/9/47	Oxley
3/2/48	Old Oak shops **R**
7/5/48	Swindon Works **G**
29/1/49	Tyseley
9/11/49	Swindon Works **HG**
28/2/50	Tyseley shops **U**
7/5/51	Old Oak shops **U**
18/1/52	Swindon Works **HI**
9/10/53	Pontypool Road shops **U**
4/12/53	Tyseley shops **U**
29/6/54	Swindon Works **HG**
29/7/55	Tyseley shops **LC**
4/8/55	Tyseley shops **U**
3/12/55	Canton
29/10/56	Swindon Works **HI**
2/11/57	Banbury
30/7/58	Swindon Works **HG**
7/10/59	Caerphilly Works **U**
27/2/60	Tyseley shops **U**
5/12/60	Swindon Works **HI**
13/7/61	Wolverhampton Works **U**
14/7/62	Stafford Road
6/10/62	Pontypool Road
25/4/63	Wolverhampton Works **U**
30/5/63	Wolverhampton Works **U**

Tenders

From new	2448
20/3/31	2532
26/6/32	2562
16/4/34	2414
15/1/36	2261
7/8/37	2229
5/11/37	2341
27/11/41	2558
4/7/43	2374
4/7/44	2180
1/6/46	2879
12/3/45	2822
23/9/49	2691
14/12/51	2926
28/5/54	2672
28/6/56	2649
30/7/58	2755
5/12/60	4094

Mileage 1,229,929

Withdrawn 15/10/63 Sold to Messrs Coopers ltd Swindon 31/12/63

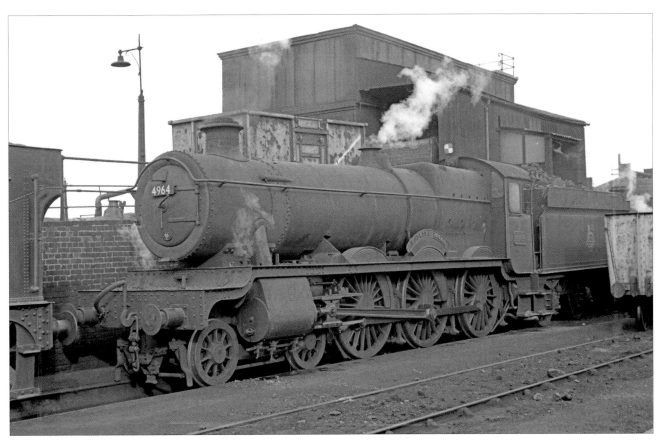

4964 RODWELL HALL at Shrewsbury shed in 1954. D.K. Jones Collection.

4964 was less widely travelled than many Halls, though it did manage to be one of the few repaired at Caerphilly – here it is after arrival there for an Unclassified repair on 20 September 1959. J. Davenport, Initial Photographics.

4965 ROOD ASHTON HALL

Built in 1929 to Lot no.254 at Swindon Works
To traffic 6/12/29

Mileages and Boilers

From new	4964
29/5/31	63,434 C4964
2/10/33	177,613 C4428
7/5/35	263,971 C4428
19/1/37	349,360 C4428
30/6/38	412,081 C4985
3/2/40	481,641 C4985
24/1/42	548,738 C4985
23/9/43	601,221 C4033
8/12/45	673,846 C4425
31/8/48	746,149 C8223
13/2/51	835,890 C9218
30/4/53	932,719 R6216
3/6/55	1,022,629 R6216
10/4/57	1,088,093 C7223
18/8/59	1,168,515 C8229

Sheds and Works history

10/1929	Swindon Works **ATC**
6/12/29	Oxley
2/6/30	Old Oak shops **R**
29/5/31	Swindon Works **I**
6/6/31	Old Oak
27/8/32	Worcester
22/10/32	Old Oak
1933	Neyland
1933	Canton
25/5/33	Canton shops **R**
18/7/33	Stourbridge shops **R**
2/10/33	Swindon Works **G**
7/5/35	Swindon Works **I**
1/6/35	Goodwick
13/11/35	Carmarthen shops **L**
19/1/37	Swindon Works **I**
30/6/38	Swindon Works **G**
23/7/38	St Philips Marsh
3/2/40	Swindon Works **I**
5/2/41	St Philips Marsh shops **R**
24/1/42	Swindon Works **I**
23/9/43	Swindon Works **L**
13/12/44	Llanelly shops **R**
8/12/45	Swindon Works **G**
6/12/46	St Philips Marsh shops **R**
2/6/47	Swindon Works **L**
31/8/48	Swindon Works **I**
19/10/49	St Philips Marsh **U**
3/12/49	Laira
22/2/50	Newton Abbot Works **U**
20/5/50	Penzance
22/9/50	Penzance shops **U**
13/12/51	Swindon Works **HI**
14/9/51	Newton Abbot Works **LC**
15/5/52	Newton Abbot Works **U**
30/4/53	Swindon Works **HG**
24/4/54	Westbury
22/5/54	Weymouth
14/8/54	Landore
6/11/54	Oxford
1/1/55	Laira
20/1/55	Laira shops **U**
3/6/55	Newton Abbot Works **HI**
8/10/55	Oxley
14/7/56	Old Oak
6/10/56	Reading
10/10/56	Old Oak shops U
10/4/57	Swindon Works **HG**
25/1/58	Didcot
18/8/59	Swindon Works **HI**
30/10/61	Old Oak shops **U**

Tenders

From new	2530
9/4/31	2561
18/3/35	2626
11/12/36	2443
19/1/37	2437
30/6/38	2613
3/2/40	2546
1/12/41	2386
6/4/43	2440
20/9/48	2778
6/2/47	2568
24/6/48	2548
3/10/49	2727
12/1/51	2844
30/4/53	2766
10/4/57	2923
18/5/57	2674

Mileage 1,243,444

Withdrawn 26/3/62, Engine preserved

Lined black 4965 ROOD ASHTON HALL crosses the 4ft 6in tracks of the Lee Moor Tramway at Laira in 1953. D.K. Jones Collection.

ROOD ASHTON HALL with six coaches west of Newton Abbot, August 1955. The train is approaching Aller Junction, where the Torbay branch diverges from the main line to Plymouth. 4965 is signalled for Plymouth and Cornwall; if it was for Torbay the train would be on the line closest to the wall. Behind the wall is the heavily used A380 which is just now (2015) about to be replaced by a bypass. The train is the Plymouth portion of a train that divided at Newton Abbot and will probably stop at Totnes en route. W. Hermiston, transporttreasury

4966 SHAKENHURST HALL
Built in 1929 to Lot no.254 at Swindon Works
To traffic 5/12/29

Mileages and Boilers

From new	4968
26/5/31	66,290 C4968
12/4/33	153,005 C4968
13/4/34	200,803 C4484
19/11/35	291,600 C4484
13/9/37	380,103 R2954
20/4/39	464,008 R2954
4/4/41	548,015 R2954
20/9/43	648,622 C4489
3/12/46	755,436 C3002
5/11/48	818,057 C4066
7/2/51	906,844 C4990
4/6/53	994,465 C8256
12/8/55	1,085,879 C8256
4/11/57	1,140,349 C8207
29/1/59	1,184,306 C4425
12/10/61	1,271,069 C2988

Sheds and Works history

8/1929	Swindon Works **ATC fitted**
5/12/29	Reading
26/5/31	Swindon Works I
6/6/31	Laira
17/11/31	Laira shops R
24/9/32	Newton Abbot
22/10/32	Laira
12/4/33	Swindon Works I
1933	Laira
1/12/33	Laira shops R
13/4/34	Swindon Works G
16/11/34	Newton Abbot Works L
1/6/35	Newton Abbot
10/7/35	Newton Abbot Works L
24/8/35	Laira
19/11/35	Swindon Works I
25/11/36	Laira shops L
19/1/37	Newton Abbot Works L
13/9/37	Swindon Works G
7/12/38	Laira shops R
20/4/39	Swindon Works I
19/6/39	Taunton
3/1940	Truro
1/8/40	Truro shops R
8/1940	Laira
4/4/41	Swindon Works I
21/8/42	Newton Abbot Works L
20/9/43	Swindon Works G
16/10/44	Newton Abbot Works R
16/1/45	St Blazey shops R
18/5/45	Newton Abbot Works L
31/10/45	Newton Abbot Works L
2/5/46	Laira shops R
31/7/46	Laira shops R
3/12/46	Swindon Works I
28/6/47	Newton Abbot Works L
23/8/47	Laira shops R
24/6/48	Newton Abbot Works L
	Tender work only
5/11/48	Swindon Works G
12/8/49	Newton Abbot shed U
13/8/49	Newton Abbot
3/11/49	Newton Abbot Works LC
5/11/49	Laira
4/5/50	Swindon Works U
7/2/51	Swindon Works HI
26/2/52	Laira shops U
14/7/52	Laira shops U
10/12/52	Laira shops U
12/1/53	Laira shops U
24/3/53	Laira shops U
4/6/53	Swindon Works HG
9/10/54	Oxley
25/4/55	Oxley shops LI
12/8/55	Wolverhampton Works HI
15/9/55	Banbury shops U
7/12/55	Stafford Road shed U
24/9/56	Oxley shops U
7/5/57	Gloucester shops U
4/11/57	Swindon Works HC
7/8/58	Taunton shops U
29/1/59	Swindon Works HG
20/7/60	Oswestry shops U
4/11/60	Wolverhampton Works LC
12/10/61	Swindon Works HI
6/10/62	Neath
28/2/63	Neath shops U
2/11/63	Oxford (see note opposite)

Tenders

From new	2442
17/4/31	2530
11/2/33	2409
12/4/33	2535
26/2/34	2405
1/10/35	2234
15/10/36	2259
9/3/39	2709
3/2/41	2602
6/8/43	2349
16/7/46	2688
17/10/46	2806
28/9/48	4012
20/3/50	2426
3/1/51	2684
4/11/57	2345
29/1/59	2673
12/10/61	2925

Mileage 1,329,611

Withdrawn 1/11/63 Sold to J Cashmore Newport 30/1/64

A careworn 4966 at Shrewsbury shed; lined black turning now to barely-lined overall grey. ColourRail

4966 SHAKENHURST HALL on 2 October 1963 at Neath shed, where it had gone in October the year before. It would soon be transferred to Oxford and it is interesting to look at the dates and wonder at how, in those fast-moving times, the paperwork didn't really seem to match what happened on the ground. It's official transfer date to Oxford was 2/11/63 and official withdrawal 1/11/63! So one wonders, did it really make the journey east, to then be sold as scrap to a Newport firm? J.L. Stevenson, courtesy Hamish Stevenson.

4967 SHIRENEWTON HALL

Built in 1929 to Lot no.254 at Swindon Works
To traffic 9/12/29

Mileages and Boilers

From new	4965
19/6/31	62,678 C4965
24/11/32	135,069 C4965
29/6/34	209,983 C4938
17/3/36	284,395 C4938
1/12/37	363,690 R7246
19/9/39	448,423 R7246
29/5/42	536,225 R7246
15/10/42	547,582 C2904
10/1/45	614,746 C2913
1/1/48	715,221 C4980
20/6/49	780,992 C2977
8/5/51	843,958 C4425
15/5/53	926,644 C8230
5/10/55	1,021,237 C4435
13/1/58	1,120,551 C4208
4/11/60	1,233,013 C4962

Sheds and Works history

12/1929	Swindon Works **ATC fitted**
9/12/29	Tyseley
9/1/30	Old Oak shops **I**
19/6/31	Swindon Works **I**
4/7/31	Oxford
26/9/31	Old Oak
30/7/32	Newton Abbot
27/8/32	Exeter
24/11/32	Swindon Works **I**
17/12/32	Old Oak
29/6/34	Swindon Works **G**
28/7/34	Shrewsbury
20/10/34	Chester
17/12/34	Chester shops **R**
17/3/36	Swindon Works **I**
31/8/37	Swindon Works **L**
1/12/37	Swindon Works **G**
22/9/38	Shrewsbury shops **R**
19/9/39	Swindon Works **I**
14/10/39	Tyseley
8/1940	Leamington Spa
10/1940	Tyseley
18/3/41	Swindon Works **L**
28/5/42	Swindon Works **I**
15/10/42	Swindon Works **L**
11/10/43	Tyseley shops **R**
28/9/44	Tyseley shops **R**
10/1/45	Swindon Works **I**
19/9/46	Swindon Works **L**
7/3/47	Tyseley shops **R**
1/1/48	Swindon Works **G**
30/10/48	St Philips Marsh
7/12/48	Swindon shed **L**
	Tender work only
20/6/49	Swindon Works **HG**
21/10/50	St Philips Marsh shops **U**
8/5/51	Swindon Works **HI**
27/12/52	Old Oak
15/5/53	Swindon Works **HI**
23/10/53	Old Oak shed **U**
25/3/54	Old Oak shed **LC**
11/3/55	Old Oak shops **U**
5/10/55	Swindon Works **HI**
8/3/56	Wolverhampton Works **LC**
16/6/56	Newton Abbot
13/7/57	Exeter
5/10/57	Penzance
2/11/57	Newton Abbot
13/1/58	Swindon Works **HG**
28/11/59	Laira
4/11/60	Swindon Works **HI**
25/3/61	Exeter
14/11/61	Exeter shops **U**
14/7/62	Neath

Tenders

From new	2407
27/9/32	2531
14/5/34	2404
8/1/36	2379
9/8/39	2665
23/1/41	2657
15/10/42	2746
10/1/45	2684
2/8/46	2268
19/9/46	2718
1/1/48	2600
5/4/51	2553
7/4/53	2592
5/10/55	2639
13/1/58	2898
4/11/60	2613
4/1961	2560

Mileage 1,274,429

Withdrawn 13/9/62 Sold to
R S Hayes Ltd Bridgend 26/8/63

4967 SHIRENEWTON HALL at
Bridgend, 7 July 1962. S.Rickard/J&J
Collection.

Old Oak's 4967 SHIRENEWTON HALL brings a down train into Exeter St David's on 7 August 1954; E1R 0-6-2T banking engine at left. J. Robertson, transporttreasury

Days after its transfer to Exeter, SHIRENEWTON HALL on 22 July 1957 finds itself at Penzance shed, where it in turn took up residence a few months later. J. Davenport, Initial Photographics.

4968 SHOTTON HALL

Built in 1929 to Lot no.254 at Swindon Works
To traffic 12/12/29

Mileages and Boilers

From new	4966
17/6/31	64,064 C4966
9/9/32	105,731 C4966
22/3/34	172,575 C4416
24/12/35	255,528 C4416
1/2/38	341,260 C4421
29/2/40	423,854 C4421
19/5/42	486,210 C4445
1/10/43	532,857 C4445
2/8/45	600,920 C2866
5/5/47	654,402 C4938
8/3/49	690,483 C8232
28/9/50	752,008 C7219
17/10/52	840,469 C9289
22/4/55	944,340 C8202
25/4/57	1,037,389 C8202
10/5/60	1,126,971 C9205

Sheds and Works history

12/1929	Swindon Works **ATC**
12/12/29	Old Oak
17/6/31	Swindon Works **I**
9/9/32	Swindon Works **I**
22/10/32	Exeter
1933	Old Oak
23/3/34	Swindon Works **G**
19/4/34	Old Oak shops **R**
5/5/34	Laira
5/4/35	Newton Abbot Works **L**
6/4/35	Newton Abbot
4/5/35	Laira
10/7/35	Swindon Works **L**
24/12/35	Swindon Works **I**
11/1/36	Penzance
3/11/36	Penzance shops **R**
26/1/37	Newton Abbot Works **L**
19/5/37	Penzance shops **R**
4/8/37	Newton Abbot Works **L**
23/11/37	Penzance shops **R**
1/2/38	Swindon Works **G**
19/11/38	Penzance shops **R**
8/2/39	Penzance shops **R**
29/4/39	Truro
22/6/39	Newton Abbot Works **L**
29/2/40	Swindon Works **I**
4/4/40	Swindon Works **L**
4/1940	Severn Tunnel Jct
3/9/41	Swindon Works **L**
19/5/42	Swindon Works **L**
27/2/43	Severn Tunnel Jct shops **R**
29/6/43	Newton Abbot Works **R**
1/10/43	Swindon Works **I**
7/1944	Westbury
2/8/45	Swindon Works **I**
5/7/46	Westbury shops **R**
22/11/46	Didcot shops **R**
5/5/47	Swindon Works **G**
25/4/57	**Renumbered 3900**
17/5/47	St Philips Marsh
5/8/48	Bath Road shops **R**
14/10/48-7/2/49 stored at Swindon	
29/1/49	**Renumbered 4968 from 3900**
8/3/49	Swindon Works **HC**
3/12/49	Laira
15/2/50	Laira shops **U**
18/7/50	Laira shops **U**
28/9/50	Swindon Works **HG**
9/10/50-6/11/50 stored at Swindon	
2/12/50	Canton
26/1/52	Penzance
23/2/52	St Blazey
23/3/52	Canton

17/10/52	Swindon Works **HI**
16/6/53	Swindon Works **LC**
22/4/55	Swindon Works **HG**
25/4/57	Swindon Works **HI**
25/1/58	Pontypool Road
22/3/58	Shrewsbury
15/9/58-22/12/58 stored at Shrewsbury shed	
5/1/59-24/3/59 stored at Shrewsbury and Wellington sheds	
7/4/59-10/5/59 stored at Wellington shed	
31/10/59	St Philips Marsh
7/1/60	St Philips Marsh shops **U**
10/5/60	Swindon Works **HG**

Tenders

From new	2409
22/4/31	2445
30/5/32	2433
28/6/325	2256
23/12/37	2261
29/2/40	2403
21/3/40	2537
11/3/42	2626
26/1/43	2567
31/8/43	2682
11/6/45	2387
2/8/45	2449
4/5/47	2840
8/3/48	2682
19/9/52	2559
4/5/53	2545
23/6/54	4066
22/4/55	2682
25/4/57	2615
10/5/60	2599

Mileage 1,205,525

Withdrawn 13/7/62 Sold to John Cashmore Ltd Newport 4/9/62

4968 SHOTTON HALL brings an up train into Dawlish station about 1960. J. Davenport, Initial Photographics.

SHOTTON HALL with a Wolverhampton train, at Stratford on Avon on 16 August 1958. R.Wilson, transporttreasury

4969 SHRUGBOROUGH HALL

Built in 1929 to Lot no.254 at Swindon Works
To traffic 14/12/29

Mileages and Boilers

From new	4967
15/4/31	64,443 C4967
8/2/33	151,685 C4967
7/12/34	225,297 C4936
4/4/36	308,845 C4936
16/2/38	392,972 C4967
28/2/40	477,144 C4967
28/10/42	567,631 C4967
14/4/44	604,656 C4490
29/3/46	662,462 C4994
31/12/47	715,290 C4909
3/3/50	785,589 C4956
10/9/52	883,641 C4466
13/4/55	969,011 C9283
22/11/57	1,063,270 C9283
6/9/60	1,153,065 C9208

Sheds and works history

12/1929	Swindon Works **ATC**
14/12/29	Old Oak
25/10/30	Bath Road **L**
15/4/31	Swindon Works **I**
8/2/33	Swindon Works **I**
7/12/34	Swindon Works **G**
15/12/34	Laira
29/6/35	Newton Abbot
21/9/35	Truro
16/11/35	Laira
4/4/36	Swindon Works **I**
2/5/36	St Philips Marsh
19/5/37	St Philips Marsh shops **R**
16/2/38	Swindon Works **G**
13/12/38	St Philips Marsh shops **R**
18/5/39	Hereford shops **R**
28/2/40	Swindon Works **I**
19/11/41	St Philips Marsh shops **R**
28/10/42	Swindon Works **I**
28/1/43	St Philips Marsh shops **R**
14/4/44	Swindon Works **L**
19/2/45	Slough shops **R**
29/3/46	Swindon Works **I**
12/9/46	Old Oak shops **R**
23/10/46	St Philips Marsh shops **R**
29/9/47	St Philips Marsh shops **R**
31/12/47	Swindon Works **L**
18/7/49	Chester shops **U**
3/3/50	Swindon Works **HG**
21/4/51	Swindon
30/8/51	Swindon Works **LC**
6/2/52	Bath Road shops **U**
12/7/52	Oxford
10/9/52	Swindon Works **HI**
4/9/53	Old Oak shops **U**
15/11/54	Old Oak shops **U**
13/4/55	Swindon Works **HG**
25/2/56	Reading
16/5/56	Old Oak shops **U**
21/3/57	Reading shops **U**
22/11/57	Swindon Works **HI**
7/1/59	Taunton shops **U**
21/2/59	Didcot
6/9/60	Swindon Works **HG**
2/12/61	Southall

Tenders

From new	2430
2/10/30	2480
16/10/34	2655
26/2/36	2319
6/2/37	2400
10/1/38	2736
29/2/40	2421
19/11/41	2647
6/1/43	2604
6/10/43	2613
7/1/46	2403
31/12/47	2912
3/3/50	2441
18/7/51	2538
7/8/52	2687
9/3/55	2706
22/11/57	2575
29/11/58	2660
6/9/60	4064

Mileage 1,214,340

Withdrawn 13/9/62 Cut up 3/11/62

4969 SHRUGBOROUGH HALL on a down goods at Westerleigh, 10 June 1956; this is the West Junction, with 4969 heading west for Winterbourne and the junctions at Filton/Patchway. transporttreasury

4969 comes into Gloucester Central past East Box about 1962. D.K. Jones Collection.

4970 SKETTY HALL

Built in 1929 to Lot no.254 at Swindon Works
To traffic 21/12/29

Mileages and Boilers

Date	Mileage/Boiler
From new	4960
2/4/31	64,131 C4960
13/4/33	157,481 C4960
8/6/34	209,804 C4950
27/3/36	300,758 C4950
12/10/37	374,857 C2943
21/6/39	451,336 C2943
30/3/42	544,330 C2943
31/8/44	627,812 C4442
31/3/47	720,612 C7268
28/10/49	821,728 C8202
25/4/52	927,581 C7275
3/6/54	1,009,029 C4957
20/9/56	1,103,084 C7267
16/12/58	1,190,210 C8220
7/6/61	1,281,916 C8215

Sheds and Works history

12/1929	Swindon Works **ATC**
21/12/29	Old Oak
17/4/30	Stafford Road shed **R**
2/4/31	Swindon Works **I**
9/5/31	Laira
24/9/31	Laira shops **R**
25/1/32	Newton Abbot shed **L**
12/7/32	Laira shops **R**
13/4/33	Swindon Works **I**
1933	St Philips Marsh
8/6/34	Swindon Works **G**
30/6/34	Bristol Bath Road
1/10/34	Weymouth shops **R**
20/10/34	Swindon
13/12/34	Swindon Works **L**
27/3/36	Swindon Works **I**
9/4/36	Wolverhampton Works **L**
2/5/36	Reading
12/10/37	Swindon Works **R**
21/6/39	Swindon Works **I**
22/7/39	Gloucester
11/11/39	Ebbw Jct
21/11/40	Swindon Works **L**
12/1941	Laira
30/3/42	Swindon Works **I**
6/8/42	Swindon Works **L**
9/9/42	Laira shops **R**
13/3/43	Newton Abbot Works **L**
7/6/43	Laira shops **R**
5/11/43	Laira shops **R**
24/4/44	Laira shops **R**
31/8/44	Swindon Works **G**
11/1944	Penzance
15/6/45	Penzance shops **R**
23/10/45	Penzance shops **R**
28/1/46	Newton Abbot Works **L**
9/10/46	Penzance shops **R**
31/3/47	Swindon Works **I**
2/12/47	Penzance shops **R**
30/4/48	Newton Abbot Works **L** Tender work only
22/12/48	Newton Abbot Works **L**
28/10/49	Swindon Works **HG**
20/5/50	Taunton
7/7/50	Taunton shops **U**
24/3/51	Severn Tunnel Jct
21/4/51	Taunton
18/9/51	Newton Abbot Works **U**
6/1/52	Taunton shops **U**
25/4/52	Swindon Works **HI**
3/11/52	Taunton shops **U**
19/3/53	Newton Abbot Works **LC**
3/6/54	Swindon Works **HG**
17/1/55	Taunton shops **U**
20/9/56	Swindon Works **HI**
19/9/57	Newton Abbot Works **LC**
16/12/58	Swindon Works **HG**
7/6/61	Swindon Works **HI**
21/5/62	Taunton shops **U**
17/6/61	Exeter
14/7/62	Old Oak
6/10/62	Duffryn Yard
12/11/62	Duffryn Yard shops **U**
14/6/63	Duffryn Yard shops **U**

Tenders

Date	Tender
From new	2532
26/2/31	2432
4/6/32	2535
5/1/33	2447
24/4/34	2437
9/1/37	2413
12/11/37	2242
21/6/39	2654
6/8/42	2738
18/4/44	1831
31/8/44	2392
31/3/47	2579
16/9/49	2602
25/3/52	2703
30/4/54	2731
3/6/54	2863
20/9/56	2665
16/12/58	2694
7/6/61	2722

Mileage 1,344,048

Withdrawn 29/7/63 Sold to G Cohen ltd Morriston 1/1/64

4970 SKETTY HALL at Temple Meads in 1959. The Halls were truly ubiquitous and while the 57XX panniers were more numerous at least they had some obvious detail differences. D.K. Jones Collection.

4970 SKETTY HALL again at Bristol Temple Meads, 17 June 1961. D. Preston, ColourRail

4971 STANWAY HALL

Built in 1930 to Lot no.254 at Swindon Works
To traffic 1/1930

Mileages and Boiler

From new	4970
17/3/31	64,729 C4970
19/8/32	130,123 C4970
29/3/34	201,205 C2883
13/1/36	283,209 C2883
10/8/37	355,108 C4448
24/5/39	438,785 C4448
12/7/41	515,987 C4448
14/8/42	550,044 C2816
28/1/44	599,145 C2816
4/8/45	648,674 C7242
9/5/47	709,310 C8285
26/4/49	759,162 C4996
24/5/51	835,954 C4443
15/6/53	917,152 C4979
21/9/55	1,005,927 C2933
16/12/57	1,102,097 C8281
28/9/60	1,211,288 C8275

Sheds and Works history

1/1930	Swindon Works **ATC fitted**
18/1/30	Old Oak
17/3/31	Swindon Works **I**
19/8/32	Swindon Works **I**
24/9/32	Stafford Road
1933	Oxley
29/3/34	Swindon Works **G**
7/4/34	Tyseley
3/8/34	Tyseley shops **R**
5/6/35	Tyseley shops **R**
22/8/35	Wolverhampton Works **L**
13/1/36	Swindon Works **I**
7/3/36	Oxley
28/12/36	Wolverhampton Works **L**
10/8/37	Swindon Works **G**
24/5/39	Swindon Works **I**
9/10/40	Swindon Works **L**
12/7/41	Swindon Works **I**
14/8/42	Swindon Works **L**
28/1/44	Swindon Works **I**
11/5/45	Stourbridge shops **R**
4/8/45	Swindon Works **L**
19/4/47	**Renumbered 3901**
9/5/47	Swindon Works **G**
29/7/47	Laira shops **R**
20/3/48	Old Oak
3/3/48	Old Oak shops **R**
21/6/48	Old Oak shops **R**
14/10/48-28/3/49 stored at Swindon	
29/1/49	**Renumbered 4971 from 3901**
23/4/49	Taunton
26/4/49	Swindon Works **HG**
6/4/50	Taunton shops **U**
14/8/50	Taunton shops **U**
26/10/50	Taunton shops **U**
24/5/51	Swindon Works **HI**
27/2/53	Swindon Works **U**
15/6/53	Swindon Works **HG**
24/1/55	Taunton shops **U**
21/9/55	Swindon Works **HG**
15/2/56	Taunton shops **U**
16/12/57	Swindon Works **HG**
11/9/59	Taunton shops **U**
28/9/60	Swindon Works **HI**
8/10/60	Canton
17/1/62	Ebbw Jct shops **U**

Tenders

From new	2534
24/1/31	2375
17/3/31	2431
19/8/32	2415
25/11/35	2581
17/5/41	2414
18/6/42	2812
14/8/42	2558
19/11/43	2592
28/5/45	2801
24/3/47	2809
31/3/49	1582
4/11/50	2399
22/4/51	2414
27/2/53	2811
12/5/53	2870
21/9/53	2816
29/12/56	2585
16/12/57	2411
28/9/60	4108

Mileage 1,281,229

Withdrawn 13/8/62 Sold to R S Hayes Ltd Bridgend 26/8/63

4971 STANWAY HALL at Shrewsbury shed in the 1950s when it was a Taunton engine; that tender has all the looks of an intermediate type, but there is not one listed in the record for this period. It is hardly surprising that some tender matches eluded the Clerks' notice; as it happened, locos generally did not have an 'allotted' tender and a swap could occur at any works visit or even at a shed. Moreover a temporary change at a shed would not reach the ear of HQ, nor did it need to. Actually there were more tender engines than there were tenders, which was not a problem as it took much longer to repair a loco than a tender. So it was that an engine rarely emerged from overhaul with the tender it came in with – unless by chance. ColourRail

4971 with a down Torquay service, leaving the station at Newton Abbot at 10.30am, 2 April 1956. Peter Kerslake, transporttreasury

4972 SAINT BRIDES HALL

Built in 1929 to Lot no.254 at Swindon Works
To traffic 1/1930

Mileages and Boilers

From new	4971
23/3/31	65,339 C4971
14/12/32	135,701 C4953
11/7/34	211,302 C4953
27/4/36	299,271 C4099
22/11/37	286,922 C4099
18/12/39	469,723 C4099
2/1/45	631,645 C8207
30/5/47	714,217 C7242
21/10/48	750,642 C7215
16/12/49	803,035 C7205
27/2/52	896,361 C2807
18/6/54	990,488 C7210
22/8/56	1,072,212 C7210
31/12/58	1,162,239 C8250
19/5/61	1,237,160 C4073

Sheds and Works history

1/1930	Swindon Works **ATC**
18/1/30	Old Oak
23/3/31	Swindon Works **I**
14/4/31	Swindon Works **L**
9/5/31	St Philips Marsh
1/7/32	St Philips Marsh shops **R**
14/12/32	Swindon Works **G**
17/12/32	Old Oak
1933	St Philips Marsh
6/11/33	Bath Road shops **R**
11/7/34	Swindon Works **I**
25/8/34	Old Oak
27/8/34	Swindon Works **Hot Box**
2/11/35	Swindon Works **L**
27/4/36	Swindon Works **G**
30/5/36	Carmarthen
22/11/37	Swindon Works **I**
8/11/38	Swindon Works **L**
10/12/38	Landore
18/12/39	Swindon Works **I**
15/9/41	Swindon Works **L**
2/1/45	Swindon Works **G**
28/2/46	Ebbw Jct shops **L**
9/9/46	Landore shops **L**
17/2/47	Bath Road shops **R**
16/5/47	**Renumbered 3904**
30/5/47	Swindon Works **I**
18/6/47	Laira shops **R**
12/7/47	Laira
8/9/47	Swindon Works **R**
13/10/47	Swindon Works **R**
29/11/47	Swindon
21/10/48	**Renumbered 4972 from 3904**
21/10/48	Swindon Works **L**
11/8/49	Swindon shed **U**
16/12/49	Swindon Works **HG**
4/7/50	Bath Road shops **LC**
27/2/52	Swindon Works **HI**
28/11/53	Bath Road
26/12/53	Swindon
18/6/54	Swindon Works **HG**
22/8/56	Swindon Works **HI**
31/12/58	Swindon Works **HG**
26/3/59	Swindon Works **LC**
14/6/60	Aberdare shops **U**
30/9/60	Old Oak shops **U**
19/5/61	Swindon Works **HI**
14/7/62	Westbury
26/1/63	Worcester shops **U**

Tenders

From new	2431
5/2/31	2408
17/10/32	2537
2/11/35	2422
13/3/36	2592
18/12/39	2582
7/8/41	2683
24/11/42	2401
6/11/44	2735
2/1/45	2737
17/8/46	2848
30/2/47	2918
25/1/52	2560
2/7/52	2773
18/6/54	2896
22/8/56	2568
9/1/58	2613
31/12/58	2898
14/6/60	2698
31/5/61	2404

Mileage 1,315,534 as at 28/12/63

Withdrawn 14/2/64 Sold to R S Hayes Bridgend 24/4/64

Parked at Weymouth shed in August 1963; Weymouth's stud of Halls, which had been there since the first, were exchanged for BR Standard 4-6-0s more suited to SR route restrictions, when the shed transferred to the Southern Region in 1958. RailOnline

4972 at Leamington Spa, 1963. The little rectangular covers on the curved running plate behind the lamp irons lifted up to give clearance for the dummy glands bolted to the valve chest covers. When the valves were taken out for attention the curved front plates were removed. D.K. Jones Collection.

4973 SWEENEY HALL

Built in 1930 to Lot no.254 at Swindon Works
To traffic 1/1930

Mileages and Boilers

From new	4972
24/4/31	63,481 C4972
6/10/32	131,397 C4926
16/4/34	206,151 C4926
8/8/35	280,151 C4975
12/3/37	368,943 C4975
4/10/38	464,485 C4021
21/11/39	528,298 C4021
12/2/42	602,937 C4021
6/11/44	687,743 C4423
30/11/46	756,977 C4066
14/10/48	823,888 C4990
18/1/51	900,942 C4096
28/9/53	1,000,604 C7205
10/12/55	1,081,752 C7205
8/4/58	1,164,889 C4435
20/5/60	1,245,843 C4435

Sheds and Works history

1/1930	Swindon Works **ATC**
18/1/30	Penzance
30/4/30	Penzance shops **L**
3/12/30	Penzance shops **L**
24/4/31	Swindon Works **I**
9/5/31	Old Oak
11/3/32	Old Oak shops **L**
6/10/32	Swindon Works **G**
1933	Swindon
16/4/34	Swindon Works **I**
5/5/34	Carmarthen
8/8/35	Swindon Works **G**
24/8/35	Landore
14/11/36	Goodwick
12/3/37	Swindon Works **I**
4/10/38	Swindon Works **G**
21/11/39	Swindon Works **I**
9/12/39	Old Oak
3/1940	Oxford
12/2/42	Swindon Works **I**
16/6/43	Swindon Works **L**
6/11/44	Swindon Works **G**
16/10/46	Oxford shops **R**
30/11/46	Swindon Works **I**
14/10/48	Swindon Works **I**
25/12/48	Swindon
18/8/50	Bath Road shops **U**
18/1/51	Swindon Works **HI**
20/8/52	Bath Road shops **U**
4/3/53	Oxford shops **U**
28/9/53	Swindon Works **HG**
10/12/55	Newton Abbot Works **HI**
24/3/56	Canton
11/1/57	Canton shops **U**
5/2/57	Hereford shops **U**
27/3/57	Ebbw Jct shops **LC**
31/5/57	Caerphilly Works **HC**
8/4/58	Swindon Works **HG**
3/12/59	Westbury shops **U**
20/5/60	Caerphilly Works **HI**
24/11/60	Caerphilly Works **LC**
26/4/62	Ebbw Jct shed **LC**

Tenders

From new	2421
4/3/31	2393
1/1/32	2435
11/3/32	2537
6/10/32	2616
26/2/34	2568
27/5/35	2443
4/12/36	2626
12/3/37	2704
4/10/38	2538
21/11/39	1838
18/9/44	2572
14/10/48	2420
8/12/49	2835
18/1/51	2422
25/8/53	2884
31/3/55	2650
8/4/58	2913
22/3/60	2626
15/3/61	4093

Mileage 1,314,618

Withdrawn 13/7/62 Sold to R S Hayes ltd Bridgend 1/10/62

4973 SWEENEY HALL at Old Oak Common in 1932; badge and **GREAT WESTERN** visible on tender on original print but no trace of lining, though apparently the film of the time sometimes did not pick it up. The stepladders highlight the absence of footsteps at the front of GWR locos, at a place where really there should have been steps.

SWEENEY HALL ready for work at Canton shed late in the 1950s, in lined green with Hawksworth tender. Modified Hall 7916 **MOBBERLEY HALL** alongside – see Part 3. ColourRail

4974 TALGARTH HALL

Built in 1930 to Lot no.254 at Swindon Works
To traffic 1/1930

Mileages and Boilers

From new	4973
2/6/31	64,983 C4973
4/8/33	141,371 C2822
20/11/34	208,083 C2822
1/7/36	277,649 C4920
29/3/38	361,935 C4920
9/2/40	442,027 C4920
24/10/42	532,562 C4092
31/10/45	635,291 C7267
14/6/47	703,692 C8290
17/3/49	778,418 C4028
5/6/51	865,021 C2962
27/5/53	952,964 C2962
21/3/55	1,025,202 C6205
15/4/57	1,117,568 C4050
15/7/59	1,197,404 C4965

Sheds and Works history

18/1/1930	Penzance
2/1930	Swindon Works **ATC**
9/5/30	Penzance shops **L**
18/8/30	Penzance shops **L**
19/12/30	Penzance shops **L**
7/1/31	Newton Abbot Works **L**
2/6/31	Swindon Works **I**
4/7/31	Taunton
24/10/31	Newton Abbot
19/12/31	Truro
24/11/32	Taunton shops **R**
1933	Oxford
4/8/33	Swindon Works **G**
20/11/34	Swindon Works **I**
1/7/36	Swindon Works **G**
19/9/36	Worcester
12/12/36	Hereford
1/6/37	Worcester shops **L**
29/3/38	Swindon Works **I**
28/2/39	Worcester shops **L**
27/10/39	Hereford shops **R**
9/2/40	Swindon Works **I**
9/9/40	Worcester shops **R**
18/8/41	Worcester shops **R**
20/4/42	Hereford shops **R**
5/1942	Canton
24/10/42	Swindon Works **G**
2/3/43	Swindon Works **L**
10/9/43	Canton shops **L**
19/1/44	Exeter shops
9/6/44	Swindon Works **L**
6/11/44	Shrewsbury shops **R**
31/10/45	Swindon Works **I**
14/6/47	Swindon Works **G**
17/3/49	Swindon Works **HG**
12/11/49	Swindon Works **U**
19/4/50	Canton shops **U**
5/6/51	Swindon Works **HG**
27/5/53	Caerphilly Works **HI**
23/6/53	Severn Tunnel Jct shops **U**
14/10/53	Ebbw Jct shops **LC**
18/5/54	Ebbw Jct shops **LC**
30/7/54	Canton shops **U**
21/3/55	Swindon Works **HG**
20/9/55	Ebbw Jct shops **LC**
15/4/57	Swindon Works **HI**
13/5/58	Swindon Works **U**
17/5/58	Pontypool Road
10/7/58	Pontypool Road shops **U**
29/11/58	Tyseley
15/7/59	Swindon Works **HG**
23/4/60	Stourbridge
1/9/60	Wolverhampton Works **LC**
8/2/61	Stourbridge shops **U**
7/10/61	Gloucester
27/1/62	Gloucester shops **U**

Tenders

From new	2535
7/4/31	2409
11/2/33	2530
26/3/33	1575
8/10/34	2614
16/11/34	2248
25/5/36	2419
17/2/38	2537
2/1/40	2575
25/8/42	1509
21/4/44	2717
30/8/45	2916
14/6/47	2864
12/2/49	2730
6/5/51	4074
7/2/55	2385
15/4/57	2831
10/7/58	2764

Mileage 1,273,651

Withdrawn 13/4/62 Cut up 6/10/62

4974 TALGARTH HALL at Cardiff General; lined green, vacuum pump lubricator in front of leading splasher. H.C. Casserley, courtesy R.M. Casserley.

A tired TALGARTH HALL at home shed Stourbridge Junction in 1960. J. Davenport, Initial Photographics.

4975 UMBERSLADE HALL

Built in 1930 to Lot no.254 at Swindon Works
To traffic 2/1930

Mileages and Boilers

From new	4974
9/1/31	46,665 C4974
15/11/32	133,311 C4974
3/2/34	179,746 C4943
4/12/35	269,307 C4943
19/8/37	345,681 R2955
1/6/39	427,449 R2955
4/11/41	517,276 R2955
20/3/44	605,270 C4484
24/5/46	684,512 C4484
28/10/48	760,673 C7228
13/4/51	852,814 C8230
5/5/53	936,967 C7222
10/8/55	1,021,849 C2920
31/10/57	1,101,501 C2920
15/11/60	1,219,617 C9286

Sheds and Works history

2/1930	Swindon Works **ATC**
2/1930	Penzance
17/5/30	Penzance shops **L**
2/9/30	Penzance shops **L**
9/1/31	Swindon Works **I**
14/2/31	Laira
4/11/31	Newton Abbot shed **R**
15/11/32	Swindon Works **I**
17/12/32	Old Oak
15/8/33	Swindon Works **L**
3/2/34	Swindon Works **G**
20/4/34	Swindon Works **R**
8/4/35	Old Oak shops **R**
4/12/35	Swindon Works **I**
14/12/35	Reading
19/8/37	Swindon Works **G**
18/9/37	Chester
1/6/39	Swindon Works **I**
24/6/39	Westbury
11/11/39	Canton
31/5/40	Ebbw Jct shops **R**
4/11/41	Swindon Works **I**
2/12/42	Canton shops **R**
19/3/43	Canton shops **R**
20/3/44	Swindon Works **G**
11/10/44	Swindon Works **R**
24/5/46	Swindon Works **I**
13/11/46	Wolverhampton Works **R**
31/10/47	Swindon Works **L**
28/10/48	Swindon Works **G**
26/9/50	Canton shops **U**
13/1/51	Southall shops **U**
13/4/51	Swindon Works **HG**
25/6/52	Canton shops **U**
5/5/53	Swindon Works **HI**
31/10/53	Hereford
10/8/55	Swindon Works **HG**
5/9/56	Worcester shops **U**
31/10/57	Swindon Works **HI**
14/6/58	Laira
27/12/58	Newton Abbot
21/11/59	Reading shops **U**
15/11/60	Swindon Works **HG**
9/10/61	Laira shops **LC**
2/12/61	Reading
24/5/62	Reading shops **LC**
29/6/63	Oxford

Tenders

From new	2444
18/1/30	2385
25/7/33	2582
10/11/33	2399
26/6/37	2639
22/4/39	2615
18/5/40	2542
19/9/41	2627
11/1/44	2442
11/10/44	2248
6/9/47	2389
31/10/47	2438
2/10/48	2597
28/10/48	2806
13/3/51	2621
27/3/53	2739
20/6/55	4041
31/10/57	2900
15/11/60	2409

Mileage 1,298,925

Withdrawn 30/9/63 Sold to Messrs Coopers ltd Swindon 31/12/63

4975 UMBERSLADE HALL heads Warship D806 CAMBRIAN at the summit of Dainton, momentarily to enter the west end of the tunnel, 3 June 1960. Behind Dainton box are banking engine spurs frequently occupied by 51XX 2-6-2Ts that having banked westbound trains, would await a path back to Newton Abbot. Les Elsey.

Scruffy now, 4975 UMBERSLADE HALL prepares to back down to Paddington at Old Oak sidings, 27 April 1963. B.W.L. Brooksbank, Initial Photographics.

4976 WARFIELD HALL
Built in 1930 to Lot no.254 at Swindon Works
To traffic 1/1930

Mileages and Boilers

From new	4975
25/4/31	61,668 C4975
15/6/33	155,317 C4910
18/1/35	232,549 C4961
4/4/36	304,485 C4961
4/4/38	390,904 C4938
27/2/40	469,382 C4938
25/7/42	552,680 C4097
9/9/44	629,565 C4097
19/6/47	700,478 C8281
17/9/48	744,119 C4905
10/2/50	792,045 C2826
29/5/52	862,634 C8251
18/8/54	946,751 C8251
11/10/56	1,032,360 C4920
28/1/59	1,141,481 C4920
17/11/61	1,220,934 C8224

Sheds and Works history

18/1/30	Penzance
2/1930	Swindon Works **ATC**
20/5/30	Penzance shops **L**
9/9/30	Penzance shops **L**
25/4/31	Swindon Works **I**
19/5/31	Laira
1/10/31	Newton Abbot shed **R**
30/1/32	Laira shops **R**
27/5/32	Newton Abbot Works **R**
25/7/32	Laira shops **R**
18/12/32	Laira shops **R**
15/6/33	Swindon Works **G**
12/10/33	Swindon Works **R**
15/5/34	Newton Abbot shed **L**
18/1/35	Swindon Works **G**
9/2/35	Carmarthen
4/4/36	Swindon Works **I**
2/5/36	Chester
4/4/38	Swindon Works **G**
17/8/39	Bath Road shops **L**
27/2/40	Swindon Works **I**
1/4/42	Chester shops **R**
25/7/42	Swindon Works **G**
9/9/44	Swindon Works **I**
11/1/45	Newton Abbot Works **L**
26/6/45	Chester shops **R**
21/2/46	Wolverhampton Works **L**
6/9/46	Wolverhampton Works **L**
7/9/46	Stafford Road
5/10/46	Chester
11/12/46	Shrewsbury shops **R**
2/3/47	Shrewsbury shops **R**
13/4/47	Chester shops **R**
19/6/47	Swindon Works **G**
17/9/48	Swindon Works **L**
10/2/50	Swindon Works **HG**
16/8/50	Chester shops **U**
26/4/51	Swindon Works **LC**
31/8/51	Oswestry shops **LC**
29/5/52	Swindon Works **HG**
16/6/52	Swindon Works **U**
29/1/53	Croes Newydd shops **U**
31/10/53	Hereford
18/8/54	Swindon Works **HI**
25/2/56	Worcester
16/6/56	Laira
11/10/56	Swindon Works **HG**
29/1/57	Laira shops **U**
5/11/57	Laira shops **U**
21/3/58	Bath Road shops **U**
5/8/58	Laira shops **U**
15/9/58-16/10/58 stored at Laira shed	
1/11/58	Penzance

28/1/59	Swindon Works **HI**
23/2/59-13/6/59 stored at Penzance shed	
11/7/59	Laira
19/11/59	Newton Abbot Works **LC**
17/5/60	Swindon Works **HC**
8/10/60	Didcot
17/11/61	Swindon Works **HG**
21/4/62	Southall
8/3/62	Duffryn Yard shops **U**
12/10/62	Southall shops **U**
6/4/63	Oxford
31/10/63	Old Oak shops **U**

Tenders

From new	2406
10/3/31	2535
4/6/32	2432
12/4/34	1948
28/11/34	2544
15/2/36	3404
21/2/38	2740
17/8/39	2440
27/4/40	2689
4/6/42	2811
18/7/44	2441
19/6/47	2390
17/9/48	2398
10/2/50	2919
21/3/51	2737
29/4/52	2550
8/6/54	2626
5/9/56	2416
11/10/56	2928
28/1/59	2749
17/5/60	2713
17/11/61	2639
2/1964	2751

Mileage 1,280,182 as at 28/12/63

Withdrawn 6/5/64 Sold to Central Wagon Co Wigan 22/6/64

4976 WARFIELD HALL on the 3.40pm stopping train from Plymouth North Road to Penzance, near Menheniot on 16 July 1956. R.C. Riley, transporttreasury

Passing through the remains of Mutley station again (see 4959 also): WARFIELD HALL heads 4087 CARDIGAN CASTLE out of Plymouth North Road, 18 August 1960. Across the road on the right is the Royal Eye Infirmary which had treated in its time a number of enginemen with 'smuts' in their eyes. On the railings for many years there was a notice which read ENGINEMEN. REMEMBER THE HOSPITAL PATIENTS. KEEP ENGINES QUIET AND AVOID SMOKE. 4976 will assist to Newton Abbot over Hemerdon and Dainton banks, as was necessary when the load was in excess of that laid down for a Castle or King. Withdrawn in May 1964 from Oxford shed, 4976 was one of the small fleet of Halls to languish there over the ensuing weeks. ColourRail

4977 WATCOMBE HALL

Built in 1930 to Lot no.254 at Swindon Works
To traffic 2/1930

Mileages and Boilers

From new	4976
7/3/31	56,797 C4976
22/9/32	125,037 C4976
15/12/33	177,766 C2943
7/3/36	284,793 C2943
29/5/37	349,203 C4418
16/2/39	422,904 C4418
17/5/41	511,279 C4418
8/5/44	600,685 C4438
2/5/46	672,562 C4438
25/8/48	744,594 C2842
5/10/50	824,215 C7216
27/1/53	904,753 C9208
5/5/55	993,326 C8207
5/6/57	1,071,539 C4026
19/10/59	1,168,978 C8269

Sheds and Works history

15/2/30	Penzance
2/1930	Swindon Works **ATC**
31/5/30	Penzance shops **L**
24/9/30	Penzance shops **L**
11/4/31	Old Oak
7/3/31	Wolverhampton Works **R**
16/1/32	Old Oak shops **R**
22/9/32	Swindon Works **I**
15/12/33	Swindon Works **G**
12/2/35	Banbury shops **R**
20/11/35	Ebbw Jct shops **R**
7/3/36	Swindon Works **I**
29/5/37	Swindon Works **G**
26/6/37	Worcester
18/9/37	Hereford
12/4/38	Worcester shops **L**
16/2/39	Swindon Works **I**
20/6/40	Worcester shops **L**
17/5/41	Swindon Works **I**
1/10/41	Hereford shops **R**
12/11/41	Hereford shops **R**
3/2/42	Hereford shops **R**
4/1942	Gloucester
2/6/43	Newton Abbot Works **L**
8/5/44	Swindon Works **G**
30/10/44	Worcester shed **R**
12/2/45	Gloucester shops **R**
2/5/46	Wolverhampton Works **I**
29/7/47	Wolverhampton Works **L**
16/9/47	Hereford shops **R**
5/3/48	Worcester shops **R**
25/8/48	Swindon Works **G**
5/10/50	Swindon Works **HG**
2/12/50	Oxley
26/1/52	Banbury
2/9/52	Banbury shops **U**
27/1/53	Swindon Works **HI**
5/5/55	Swindon Works **HG**
16/6/56	Laira
16/8/56	Laira shops **U**
6/10/56	Old Oak
5/6/57	Swindon Works **HG**
26/2/58	Old Oak shops **U**
16/4/58	Newton Abbot Works **LC**
27/12/58	Reading
19/10/59	Swindon Works **HI**
20/5/61	Canton
26/6/61	Southall shops **U**
14/8/61	Hereford shops **U**

Tenders

From new	2536
21/1/31	2433
6/6/32	2592
11/10/33	2167
15/12/33	2636
18/1/36	2562
2/4/37	2617
12/1/39	2387
28/2/41	2531
23/3/44	2921
9/8/47	1666
25/8/48	2544
8/9/50	2714
16/12/52	2821
28/3/55	2761
5/6/57	2821
6/1961	2568
6/1961	2448
6/1961	2738

Mileage 1,260,721

Withdrawn 10/5/62 Cut up11/8/62

Reading's 4977 WATCOMBE HALL about 1960, climbing out of Patchway Tunnel towards Patchway Station. The Up and Down lines diverge at this point with the later Up line being built on an easier gradient of 1 in 100 through the Up tunnel. The original Down line has a steeper 1 in 80 gradient through a separate tunnel set at a higher level than the Up tunnel. Trains requiring assistance from Severn Tunnel Junction would have the extra engine in front of the train engine to Patchway or through to Stoke Gifford. A small number of banking engines were held at Pilning and on some workings the leading assisting engine was detached at Pilning and returned to Severn Tunnel Junction and a Pilning banker provided at the rear of the train to assist to Patchway. In this photograph the banker is on the rear and would have banked from Pilning. The Up Refuge Siding can be seen on the right. The double signal behind the train would be (right-hand) for Bristol Temple Meads and (left-hand) for the Badminton route.

4977 WATCOMBE HALL at Oxford shed at an unknown date. The cleaning on the tender looks suspiciously as if someone has chalked GWR, only for it to be subsequently expunged – so the view is probably quite late, in less deferential times. J. Davenport, Initial Photographics.

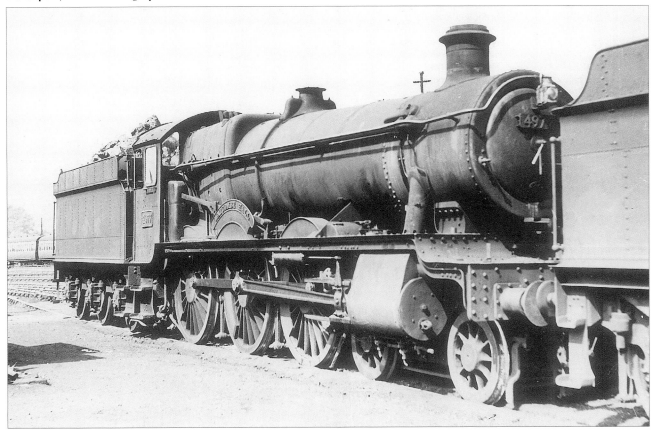

4978 WESTWOOD HALL

Built in 1930 to Lot no.254 at Swindon Works
To traffic 2/1930

Mileages and Boilers

From new	4977
24/3/31	61,501 C4977
20/6/33	148,844 C4977
22/1/35	222,660 C4480
15/5/36	301,021 C4480
8/3/37	342,267 C4445
3/3/38	386,818 C4445
11/10/39	462,616 C4445
23/2/42	545,219 C2940
19/6/44	632,227 C2940
28/10/46	717,212,C7217
8/10/48	788,298 C8287
15/2/51	872,216 C7218
17/9/53	964,341 C4413
7/11/55	1,066,481 C2939
5/2/58	1,164,215 C4962
29/8/60	1,259,373 C4460

Sheds and Works history

2/1930	Swindon Works **ATC**
15/2/30	Laira
11/9/30	Laira shops **L**
24/3/31	Swindon Works **I**
11/4/31	Old Oak
6/6/31	Truro
22/3/32	Truro shops **R**
15/7/32	Newton Abbot shed **R**
20/6/33	Swindon Works **I**
1933	Chester
1933	Banbury
19/12/33	Banbury shops **R**
22/1/35	Swindon Works **G**
31/7/35	Swindon Works **L**
28/8/35	Carmarthen
19/11/35	Carmarthen shops **R**
15/5/36	Swindon Works **I**
30/5/36	Old Oak
8/3/37	Swindon Works **L**
3/3/38	Swindon Works **I**
1/2/39	Old Oak shops **L**
11/10/39	Swindon Works **I**
21/3/40	Swindon Works **L**
7/6/41	Wolverhampton Works **L**
23/2/42	Swindon Works **G**
19/6/44	Swindon Works **I**
9/6/45	Swindon Works **L**
6/7/46	Old Oak shops **R**
28/10/46	Swindon Works **G**
5/5/48	Old Oak shed **R**
26/7/48	Reading shops **R**
8/10/48	Swindon Works **I**
26/2/49	Southall
26/3/50	Southall shops **U**
25/5/50	Southall shops **U**
15/2/51	Swindon Works **HG**
3/3/51-16/3/51 stored at Swindon	
24/3/51	Old Oak
11/8/51	Landore
21/2/53	Laira
18/3/53	Laira shops **U**
17/9/53	Swindon Works **HI**
9/12/54	Laira shops **U**
31/3/55	Laira shops **U**
7/11/55	Swindon Works **HG**
24/2/56	Newton Abbot Works **LC**
19/5/56	Taunton
22/6/56	Taunton shops **U**
14/8/56	Taunton shops **U**
5/2/58	Swindon Works **HG**
5/12/58	Newton Abbot Works **LC**
29/8/60	Swindon Works **HI**

4/8/61	Swindon Works **LC**
7/10/61	Swindon
4/11/61	Newton Abbot
23/9/62	Laira shops **U**
6/10/62	Laira
31/10/62	Caerphilly Works **LC**
11/2/63	Laira shops **U**
1/8/63	Exeter shops **U**
27/12/63	Worcester shops **U**
22/6/64	Westbury
24/8/64	Severn Tunnel Jct

Tenders

From new	2408
10/2/31	2417
6/3/33	2589
31/3/36	2397
9/2/37	2565
10/1/38	2665
9/9/39	2684
3/2/40	1906
21/3/40	2697
18/5/41	2634
24/11/41	2696
29/4/44	2374
28/10/46	2734
8/10/48	2673
8/1/51	2545
1/12/51	2719
6/8/53	2781
7/11/55	2642
5/2/58	2549
29/8/60	2786
4/8/61	2822

Mileage 1,331,101 as at 28/12/63

Withdrawn 9/1964

Relatively gleaming, 4978 WESTWOOD HALL stands by the coal stage at Oxley shed in the late 1950s, when it was a Taunton engine. J. Davenport, Initial Photographics.

4979 WOOTTON HALL

Built in 1930 to Lot no.254 at Swindon Works
To traffic 2/1930

Mileages and Boilers

From new	4978
31/3/31	62,340 C4978
9/3/33	132,210 C2885
11/7/34	196,738 C2885
7/4/36	281,410 C2952
7/12/37	368,746 C2952
24/2/40	447,394 C2952
29/10/41	495,361 C4027
29/4/43	548,133 C4027
10/8/45	620,463 C9217
19/12/47	693,444 C4035
14/10/49	761,733 C4035
10/4/52	846,838 C4071
31/5/54	926,283 C4424
16/10/56	1,014,215 C4424
20/4/59	1,097,640 C4981
3/10/61	1,171,472 C4988

Sheds and Works history

15/2/30	Laira
2/1930	Swindon Works **ATC**
2/6/30	Laira shops **L**
8/9/30	Laira shops **L**
25/12/30	Laira shops **L**
31/3/31	Swindon Works **I**
9/5/31	Penzance
18/2/32	Swindon Works **L**
5/7/32	Swindon Works **L**
30/7/32	Laira
9/3/33	Swindon Works **G**
7/7/33	Newton Abbot shed **R**
10/11/33	Laira shops **R**
21/2/34	Laira shops **R**
11/7/34	Swindon Works **I**
28/7/34	Tyseley
20/3/35	Tyseley shops **R**
7/4/36	Swindon Works **G**
7/12/37	Swindon Works **I**
24/2/40	Swindon Works **I**
3/1940	Severn Tunnel Jct
22/5/41	Severn Tunnel Jct shops **R**
24/6/41	Swindon Works **R**
29/10/41	Swindon Works **L**
29/4/43	Swindon Works **I**
1/8/44	Severn Tunnel Jct shops **L**
23/11/44	Oxley shops **R**
10/8/45	Swindon Works **I**
28/12/45	Didcot shops **R**
13/1/47	Danygraig shops **R**
28/4/47	Old Oak shops **R**
19/12/47	Swindon Works **G**
27/12/47	Canton
14/10/49	Swindon Works **HI**
18/8/50	Ebbw Jct shops **U**
10/5/51	Ebbw Jct shops **U**
19/7/51	Worcester shops **U**
10/4/52	Swindon Works **HI**
12/9/52	Swindon Works **LC**
21/3/53	Southall
2/9/53	Southall shops **U**
14/12/53	Old Oak shops **U**
31/5/54	Swindon Works **HG**
8/10/55	Didcot
23/11/55	Didcot shops **U**
16/10/56	Swindon Works **HI**
11/5/57	Didcot shops **U**
5/10/57	Reading
1/2/58	Reading shops **LC**
4/7/58	Reading shops **LC**
12/7/58	Oxford
7/1/59	Old Oak shops **U**
20/4/59	Swindon Works **HG**
20/4/60	Wolverhampton Works **LC**
17/3/61	Didcot shops **U**
15/6/61	Old Oak shops **U**
3/10/61	Swindon Works **HI**

Tenders

From new	2417
31/3/31	2405
5/7/32	2431
9/3/33	2542
7/4/36	2385
24/2/40	2746
29/10/41	2542
29/4/43	2691
10/8/45	1513
4/9/46	2609
10/4/52	2758
12/9/52	1766
31/5/54	2745
8/9/56	2428
16/10/56	2891
20/4/59	2565
6/1961	2574
3/10/61	2420

Mileage 1,233,801

Withdrawn 28/12/63 Engine preserved

4979 WOOTTON HALL passing Twyford East box, 30 August 1955; lined black. J. Robertson, transporttreasury

4979 at Reading shed, 12 September 1960. D.K. Jones Collection.

4980 WROTTESLEY HALL

Built in 1930 to Lot no.254
To traffic 11/2/30

Mileages and Boilers

From new	4979
12/6/31	64,582 C4979
18/1/33	131,444 C4956
11/4/34	193,895 C4956
9/1/36	276,929 C4956
21/12/36	319,676 C2820
10/2/38	367,769 C2820
16/5/41	465,570 C2820
23/9/41	469,278 C2886
24/11/44	576,590 C2922
29/10/47	671,609 C4429
1/11/49	744,406 C2927
11/1/52	833,627 C2927
4/10/54	915,472 C2801
5/2/57	997,197 C2801
10/3/59	1,073,390 C8258
20/9/61	1,166,288 C8258

Sheds and Works history

2/1930	Swindon works **ATC**
11/2/30	Penzance
7/6/30	Penzance shops **L**
2/10/30	Penzance shops **L**
12/6/31	Newton Abbot Works **I**
4/7/31	Taunton
21/11/31	Penzance
6/7/32	Penzance shops **R**
21/9/32	Penzance shops **R**
18/1/33	Swindon Works **G**
1933	Laira
10/11/33	Newton Abbot shed **R**
11/4/34	Swindon Works **I**
2/6/34	Gloucester
9/1/36	Swindon Works **I**
8/2/36	Penzance
21/12/36	Swindon Works **G**
5/2/37	Newton Abbot shed **R**
30/7/37	Penzance shops **R**
10/2/38	Swindon Works **I**
22/10/38	Penzance shops **R**
3/12/38	Newton Abbot shed **R**
12/1/39	Newton Abbot shed **R**
10/2/39	Newton Abbot shed **R**
1/4/39	Newton Abbot
11/7/39	Newton Abbot shed **L**
15/1/40	Newton Abbot shed **L**
24/4/40	Swindon Works **L**
16/5/41	Swindon Works **I**
30/6/41	Newton Abbot shed **R**
23/9/41	Swindon Works **L**
11/1941	Worcester
24/3/43	Old Oak shops **R**
18/6/44	Worcester shed **R**
24/11/44	Swindon Works **G**
26/3/45	Worcester shops **R**
1/6/46	Worcester shops **L**
2/9/46	Worcester shops **R**
29/10/47	Swindon Works **I**
1/11/49	Swindon Works **HG**
26/2/49	Oxley
26/3/49	Tyseley
2/12/50	Banbury
11/1/52	Wolverhampton Works **HI**
26/9/52	Wolverhampton Works **U**
18/11/53	Banbury shops **U**
4/10/54	Swindon Works **HG**
31/12/55	St Philips Marsh
19/5/56	Bath Road
16/6/56	St Philips Marsh
5/2/57	Swindon Works **HI**
11/7/58	St Philips Marsh shops **LC**
10/3/59	Swindon Works **HG**
20/9/61	Caerphilly Works **HI**
1/5/62	Taunton shops **U**
9/8/62	St Philips Marsh shops **LC**
10/3/63	Laira shops **U**
10/5/63	St Philips Marsh shops **U**
29/6/63	Swindon

Tenders

From new	2397
13/4/31	2422
12/8/32	2259
18/1/33	2541
11/11/35	2415
21/12/36	2669
8/1/38	2365
28/2/40	2427
18/3/41	2780
11/8/41	2549
24/11/44	2910
27/10/47	2783
30/9/49	2643
30/8/54	2783
5/2/57	2869
10/3/59	2575
30/1/60	2611
7/10/61	4097

Mileage 1,213,359

Withdrawn 4/7/63

4980 WROTTESLEY HALL at Chester shed in lined black, about 1950; BR 84E Tyseley plate, GW TYS still stencilled behind buffer beam. J. Davenport, Initial Photographics.

4980 WROTTESLEY HALL still in lined black, all shiny black, coppery and brass, at Banbury station on 18 March 1955. H.C. Casserley, courtesy R.M. Casserley.

4981 ABBERLEY HALL

Built in 1931 to Lot no.268 at Swindon Works
To traffic 29/12/30

Mileages and Boilers

From new	4471
23/12/32	100,047 C4471
9/7/34	176,954 C4952
9/5/36	265,722 C4952
18/5/38	355,155 C4472
28/5/40	436,016 C4472
21/11/42	525,408 C4472
5/9/44	590,192 C7258
30/10/45	626,487 C7258
11/3/47	675,829 C7202
8/9/49	777,870 C4480
14/12/51	856,639 C7273
26/2/54	935,695 C4920
14/6/56	1,019,395 C2983
3/10/58	1,119,921 C2983
30/3/61	1,195,507 C2832

Sheds and Works history

1/1931	Swindon Works **ATC**
17/1/31	Oxley
29/8/31	Stafford Road
21/11/31	Tyseley
16/1/32	Stafford Road
13/2/32	Oxley
23/12/32	Swindon Works **I**
1933	Laira
22/9/33	Laira shops **R**
31/12/33	Newton Abbot Works **L**
9/7/34	Swindon Works **G**
28/7/34	Bath Road
29/11/34	Danygraig shops **L**
6/3/35	Bath Road shops **R**
28/5/35	Swindon Works **L**
29/10/35	Swindon Works **L**
16/11/35	St Philips Marsh
9/5/36	Swindon Works **I**
30/5/36	Old Oak
30/11/36	Old Oak shops **R**
25/9/37	Old Oak shops **R**
18/5/38	Swindon Works **G**
6/7/38	Ebbw Jct shops **R**
5/10/38	Old Oak shops **R**
14/4/39	Bath Road shops **R**
28/5/40	Swindon Works **I**
31/12/41	Banbury shops **R**
1/1942	Carmarthen
14/10/42	Carmarthen shops **R**
21/11/42	Swindon Works **I**
3/11/43	Carmarthen shops **R**
5/9/44	Swindon Works **L**
30/10/45	Swindon Works **I**
11/3/47	Swindon Works **G**
18/1/49	Carmarthen shops **U**
8/9/49	Swindon Works **HG**
3/8/51	Carmarthen shops **U**
14/12/51	Swindon Works **HI**
16/5/53	Landore
26/2/54	Swindon Works **HI**
25/4/55	Llanelly shops **U**
3/12/55	Llanelly
14/6/56	Swindon Works **HG**
26/1/57	Goodwick
3/10/58	Caerphilly Works **HI**
30/3/61	Swindon Works **HG**
28/11/61	Carmarthen shops **U**
11/6/63	Carmarthen shops **U**
29/9/63	Oxford

Tenders

From new	2564
5/5/34	2257
9/7/34	2531
13/9/35	2661
17/3/36	2599
1/4/38	2743
20/4/40	2624
14/10/42	2394
5/9/44	2748
3/9/45	2731
18/1/49	2618
10/8/49	2857
15/11/51	2556
19/6/54	2571
5/5/56	4035
14/6/56	2856
30/3/61	2847

Mileage 1,274,585

Withdrawn 3/10/63 Sold to Messrs Coopers ltd Swindon 31/12/63

4981 ABBERLEY HALL at Whitland with one van on 1 June 1961, presumably forming up a train. R.C. Riley, transporttreasury

ABBERLEY HALL in the rain at Swansea High Street on 16 April 1959. S.Rickard/J&J Collection.

4982 ACTON HALL

Built in 1930 to Lot no.268 at Swindon Works
To traffic 7/1/31

Mileages and Boilers

From new	4472
9/2/33	97,277 C4472
12/7/34	160,463 C4482
19/2/36	250,197 C4482
13/11/37	339,207 R2992
11/8/39	430,098 R2992
4/2/42	524,489 R2992
14/12/43	588,123 C2957
7/12/45	656,039 C4404
9/8/47	723,808 C2980
19/1/50	814,959 C7245
10/4/52	901,853 C8206
20/10/54	992,309 C7224
3/4/57	1,080,875 C7224
6/11/59	1,163,462 C4048

Sheds and Works history

1/1931	Swindon Works **ATC fitted**
7/1/31	Weymouth
8/3/32	Weymouth shops **R**
9/2/33	Swindon Works **I**
1933	Swindon
1933	Westbury
12/7/34	Swindon Works **G**
25/8/34	Worcester
20/10/34	Hereford
1/5/35	Worcester shops **L**
19/2/36	Swindon Works **I**
7/3/36	Laira
4/1/37	Swindon Works **L**
30/7/37	Newton Abbot shed **L**
13/11/37	Swindon Works **G**
11/8/39	Swindon Works **I**
16/9/39	Goodwick
31/10/40	Swindon Works **L**
15/10/41	Landore shops **R**
4/2/42	Swindon Works **I**
14/12/43	Swindon Works **G**
29/1/44	Swindon Works **L**
28/4/45	St Blazey shops **R**
5/6/45	Bath Road shops **R**
7/12/45	Swindon Works **I**
9/8/47	Swindon Works **G**
4/10/47	Llanelly
1/11/47	Goodwick
7/8/48	Landore
9/8/48	Danygraig shops **L**
2/5/49	Newton Abbot Works **LC**
19/1/50	Swindon Works **HG**
22/4/50	St Philips Marsh
17/6/50	Neyland
9/7/51	Neath shops **U**
14/7/51	Ebbw Jct shops **LC**
10/4/52	Swindon Works **HI**
31/10/53	Ebbw Jct
7/5/54	Ebbw Jct **U**
20/10/54	Swindon Works **HG**
23/6/55	Ebbw Jct shops **LC**
3/4/57	Swindon Works **HI**
30/8/57	Old Oak shops **U**
19/4/58	Canton
10/6/58	Ebbw Jct shops **LC**
15/9/58-25/9/58	stored at Canton
29/11/58	Tyseley
6/11/59	Swindon Works **HG**
27/1/60	Tyseley shops **U**
25/2/61	Old Oak
22/3/61	Old Oak shops **U**
9/9/61	Laira
6/1/62	Laira shops **U**
1/2/62	Laira shops **U**

Tenders

From new	2566
29/5/34	2580
1/1/36	2597
30/9/37	2582
20/6/39	2587
31/10/40	2766
22/12/41	2403
27/3/43	2262
14/12/43	2413
7/12/45	2846
9/8/47	2531
19/1/50	2445
25/5/50	2809
15/9/54	4105
6/10/56	2607
23/2/57	2555
3/4/57	2720
6/11/59	2403
1/1962	2655

Mileage 1,245,012

Withdrawn 11/5/62 cut up11/8/62

Lined black 4982 ACTON HALL with Hawksworth tender at Salisbury with a train for the Bristol direction, 27 June 1956. D.K. Jones Collection.

4982 ACTON HALL at Penzance shed in 1961; Warship Type 4 in the shed behind. On the front running plate are supplies/provisions either conveyed from the station or about to be taken there with the Hall's next job. D.K. Jones Collection.

4983 ALBERT HALL

Built in 1930 to Lot no.268 at Swindon Works
To traffic 13/1/31

Mileages and Boilers

From new	4473
16/3/33	99,699 C4473
9/7/34	166,079 C4473
30/1/36	238,709 C2839
27/5/37	321,041 C2839
28/2/39	404,436 C2839
12/8/41	490,476 C2809
22/1/45	590,645 C3003
5/11/47	665,015 C2846
5/1/50	732,477 C8207
9/7/52	821,563 C2941
5/11/54	899,571 C2941
3/10/56	975,049 C9202
10/10/58	1,058,409 C9202
13/4/61	1,122,505 C2800

Sheds and Works history

1/1931	Swindon Works **ATC**
13/1/31	Goodwick
10/2/31	Canton shops **R**
1/12/31	Goodwick shops **R**
14/3/32	Goodwick shops **R**
24/3/32	Swindon Works **L**
16/3/33	Swindon Works **I**
1933	Laira
12/10/33	Laira shops **R**
1/3/34	Newton Abbot shed **L**
9/7/34	Swindon Works **I**
28/7/34	Bath Road
17/11/34	Weymouth
14/8/35	Weymouth shops **R**
12/11/35	Banbury shops **R**
30/1/36	Swindon Works **G**
23/12/36	Weymouth shops **R**
6/2/37	Weymouth shops **R**
27/5/37	Swindon Works **I**
26/6/37	Oxford
6/5/38	Reading shops **R**
29/7/38	Old Oak shops **R**
28/2/39	Swindon Works **I**
1/4/39	Newton Abbot
27/1/40	Newton Abbot shed **R**
31/8/40	Newton Abbot shed **L**
31/3/41	Newton Abbot shed **R**
12/8/41	Swindon Works **G**
4/3/43	Newton Abbot Works **L**
18/12/43	Newton Abbot Works **L**
22/1/45	Swindon Works **I**
1/1/46	Newton Abbot shed **R**
1/3/47	Newton Abbot Works **L**
5/11/47	Swindon works **G**
4/8/49	Newton Abbot shed **U**
5/1/50	Swindon Works **HG**
22/4/50	Swindon
24/1/51	Ebbw Jct
24/3/51	Carmarthen
17/7/51	Weymouth shops **U**
29/12/51	St Philips Marsh
9/7/52	Swindon Works **HG**
5/7/53	Bath Road shops **U**
6/11/53	Bath Road shops **U**
5/11/54	Swindon Works **HI**
26/3/55	Bath Road
3/10/56	Swindon Works **HG**
1/12/56	St Philips Marsh
14/6/58	Carmarthen
19/7/58	Carmarthen shops **U**
10/10/58	Caerphilly Works **HI**
6/10/58-22/12/58	Stored at Carmarthen
6/1/59-23/3/59	Stored at Carmarthen
8/4/59-11/5/59	Stored at Llanelly
18/4/59	Canton
11/7/59	Pontypool Road
26/8/60	Bath Road shops **U**
5/11/60	Old Oak
13/4/61	Swindon Works **HG**
19/9/61	continuation of previous **HG**
25/5/62	Swindon Works **LC**
6/11/62	Duffryn Yard
9/3/63	Neyland
13/6/63	Ebbw Jct shops **LC**
9/9/63	Severn Tunnel Jct
30/11/63	St Philips Marsh

Tenders

From new	2563
15/3/32	2418
4/12/35	2580
14/4/37	2534
25/6/37	2232
16/1/39	2692
6/6/41	2388
10/11/44	2569
22/1/45	2746
5/11/47	2722
18/5/49	2444
25/11/49	2420
20/4/51	2616
9/6/52	2912
31/10/53	2565
25/9/54	2928
30/11/56	2670
7/9/57	2602
13/4/61	2916
19/9/61	2634
25/5/62	4084

Mileage 1,199,562

Withdrawn 28/12/63 Sold to Woodham Brothers Barry 30/4/64

Fresh off 'AE' Shop, ready for firing up and its trial trips, 4983 ALBERT HALL stands glistening outside on 9 April 1961. H.D. Ramsey, Initial Photographics.

4983 ALBERT HALL at Llanvihangel on a North West to Torbay through train, 1 August 1953. A.W. Cawston, courtesy Brian Bailey.

4984 ALBRIGHTON HALL

Built in 1931 to Lot no.268 at Swindon Works
To traffic 16/1/31

Mileages and Boilers

From new	4474
21/9/33	102,081 C4474
4/4/35	177,452 C4904
2/1/37	259,173 C4904
8/9/38	343,620 C4961
29/5/40	427,826 C4961
13/6/42	509,741 C4961
3/11/44	601,984 C4024
30/9/47	701,206 C4445
24/3/50	797,003 C4445
26/8/52	878,803 C8234
1/10/54	956,376 C8234
3/1/56	997,192 C2851
11/3/57	1,044,069 C2848
15/10/59	1,131,989 C7223
29/5/61	1,181,322 C2985

Sheds and Works history

1/1931	Swindon Works **ATC fitted**
17/11/31	Worcester shops **L**
16/1/31	Westbury
1933	Old Oak
21/9/33	Swindon Works **I**
4/4/35	Swindon Works **G**
17/12/35	Old Oak shops **R**
25/3/36	Swindon Works **R**
2/6/36	Reading shops **R**
2/1/37	Swindon Works **I**
8/9/38	Swindon Works **G**
15/10/38	Carmarthen
29/5/40	Swindon Works **I**
13/6/42	Swindon Works **I**
2/8/42	Carmarthen shops **L**
23/10/43	Newton Abbot Works **L**
3/11/44	Swindon Works **G**
4/5/46	Swindon Works **L**
10/9/46	Newton Abbot Works **L**
30/9/47	Swindon Works **I**
3/5/49	St Blazey shops **U**
6/12/49	Carmarthen shops **U**
24/3/50	Swindon Works **HI**
1/6/51	Carmarthen shops **U**
30/1/52	Carmarthen shops **U**
26/8/52	Swindon Works **HG**
28/11/53	St Philips Marsh
26/12/53	Carmarthen
1/10/54	Swindon Works **HI**
3/1/56	Swindon Works **HC**
6/10/56	Oxley
11/3/57	Swindon Works **HG**
24/2/58	Old Oak shops **U**
17/6/58	Swindon Works **LC**
20/11/58	Oxley shops **U**
15/10/59	Swindon Works **HI**
29/5/61	Swindon Works **HI**
17/6/61	Exeter
14/7/62	Canton

Tenders

From new	2560
12/6/33	2423
17/10/33	2266
4/4/35	2660
19/11/36	2421
8/8/38	2673
1/5/42	2396
18/9/44	2895
3/11/44	2638
4/5/46	2799
20/9/47	2556
24/5/49	2920
20/2/50	2904
28/7/52	2440
21/8/54	2809
3/1/56	2556
24/3/56	2644
11/3/57	2853
17/6/58	2531
15/10/59	2633
17/9/60	2401
29/5/61	2904

Mileage 1,231,044

Withdrawn 21/9/62 Sold to R S Hayes ltd Bridgend 26/8/63

A lovely looking ALBRIGHTON HALL at Old Oak Common shed, 16 October 1960. J. Davenport, Initial Photographics.

An exceedingly scruffy and NOT TO BE MOVED 4984 ALBRIGHTON HALL undergoing attention at Shrewsbury shed. The engine behind is having the smokebox cleared, in a less-than sophisticated fashion – a sheet of scrap metal laid across the buffers of the engines to divert the char away from the pit. ColourRail

4985 ALLESLEY HALL

Built in 1931 to Lot no.268 at Swindon Works
To traffic 22/1/31

Mileages and Boilers

From new	4475
13/2/33	100,806 C4475
26/4/34	145,378 C4957
2/2/35	174,478 C4957
6/11/36	250,363 C4933
12/10/38	335,101 C4933
9/10/40	419,144 C4933
20/2/43	506,405 C8289
13/4/46	618,846 C2816
27/11/47	684,321 C2877
1/5/50	778,141 C2819
21/1/53	860,019 C4420
1/7/55	956,150 C8282
22/5/57	1,036,296 C2877
3/12/59	1,136,078 C8278
5/6/61	1,179,208 C4030

Sheds and Works history

22/1/31	Old Oak
14/2/31	Swindon Works **ATC**
1933	Laira
13/2/33	Swindon Works **I**
28/4/33	Swindon Works **L**
1933	Penzance
19/9/33	Penzance shops **R**
5/12/33	Swindon Works **L**
26/4/34	Swindon Works **L**
5/5/34	Laira
20/10/34	Penzance
20/11/34	Penzance shops **R**
2/2/35	Swindon Works **I**
19/8/35	Newton Abbot Works **L**
22/2/36	Swindon Works **L**
6/11/36	Swindon Works **G**
23/6/37	Penzance shops **R**
6/10/37	Penzance shops **R**
6/4/38	Newton Abbot Works **L**
12/10/38	Swindon Works **I**
15/10/38	Old Oak
5/4/39	Tyseley shops **R**
9/10/40	Swindon Works **I**
12/2/42	Old Oak shops **L**
20/2/43	Swindon Works **G**
14/12/44	Old Oak shops **L**
5/5/45	Old Oak shops **L**
13/4/46	Swindon Works **I**
22/3/47	Old Oak shops **R**
27/11/47	Swindon Works **G**
25/2/49	Old Oak shops **U**
13/8/49	Reading
1/5/50	Swindon Works **HG**
9/5/50-26/7/50	Stored at Swindon
12/8/50	Bath Road
4/11/50	Westbury
27/11/52	Westbury shops **U**
21/1/53	Swindon Works **HG**
13/6/53	Truro
3/10/53	Taunton
1/7/55	Swindon Works **HI**
24/9/56	Taunton shops **LC**
22/5/57	Swindon Works **HG**
13/10/58	Taunton shops **U**
3/12/59	Swindon Works **HI**
5/6/61	Swindon Works **HG**
9/2/63	Pontypool Road
21/12/63	Aberdare shops **U**
22/6/64	Gloucester
20/7/64	Neath

Tenders

From new	2435
2/32	2393
5/4/32	2386
12/12/34	2428
12/8/36	1513
13/9/39	2405
14/8/40	2764
1/1/43	1666
15/2/46	2626
27/11/47	2268
13/12/52	2727
1/7/55	2864
24/9/56	2563
22/5/57	2895
3/12/59	2744
5/6/61	4053

Mileage 1,253,139 as at 28/12/63

Withdrawn 9/64

4985 ALLESLEY HALL at Exeter St David's, 34057 BIGGIN HILL alongside, on 11 June 1960. J. Davenport, Initial Photographics.

4985 with Hawksworth tender, at Tyseley shed on 28 July 1962. ColourRail

4986 ASTON HALL

Built in 1931 to Lot no.268 at Swindon Works
To traffic 23/1/31

Mileages and Boilers

Date	Mileage	Boiler
From new	4476	
1/6/32	67,072	C4476
13/1/34	137,060	C4485
1/7/35	215,683	C4417
25/2/37	296,804	C4417
6/1/39	380,676	C4417
6/5/41	466,220	C2843
17/8/43	549,073	C2843
24/3/45	601,541	C2852
10/3/47	672,579	C8278
4/5/49	747,763	C2811
12/6/51	830,833	C7265
2/7/53	902,156	C8289
10/10/55	994,674	C8289
9/10/57	1,071,043	C7269
4/1/259	1,141,807	C6215

Sheds and Works history

23/1/31	Penzance
14/2/31	Swindon Works **ATC**
25/5/31	Penzance shops **R**
1/6/32	Swindon Works **I**
8/2/33	Newton Abbot shed **L**
27/7/33	Newton Abbot shed **L**
13/1/34	Swindon Works **G**
30/6/34	Newton Abbot
2/11/34	Newton Abbot Works **L**
1/7/35	Swindon Works **G**
27/7/35	Weymouth
16/9/36	Newton Abbot shed **L**
25/2/37	Swindon Works **I**
6/3/37	St Philips Marsh
4/3/38	St Philips Marsh shops **R**
6/1/39	Swindon Works **I**
4/3/39	Bath Road
27/5/39	Bath Road shops **L**
2/1940	St Philips Marsh
22/5/40	St Philips Marsh shops **R**
16/12/40	St Philips Marsh shops **R**
6/5/41	Swindon Works **G**
25/7/41	St Philips Marsh shops **R**
26/11/41	St Philips Marsh shops **R**
16/4/42	St Philips Marsh shops **R**
8/6/42	St Philips Marsh shops **R**
17/8/43	Swindon Works **I**
24/3/45	Swindon Works **G**
10/3/47	Swindon Works **I**
4/5/49	Swindon Works **G**
5/7/50	Swindon Works **LC**
12/6/51	Swindon Works **HI**
29/11/52	Old Oak
6/2/53	Swindon Works **LC**
2/7/53	Swindon Works **HG**
5/5/54	Old Oak shops **U**
1/12/54	St Blazey shops **U**
26/3/55	Oxley
10/10/55	Swindon Works **HI**
16/6/56	Stafford Road
2/3/57	Stafford Road shed **U**
9/10/57	Swindon Works **HG**
17/4/58	Shrewsbury shops **U**
13/6/59	Stourbridge
4/12/59	Swindon Works **HG**
26/12/59	Stafford Road
31/12/60	Reading
25/3/61	Southall
25/8/61	Exeter shops **U**
1/11/61	Southall shops **U**

Tenders

From new	2443
4/5/35	2665
19/1/37	2658
9/11/38	2707
17/3/41	2611
7/7/43	2771
7/2/45	2761
10/3/47	2432
4/5/49	2809
28/5/50	2446
5/7/50	2838
12/6/51	2432
18/5/53	2919
2/7/53	2571
24/4/54	4014
10/10/55	2651
9/10/57	2426
4/12/59	2441
6/1961	2568
6/1961	2798
6/1961	2441

Mileage 1,222,109

Withdrawn 11/5/62 Cut up 1/12/62

4986 ASTON HALL at Crewe with the North sheds over on the right and the coaling plant just peeping over the top. Engine is in lined black and the tender unlined, with the vestiges of a GWR badge but no letters. The tender might even be plain green... B.W.L. Brooksbank, Initial Photographics.

4987 BROCKLEY HALL

Built in 1931 to Lot no.268 at Swindon Works
To traffic 24/1/31

Mileages and Boilers

From new	4477
9/8/32	85,679 C4477
6/4/34	165,420 C4477
28/5/35	220,923 C4486
27/1/37	308,050 C4486
30/9/38	391,306 C4080
1/7/40	471,508 C4080
3/9/42	551,555 C4080
17/4/46	653,618 C4080
20/1/48	702,978 C4954
25/1/50	769,205 C4459
21/5/52	846,437 C7245
15/12/54	939,979 C4048
27/6/57	1,031,427 C4048
15/6/59	1,099,967 C2856

Sheds and Works history

24/1/31	Carmarthen
14/2/31	Swindon Works **ATC**
27/8/32	Old Oak
9/8/32	Swindon Works **I**
6/4/34	Swindon Works **I**
12/12/34	Old Oak shops **R**
28/5/35	Swindon Works **G**
29/6/35	Canton
27/1/37	Swindon Works **I**
10/6/38	Canton shops **R**
30/9/38	Swindon Works **G**
28/1/40	Canton shops **R**
1/7/40	Swindon Works **I**
8/1940	Oxley
3/9/42	Swindon Works **I**
24/6/43	Oxley shops **R**
10/8/43-3/2/44	Swindon Works **L** (177 days)
8/12/44	Tyseley shops **R**
17/4/46	Wolverhampton Works **I**
28/6/46	Tyseley shops **R**
14/8/46	Worcester shops **R**
20/9/47	Reading shops **R**
20/1/48	Swindon Works **G**
27/10/48	Wolverhampton Works **L**
22/9/49	Bath Road shops **U**
23/11/49	Chester
25/1/50	Swindon Works **HG**
6/3/50	Ebbw Jct shops **U**
14/7/51	Leamington Spa
22/10/51	Tyseley shops **U**
21/5/52	Swindon Works **HI**
1/11/52	Banbury
14/8/53	Banbury shops **U**
15/12/54	Swindon Works **HG**
6/6/55	Reading shops **U**
3/12/55	Reading
27/6/57	Swindon Works **HI**
10/4/58	Swindon Works **HC**
12/7/58	Oxford
9/8/58	Reading
15/6/59	Swindon Works **HG**
11/7/60	Old Oak shops **U**
12/9/60	Tyseley shops **U**
7/10/61	Southall

Tenders

From new	2416
4/4/35	2438
13/12/36	2672
29/8/38	2421
28/2/40	2829
14/7/42	1649
10/8/43	2553
1/12/47	2847
25/1/50	2885
17/4/52	2634
9/11/54	2690
27/6/57	2893
10/4/58	2539
15/6/59	2622

Mileage 1,195,979

Withdrawn 9/4/62 Cut up 21/3/64

Lined black 4987 BROCKLEY HALL at Oxford station, 15 September 1955. M. Robertson, transporttreasury

4987 BROCKLEY HALL still in lined black, at Shrewsbury station in 1955. D.K. Jones Collection.

4988 BULWELL HALL

Built in 1931 to Lot no.268 at Swindon Works
To traffic 29/1/31

Mileages and Boilers

From new	4478
22/6/32	72,094 C4478
12/2/34	150,254 C2951
30/12/35	240,066 C2951
7/12/36	280,482 C4007
5/1/38	321,766 C4007
10/2/42	454,208 C7202
1/7/44	527,954 C7202
18/10/46	597,946 C7265
12/8/48	658,798 C8209
15/8/50	723,479 C4477
11/1/52	770,115 C4490
30/10/53	832,049 C4042
15/5/56	924,411 C4428
30/9/58	1,031,321 C4428
26/6/61	1,127,508 C4982

Sheds and Works history

29/1/31	Old Oak
14/2/31	Swindon Works **ATC**
22/6/32	Swindon Works **I**
12/2/34	Swindon Works **G**
10/3/34	Tyseley
4/5/35	Stafford Road
30/12/35	Swindon Works **I**
11/1/36	Oxley
9/6/36	Wolverhampton Works **L**
7/12/36	Swindon Works **L**
6/5/37	Oxford shops **R**
5/1/38	Swindon Works **I**
18/11/38	Bath Road shops **L**
27/5/39	St Philips Marsh
29/11/39	Swindon Works **L**
19/4/40	St Philips Marsh shops **R**
8/1940	Westbury
6/4/41	Westbury shops **R**
5/7/41	Westbury shops **R**
25/10/41	Westbury shops **R**
10/2/42	Swindon Works **L**
8/10/42	Swindon Works **L**
24/4/43	Westbury shops **R**
1/7/44	Swindon Works **I**
1/2/45	Westbury shops **R**
20/4/46	Didcot shops **R**
20/7/46	Reading shops **R**
18/10/46	Swindon Works **G**
2/11/46	Weymouth
12/8/48	Swindon Works **L**
20/5/49	Weymouth shops **U**
16/1/2/49	Weymouth shops **U**
15/8/50	Swindon Works **HG**
11/1/52	Swindon Works **HC**
16/10/52	Weymouth shops **U**
6/12/52	Weymouth shops **U**
10/9/53	Oxford shops **U**
30/10/53	Swindon Works **HG**
26/3/54	Weymouth shops **U**
31/5/54	Swindon Works **LC**
16/7/55	Exeter
8/10/55	Tyseley
14/12/55	Tyseley shops **U**
15/5/56	Swindon Works **HG**
17/5/58	St Philips Marsh
30/9/58	Swindon Works **HI**
29/11/58	Bath Road
8/8/59	Severn Tunnel Jct
18/6/60	Neath
30/8/60	St Philips Marsh **U**
26/6/61	Swindon Works **HG**
15/12/62	Llanelly
29/9/63	Oxford

Tenders

From new	2444
30/11/33	2597
11/11/35	2388
7/12/36	2558
8/11/37	2424
8/6/38	2542
27/9/39	2566
11/6/40	2703
4/12/41	2552
8/10/42	2647
1/7/44	2829
18/10/46	2735
4/5/48	2615
23/4/50	2616
20/4/51	2420
23/4/51	2884
11/1/52	2661
30/10/53	2796
15/5/56	4083
30/9/58	4090
26/6/61	2618

Mileage 1,205,459

Withdrawn 14/2/64 Cut up 21/3/64

4988 BULWELL HALL; a lined black Hall at Oxford again, this time 23 June 1954. M. Robertson, transporttreasury

4989 CHERWELL HALL

Built in 1931 to Lot no.268 at Swindon Works
To traffic 3/2/31

Mileages and Boilers

From new	4479
1/9/32	72,561 C4479
5/6/34	149,266 C4011
7/2/36	229,911 C4916
11/11/37	321,181 C4916
4/9/39	406,679 C4904
3/6/42	501,225 C4904
21/3/45	595,523 C8254
2/9/47	680,507 C4991
16/3/50	768,217 C2993
21/5/52	846,948 C7203
3/3/54	907,594 C7203
30/8/56	990,989 C8285
9/12/58	1,083,256 C8285
15/12/61	1,160,251 C7206

Sheds and Works history

3/2/31	Penzance
14/2/31	Swindon Works **ATC**
29/12/31	Penzance shops **R**
1/9/32	Swindon Works **I**
24/9/32	Gloucester
6/10/33	Swindon Works **L**
22/11/33	Gloucester Shops **R**
5/6/34	Swindon Works **G**
30/6/34	Chester
6/6/35	Chester shops **R**
7/2/36	Swindon Works **G**
7/3/36	Penzance
4/4/36	Laira
25/7/36	Truro
22/8/36	Laira
19/3/37	Newton Abbot shed **L**
11/11/37	Swindon Works **I**
11/12/37	Truro
5/4/39	Newton Abbot shed **L**
4/9/39	Swindon Works **G**
16/9/39	Reading
9/2/41	Reading shops **R**
31/10/41	Reading shops **R**
3/6/42	Swindon Works **I**
26/11/43	Reading shops **R**
3/6/44	Reading shops **R**
22/8/44	Reading shops **R**
21/3/45	Swindon Works **G**
19/3/46	Reading shops **R**
2/9/46	Old Oak shops **L**
14/11/46	Reading shops **R**
2/9/47	Swindon Works **I**
30/9/47	Severn Tunnel Jct shops **R**
1/12/48	Old Oak shops **R**
16/3/50	Swindon Works **HG**
21/5/52	Swindon Works **HG**
3/3/54	Swindon Works **HI**
19/9/55	Reading shops **U**
30/8/56	Swindon Works **HG**
9/12/58	Wolverhampton Works **HI**
15/7/59	Old Oak shops **LC**
28/11/59	Gloucester
7/1/60	Gloucester shops **U**
20/10/60	Wolverhampton Works **LC**
25/11/60	Oxley shops **U**
15/3/61	Didcot shops **U**
5/12/61	Swindon Works **HG**
27/1/62	Southall
19/11/62	Southall shops **U**
29/6/63	Pontypool Road
27/7/63	Westbury
25/9/63	Worcester shops **U**
27/1/64	Taunton
3/4/64	Old Oak shops **U**
5/10/64	Severn Tunnel Jct

Tenders

From new	2419
13/4/34	2562
27/12/35	2546
23/7/38	1782
4/9/39	2579
3/6/42	2734
3/2/45	2882
2/9/47	2641
10/9/47	2748
13/2/50	2443
14/1/34	2925
2/9/55	2655
30/8/56	2685
15/12/61	2625
21/3/64	4118

Mileage 1,216,039 as at 28/12/63

Withdrawn 11/1964

In the malodorous condition so typical of the time, 4989 CHERWELL HALL (still with nameplate, remarkably) has a train at Westbury station in June 1964. B.H. Fletcher, transporttreasury

4989 CHERWELL HALL soldiers on at Banbury, doggedly hanging on to its nameplate and smokebox plate, on 13 October 1964. It was withdrawn a week or so later. K.Fairey, ColourRail

4990 CLIFTON HALL

Built in 1931 to Lot no.268 at Swindon Works
To traffic 9/2/31

Mileages and Boilers

Date	Mileage
From new	4480
9/9/32	69,453 C4480
2/7/34	138,839 C4970
28/4/36	227,454 C4970
25/9/37	296,510 C2811
15/6/39	373,710 C2811
25/9/41	458,940 C2811
29/2/44	537,553 C4968
9/2/46	607,887 C4058
3/3/49	703,363 C4900
4/4/51	786,914 C4922
4/9/53	875,153 C7233
8/8/58	1,049,099 C4433

Tenders

From new	2437
27/4/34	2646
12/3/36	2542
12/8/37	2627
2/5/39	2683
16/7/41	2256
3/1/44	2866
27/11/45	2413
25/1/47	2443
25/2/48	2899
28/1/49	2909
5/3/51	2619
26/7/53	2417
24/4/54	2647
13/1/56	2404
8/8/58	2397
25/5/59	2439

Mileage 1,150,964

Withdrawn 5/4/62 Cut up 16/6/62

Sheds and Works history

9/2/31	Penzance
14/2/31	Swindon Works **ATC**
9/9/32	Swindon Works **I**
22/10/32	Truro
28/6/33	Truro shops **R**
27/11/33	Truro shops **R**
26/1/34	Newton Abbot shed **L**
2/7/34	Swindon Works **G**
28/7/34	Westbury
29/6/35	St Philips Marsh
1/8/35	St Philips Marsh shops **R**
23/9/35	Taunton shops **R**
28/4/36	Swindon Works **I**
30/5/36	Weymouth
9/6/37	Weymouth shops **R**
25/9/37	Swindon Works **G**
3/8/38	Weymouth shops **R**
16/12/38	Swindon Works **L**
15/6/39	Swindon Works **I**
24/6/39	Worcester
14/10/39	Gloucester
11/11/39	Canton
25/9/41	Swindon Works **I**
10/1941	Worcester
2/1942	St Philips Marsh
11/4/42	Swindon Works **L**
29/2/44	Swindon Works **G**
14/6/45	Bath Road shops **R**
9/2/46	Swindon Works **I**
25/1/47	Swindon Works **L**
28/4/47	Bath Road shops **L**
30/5/47	St Philips Marsh shops **R**
10/12/47	St Philips Marsh shops **L**
8/9/48	St Philips Marsh shops **R**
3/3/49	Swindon Works **HG**
4/4/51	Swindon Works **HG**
23/2/52	Severn Tunnel Jct
1/11/52	Pontypool Road
4/9/53	Swindon Works **HG**
13/1/56	Swindon Works **HI**
29/12/56	Penzance
18/5/57	Stafford Road
25/6/57	Stafford Road shed **U**
8/8/58	Swindon Works **HG**
16/7/59	Wolverhampton Works **LC**
5/9/59	Banbury
31/10/59	Hereford
27/4/60	Caerphilly Works **HC**
2/11/60	Ebbw Jct shops **LC**
30/12/60	Hereford shops **U**
8/5/61	Hereford shops **U**
18/1/61	Banbury shops **U**

Hereford's **CLIFTON HALL** light engine, still sumptuously coaled, waits to proceed to 'Coleham' shed about 1960. The big Shrewsbury Severn Bridge box is on the left. A.Robey, transporttreasury

In black and dirt livery at Stafford Road, probably in 1957. J. Davenport, Initial Photographics.

4991 COBHAM HALL

Built in 1931 to Lot no.268 at Swindon Works
To traffic 2/1931

Mileages and Boilers

From new	4481
6/1/33	80,240 C4481
29/3/34	140,960 C4407
22/1/36	224,021 C4407
27/8/36	254,500 C4443
24/12/37	311,863 C4443
4/7/39	385,662 C4443
6/6/41	463,022 C4447
31/7/43	548,735 C4447
10/5/46	647,460 C4492
3/1/49	739,821 C7258
28/6/50	786,518 C7279
7/11/51	837,720 C4906
6/5/54	934,973 C9298
30/7/56	1,016,475 C4436
8/7/58	1,096,693 C8261
1/5/61	1,198,101 C8235

Sheds and Works history

4/2/31	Swindon Works **ATC**
14/2/31	St Philips Marsh
23/9/31	Swindon shed **L**
6/1/33	Swindon Works **I**
1933	Chester
29/3/34	Swindon Works **G**
7/4/34	Penzance
22/10/34	Penzance shops **R**
5/2/35	Newton Abbot Works **L**
31/5/35	Newton Abbot Works **L**
16/11/35	Newton Abbot
22/1/36	Swindon Works **I**
8/2/36	Truro
4/4/36	Laira
27/8/36	Swindon Works **L**
15/10/36	Laira shops **R**
14/11/36	St Philips Marsh
6/2/37	Newton Abbot Works **L**
24/12/37	Swindon Works **I**
15/6/38	Newton Abbot shed **L**
21/2/39	Newton Abbot shed **L**
4/7/39	Swindon Works **I**
7/1/41	Newton Abbot Works **L**
6/6/41	Swindon Works **G**
15/1/42	Laira shops **R**
9/12/42	Laira shops **R**
24/4/43	Newton Abbot Works **R**
31/7/43	Swindon Works **I**
2/10/44	Laira shops **R**
9/11/44	Laira shops **R**
23/3/45	Newton Abbot Works **R**
30/8/45	Laira shops **R**
18/12/45	Laira shops **R**
30/1/46	Taunton shops **R**
10/5/46	Swindon Works **G**
19/6/46	St Blazey shops **R**
28/3/47	Newton Abbot Works **L**
12/7/47	Oxley
20/11/47	Stafford Road shed **R**
8/12/47	St Philips Marsh shops **R**
12/2/48	Oxley shops **L**
	Tender work only
18/5/48	Oxley shops **R**
8/9/48	Oxley shops **R**
3/1/49	Swindon Works **HG**
2/6/49	Swindon Works **U**
18/11/49	Oxley shops **U**
4/4/50	Oxley shops **U**
28/6/50	Swindon Works **HC**
12/10/50	Shrewsbury shops ex LMR **U**
16/8/51	Reading shops **U**
7/11/51	Swindon works **HG**
9/8/52	Stafford Road
30/4/53	Southall shops **U**
31/10/53	Pontypool Road
6/5/54	Swindon Works **HI**
9/9/55	Oxley shops **U**
25/10/55	Pontypool Road shops **U**
25/2/56	Taunton
30/7/56	Swindon Works **HG**
8/7/58	Swindon Works **HG**
30/1/59	Newton Abbot Works **LC**
23/6/59	Bath Road shops **LC**
7/6/60	Newton Abbot Works **LC**
1/5/61	Swindon Works **HG**
5/10/62	Ebbw Jct **U**
6/10/62	St Philips Marsh
27/2/63	Cheltenham shops **U**
25/6/63	St Philips Marsh shops **U**
29/6/63	Swindon

Tenders

From new	2446
4/3/31	1827
18/11/33	1834
4/10/34	2581
2/12/35	2567
2/5/36	1513
27/8/36	2428
23/5/39	2389
11/11/39	2599
7/4/41	2391
31/7/43	2608
3/8/43	2659
16/3/46	2825
17/11/48	2697
28/6/50	2536
8/10/51	2587
5/4/54	2553
5/10/55	2567
30/7/56	2742
12/7/58	2407
1/5/61	2699

Mileage 1,270,339

Withdrawn 28/12/63 Sold to J Cashmore 28/2/64

Taunton's 4991 COBHAM HALL at Weston Super Mare with an up train in the later 1950s; it has come in as a stopper and is going out as an express. ColourRail

COBHAM HALL in a rarely-photographed corner of Newton Abbot shed, 29 September 1956. The turntable lies out of sight beyond the weighbridge (to the left) and the Loco Factory over on the right; 4991 is either proceeding to turn or has turned and is running back to the main part of the shed yard. RailOnline

4991 COBHAM HALL at Westbourne Park in August 1961, running back to Old Oak Common.

4992 CROSBY HALL

Built in 1931 to lot no.268 at Swindon Works
To traffic 2/1931

Mileages and Boilers

From new	4482
9/8/32	60,542 C4482
5/4/34	128,451 C4902
20/9/35	209,263 C4902
19/5/37	291,308 C2951
18/1/39	371,580 C2951
19/3/41	458,993 C2951
18/3/42	489,566 C4443
15/3/45	574,609 C4948
17/6/48	669,958 C4040
12/10/50	753,546 C2907
13/5/53	855,275 C2907
11/1/55	933,990 C4269
26/4/57	1,032,418 C4269
9/7/59	1,128,846 C6220
16/10/61	1,201,204 C8278

Sheds and Works history

14/2/31	Penzance
14/3/31	Swindon Works **ATC**
20/7/31	Penzance shops **R**
25/11/31	Penzance shops **R**
9/8/32	Swindon Works **I**
27/8/32	Weymouth
21/4/33	Weymouth shops **R**
18/12/33	Weymouth shops **R**
5/4/34	Swindon Works **G**
5/5/34	Westbury
20/9/35	Swindon Works **I**
19/10/35	Bristol Bath Road
29/5/37	Westbury
8/1/37	St Philips Marsh shops **R**
19/5/37	Swindon Works **G**
23/2/38	St Philips Marsh shops **R**
18/1/39	Swindon Works **I**
4/3/39	Reading
19/3/41	Swindon Works **I**
3/1941	Newton Abbot
18/3/42	Swindon Works **L**
6/7/43	Newton Abbot Works **L**
20/9/43	Newton Abbot Works **L**
6/4/44	Newton Abbot Works **L**
15/3/45	Swindon Works **I**
12/3/47	Newton Abbot Works **L**
14/4/47	Tyseley
17/6/48	Swindon Works **I**
30/10/48	St Philips Marsh
3/12/49	Laira
25/4/50	Laira shops **U**
12/10/50	Swindon Works **HG**
9/4/52	Penzance shops **U**
21/7/52	Laira shops **U**
25/9/52	Taunton shops **U**
7/11/52	Laira shops **U**
24/2/53	Laira shops **U**
13/5/53	Swindon Works **HI**
29/12/53	Exeter shops **U**
11/1/55	Swindon Works **HG**
28/9/55	Penzance shops **U**
15/10/56	Laira shops **U**
26/4/57	Swindon Works **HI**
2/11/57	Newton Abbot
12/7/58	Exeter
17/10/58	Newton Abbot Works **LC**
9/7/59	Swindon Works **HG**
1/3/60	Newton Abbot Works **LC**
4/5/60	Old Oak shops **U**
8/10/60	Taunton
9/6/61	Taunton shops **U**
16/10/61	Swindon Works **HG**
6/10/62	St Philips Marsh
29/6/63	Gloucester
30/11/63	St Philips Marsh
20/2/64	Worcester shops **U**
22/6/64	Barrow Road
9/1/65	Severn Tunnel Jct
10/4/65	Barrow Road

Tenders

From new	2445
6/7/31	2264
1/6/32	4159
1/2/34	2417
24/7/35	2410
31/3/37	2562
12/12/38	2530
17/1/41	2593
12/2/42	2680
25/1/45	2785
3/5/48	2628
15/7/50	2542
2/10/50	2799
8/4/53	2553
28/11/53	2580
26/12/53	2564
27/3/54	2871
11/1/55	2712
14/7/56	2831
26/4/57	2683
6/7/59	2831
3/12/60	2654
16/10/61	4035

Mileage 1,268,293 as at 28/12/63

Withdrawn 4/1965

4992 CROSBY HALL with an up train comes into the station past the wonderful signal box at Newton Abbot, 16 August 1957. J. Robertson, transporttreasury

Underneath all that grime, 4992 with a parcels in the bay (platform 5 to left) at the south end of Shrewsbury station on 7 September 1964, will have lined green. Of interest over on the right is a train of distinctive Murgatroyds Liquid Chlorine bogie wagons. RailOnline

4993 DALTON HALL

Built in 1931 to Lot no.268 at Swindon Works
To traffic 2/1931

Mileages and Boilers

From new	4483
29/7/32	67,025 C4483
26/4/34	143,012 C4974
21/12/35	225,165 C4974
21/12/37	315,220 C4950
11/11/39	392,967 C4950
21/6/42	481,784 C4950
16/3/43	500,545 C4032
23/4/45	568,071 C4032
20/9/46	621,814 C7249
19/11/48	692,654 C4484
28/3/50	743,989 C4909
29/5/51	786,889 C4909
3/12/51	802,103 C4021
17/3/54	881,862 C8185
18/4/56	954,888 C2832
20/8/58	1,039,785 C2832
9/11/60	1,115,525 C9283

Sheds and Works history

9/2/31	Penzance
14/3/31	Swindon Works **ATC**
30/5/32	Penzance shops **R**
29/7/32	Swindon Works **I**
27/8/32	Truro
12/12/32	Newton Abbot shed **R**
23/3/33	Newton Abbot shed **R**
12/10/33	Newton Abbot shed **R**
1933	Penzance
26/4/34	Swindon Works **G**
2/6/34	Old Oak
28/9/34	Old Oak shops **R**
17/9/35	Newton Abbot Works **R**
21/12/35	Swindon Works **I**
11/1/36	Tyseley
21/12/35	Swindon Works **I**
29/5/37	Swindon Works **L**
21/12/37	Swindon Works **G**
11/11/39	Swindon Works **I**
21/6/42	Swindon Works **I**
12/11/42	Swindon Works **L**
1/1943	Leamington Spa
16/3/43	Swindon Works **L**
4/1943	Tyseley
11/1943	Leamington Spa
3/1944	Tyseley
1/3/44	Tyseley shops **R**
23/4/45	Swindon Works **I**
20/9/46	Swindon Works **G**
29/5/47	Tyseley shops **R**
22/1/48	Bath Road shops **R**
19/11/48	Swindon Works **I**
28/3/49	Stourbridge shops **U**
8/7/49	Old Oak shops **U**
9/8/49	Weymouth shops **U**
5/11/49	Worcester
28/3/50	Swindon Works **HC**
29/5/51	Swindon Works **HI**
14/7/51	Hereford
3/12/51	Swindon Works **HC**
12/7/52	Reading
23/3/53	Old Oak shops **U**
30/4/53	Reading shops **LC**
17/3/54	Swindon Works **HI**
18/4/56	Swindon Works **HG**
20/8/58	Swindon Works **HI**
26/12/59	Worcester
9/11/60	Swindon Works **HG**
17/6/61	Exeter
14/7/62	Taunton
6/10/62	St Philips Marsh
29/1/63	Caerphilly Works **LC**
29/6/63	Swindon
6/11/63	Worcester shops **U**
30/11/63	St Philips Marsh
22/6/64	Barrow Road
9/1/65	Severn Tunnel Jct

Tenders

From new	2096
31/5/32	2405
29/2/34	2535
1/5/37	2430
5/11/37	2722
3/10/39	2564
18/5/42	2545
12/11/42	2418
9/2/43	2637
4/3/45	2736
7/8/46	2684
19/11/48	2572
22/4/51	2561
6/11/51	2867
9/2/54	2918
18/4/51	4017
3/9/57	2598
5/10/57	2590
20/8/58	2534
10/9/60	2560
22/4/61	2606

Mileage 1,192,446 as at 28/12/63

Withdrawn 2/1965

4993 DALTON HALL at Old Oak Common on 12 June 1949, still in plain black; old GW TYS shed code behind the buffer beam, which has been deranged somewhat in a minor collision. W. Hermiston, transporttreasury

Late on, without smokebox door number plate, DALTON HALL takes coal empties through Chalford station on 26 September 1964. It was withdrawn in February 1965. Hamish Stevenson.

4994 DOWNTON HALL

Built in 1931 to Lot no.268 at Swindon Works
To traffic 3/1931

Mileages and Boilers

From new	4484
25/10/32	72,311 C4484
30/1/34	120,112 C4916
12/9/35	192,847 C4089
24/9/37	282,026 C4089
2/5/38	304,575 C4927
27/9/39	368,933 C4927
1/5/42	462,540 C4927
24/3/43	495,865 C4912
18/10/44	550,068 C4912
20/6/47	627,052 C2986
28/6/49	799,818 C8243
7/12/51	784,098 C4483
21/4/54	865,598 C7274
14/5/56	939,094 C7274
28/8/58	1,022,681 C7274
23/6/61	1,089,669 C4907

Sheds and Works history

4/3/31	Swindon Works **ATC**
14/3/31	Penzance
23/11/31	Newton Abbot Works **R**
25/2/32	Newton Abbot Works **R**
21/6/32	Penzance shops **R**
25/10/32	Swindon Works **I**
19/11/32	St Philips Marsh
23/2/33	Swindon Works **L**
30/1/34	Swindon Works **G**
10/2/34	Penzance
11/10/34	Swindon Works **L**
29/4/35	Penzance shops **R**
12/9/35	Swindon Works **G**
21/9/35	Reading
9/12/36	Old Oak shops **R**
24/9/37	Swindon Works **I**
3/5/38	Swindon Works **L**
27/9/39	Swindon Works **I**
1/5/42	Swindon Works **I**
24/3/43	Swindon Works **L**
18/10/44	Swindon Works **I**
20/3/45	Reading shops **L**
14/6/45	Reading shops **R**
18/10/46	Old Oak shops **L**
15/2/47	Reading shops **L**
20/6/47	Swindon Works **G**
15/5/48	Reading shops **R**
6/11/48	Reading shops **R**
28/6/49	Swindon Works **HG**
3/8/50	Reading shops **U**
21/6/51	Old Oak shops **LC**
7/12/51	Swindon Works **HI**
21/2/53	Didcot
2/12/53	Old Oak shops **U**
21/4/54	Swindon Works **HG**
27/1/56	Old Oak shops **U**
14/5/56	Swindon Works **HI**
11/10/57	Didcot shops **U**
28/8/58	Swindon Works **HI**
19/6/59	Wolverhampton Works **LC**
12/11/59	Wolverhampton Works **LC**
23/6/61	Swindon Works **HI**

Tenders

From new	2418
12/11/31	2257
17/11/33	2444
22/7/35	2664
7/8/37	2504
28/3/38	2422
27/9/39	2246
8/8/42	2566
30/1/43	2842
18/10/44	2600
11/5/47	2531
20/6/47	2773
28/6/49	2403
16/6/51	2579
9/11/51	2857
12/3/54	4070
14/5/56	2585
23/6/61	2855

Mileage 1,143,348

Withdrawn 15/3/63 Sold to John Cashmore, Newport 4/11/63

4994 DOWNTON HALL having its tubes cleaned at Bath Road, 4 July 1947, with GW and badge. Plain black for Halls was dropped in 1945 and here we have a 1947 repaint; hence, plain green. The GW stencil shed code RDG for Reading is in the 'wrong' place, above the cylinder instead of behind the buffer beam. H.C. Casserley, courtesy R.M. Casserley.

With vestiges of lining (black) showing, 4994 stands in dismal external condition at the Shrewsbury coal stage, about 1958. D.K. Jones Collection.

4995 EASTON HALL

Built in 1931 to Lot no.268 at Swindon Works
To traffic 3/1931

Mileages and Boilers

From new	4485
1/6/32	65,883 C4485
26/10/33	122,263 C2817
28/5/35	205,479 C2817
24/2/37	292,000 C4979
19/10/38	377,272 C4979
11/9/40	459,252 C4979
30/11/42	537,823 C7248
1/9/45	632,342 C8211
5/1/48	702,181 C4486
28/6/50	804,689 C8282
9/1/53	887,699 C4056
2/2/55	960,089 C4056
31/7/57	1,041,065 C8248
29/4/60	1,141,779 C4443

Sheds and Works history

14/3/31	Laira
14/3/31	Swindon Works **ATC**
22/8/31	Laira shops **R**
1/6/32	Swindon Works **I**
2/7/32	Penzance
3/5/33	Penzance shops **R**
1933	Old Oak
26/10/33	Swindon Works **G**
28/5/35	Swindon Works **I**
26/10/36	Old Oak shops **R**
24/2/37	Swindon Works **G**
10/7/37	Weymouth shops **R**
19/10/38	Swindon Works **I**
12/11/38	Reading
9/12/39	Swindon Works **L**
11/9/40	Swindon Works **I**
14/9/42	Reading shops **R**
30/11/42	Swindon Works **G**
19/3/43	Reading shops **L**
2/8/44	Reading shops **R**
13/12/44	Reading shops **R**
1/9/45	Swindon Works **I**
12/9/46	Reading shops **R**
25/10/46	Old Oak shops **R**
21/5/47	Reading shops **L**
5/1/48	Swindon Works **G**
7/5/49	Reading shops **U**
17/1/50	Old Oak shops **U**
28/6/50	Swindon Works **HG**
9/1/53	Swindon Works **HG**
2/3/53	Swindon Works **LC**
2/2/55	Swindon Works **HI**
13/10/56	Reading shops **U**
31/7/57	Swindon Works **HG**
12/7/58	Oxford
25/11/58	Wolverhampton Works **LC**
27/2/60	Southall
29/4/60	Swindon Works **HI**

Tenders

From new	2414
2/3/31	2376
25/4/32	2430
27/7/33	2134
10/4/35	2584
12/1/37	2716
19/10/38	2672
30/10/39	2569
31/7/40	2713
30/11/42	2787
1/9/45	2427
11/5/47	2600
5/1/48	2677
9/12/52	2854
16/12/54	2740
11/8/56	2571
8/9/56	2605
30/7/57	2664
29/4/60	2615

Mileage 1,217,636

Withdrawn 8/6/62 Cut up 11/8/62

Reading's lined black 4995 EASTON HALL at Teignmouth on 2 August 1955; 4995 had been at Reading since before the War. J. Robertson, transporttreasury

Southall's 4995 EASTON HALL at Shrewsbury shed, relatively fresh out of works about 1960. ColourRail

4996 EDEN HALL

Built in 1931 to Lot no.268 at Swindon Works
To traffic 3/1931

Mileages and Boilers

Date	Mileage
From new	4486
27/5/33	111,727 C4486
22/2/35	190,145 C2840
11/1/37	277,591 C2840
5/5/38	332,688 C4974
4/3/39	364,996 C4974
25/7/41	443,664 C4974
10/9/43	513,696 C4995
30/11/45	583,398 C4995
23/11/48	670,189

Sheds and Works history

Date	Location
14/3/31	Old Oak
14/3/31	Swindon Works **ATC fitted**
8/1/32	Swindon Works **L**
16/1/32	Oxford
13/2/32	Old Oak
22/5/33	Swindon Works **I**
1933	Worcester
22/2/35	Swindon Works **G**
9/3/35	Banbury
5/5/36	Banbury shops **R**
11/1/37	Swindon Works **I**
29/9/37	Banbury shops **R**
5/5/38	Swindon Works **L**
4/3/39	Swindon Works **I**
28/1/41	Banbury shops **R**
25/7/41	Swindon Works **I**
8/1941	Oxford
10/9/43	Swindon Works **G**
23/6/44	Wolverhampton Works **L**
30/3/45	Worcester shops **R**
30/11/45	Wolverhampton Works **I**
29/12/45	Stafford Road
9/9/46	Newton Abbot Works **R**
22/10/46	Oxley shops **R**
13/6/47	Swindon Works **L**
18/1/48	Southall shops **R**
18/3/48	Tyseley shops **L**
20/3/48	Tyseley
17/4/48	Oxley
23/11/48	Swindon Works **G**
25/12/48	Gloucester
12/12/50	Swindon Works **HG**
16/1/51	Swindon Works **U**
2/9/52	Swindon Works **U**
27/4/53	Gloucester shops **U**
1/10/53	Swindon Works **HG**
13/9/55	Swindon Works **HI**
24/3/56	Canton
10/6/56	Canton shops **U**
20/11/57	Swindon Works **HG**
2/7/58	Newton Abbot Works **LC**
27/8/58	Bath Road shops **U**
1/11/58	Southall
6/1/59	Swindon Works **HC**
28/11/59	Worcester
24/3/60	Hereford shops **U**
6/10/60	Wolverhampton Works **HI**
6/7/61	Wolverhampton Works **LC**
15/7/61	Exeter
17/11/61	Wolverhampton Works **LC**
14/7/62	Taunton

Tenders

From new	2266
24/11/31	2589
24/1/33	1457
15/2/34	2421
22/2/35	2413
11/1/37	2438
19/3/38	2692
2/2/39	2705
17/7/43	2855
13/6/47	2683
20/10/48	1513
23/11/48	2851
13/12/50	2663
6/1/50	2835
2/9/52	2622
26/8/53	2617
11/7/54	2556
20/9/54	2925
13/9/55	2571
11/12/56	2555
29/12/56	2567
23/2/57	2607
20/11/57	2902
16/1/59	2626
11/1959	2721
9/1/60	4091
2/1962	2542

Mileage 1,185,530

Withdrawn 30/9/63 Sold to Messrs Cooper ltd Swindon 31/12/63

4996 EDEN HALL, piloting 5092 TRESCO ABBEY on a down Bristol express at Wootton Bassett, 18 September 1955. R.C. Riley, transporttreasury

Pretty in lined green at Salisbury station, 1961. D.K. Jones Collection.

4997 ELTON HALL

Built in 1931 to lot no.268 at Swindon Works
To traffic 3/1931

ColourRail

Mileages and Boilers
From new	4487
28/4/33	91,051 C4487
27/4/34	148,084 C4924
23/11/34	173,988 C4924
6/4/36	250,821 C4924
21/9/37	323,480 C4924
18/8/39	406,024 C4924
7/11/40	452,016 C4457
28/11/41	458,552 C4457
7/10/44	571,326 C4457
15/5/46	623,745 C4028
9/3/49	718,127 C2920
26/10/50	785,674 C4448
17/9/53	884,905 C2983
18/1/56	975,309 C9204
28/1/58	1,048,145 C4421
12/5/60	1,109,279 C7256

Sheds and Works history
14/3/31	Oxford
14/3/31	Swindon Works **ATC**
11/4/31	Westbury
1933	Hereford
28/4/33	Swindon Works **I**
30/1/34	Hereford shops **R**
27/4/34	Swindon Works **L**
23/11/34	Swindon Works **I**
15/12/34	Carmarthen
6/4/36	Swindon Works **I**
5/5/37	Swindon Works **L**
21/9/37	Swindon Works **I**
31/8/38	Swindon Works **L**
8/12/38	Swindon Works **L**
18/8/39	Swindon Works **I**
3/10/39	Danygraig shops **R**
7/11/40	Swindon Works **I**
2/1942	Neyland
9/7/42	Newton Abbot Works **L**
1/12/42	Newton Abbot Works **L**
3/4/43	Carmarthen shops **L**
29/5/43	Carmarthen shops **L**
8/2/44	Llanelly shops **R**
29/7/44	Neyland shops **R**
7/10/44	Swindon Works **I**
31/5/45	Neyland shops **R**
18/11/45	Neyland shops **R**
15/5/46	Swindon Works **G**
1/2/47	Neyland shops **R**
6/11/47	Swindon Works **R**
14/4/48	Carmarthen shops **L**
9/3/49	Swindon Works **HG**
7/2/50	Newton Abbot Works **LC**
26/10/50	Swindon Works **HG**
2/1/51	Carmarthen shops **U**
17/9/53	Swindon Works **HG**
26/12/53	Stafford Road
19/10/54	Stourbridge shops **U**
23/5/55	Stafford Road shed **U**
2/9/55	Southall shops **U**
8/10/55	Oxley
18/1/56	Swindon Works **HI**
14/5/57	Tyseley shops **U**
28/1/58	Swindon Works **HG**
14/5/58	Oxley shops **LC**
7/7/59	Caerphilly Works **LC**
1/10/59	Tyseley shops **U**
4/12/59	Wolverhampton Works **LC**
23/1/60	Oxley **U**
12/5/60	Wolverhampton Works **HC**
24/8/60	Wolverhampton Works **U**

Tenders
From new	1792
9/1931	2046
10/1/33	1937
6/4/34	2614
5/10/34	2530
19/2/36	2544
13/4/37	2662
10/8/37	2531
21/9/37	2536
31/8/38	2699
18/8/39	2737
11/10/40	2587
30/9/41	2449
12/8/44	2896
30/3/46	2147
6/11/47	2682
9/2/49	2732
28/1/50	2582
22/4/50	2722
26/10/50	2578
30/12/50	2538
4/8/51	4012
17/9/53	2829
18/1/56	2702
28/1/58	2267

Mileage 1,148.456

Withdrawn 30/10/61 Cut up 2/12/61

4997 ELTON HALL piloting 6016 KING EDWARD V on the up Cornish Riviera Express, at South Brent in August 1947. A.W. Cawston, courtesy Brian Bailey.

4997 ELTON HALL pilots 6908 DOWNHAM HALL on Hemerdon, 31 May 1961. Tony Cooke, ColourRail

4998 EYTON HALL

Built in 1931 to Lot no.268 at Swindon Works
To traffic 3/1931

Mileages and Boilers

From new	4488
22/11/32	84,948 C4488
15/6/34	157,638 C4947
12/3/36	254,086 C4947
2/12/37	344,314 R7247
2/8/39	428,490 R7247
23/1/42	526,026 R7247
15/2/44	604,256 C4990
10/5/46	684,406 C7236
4/5/48	763,998 C4974
14/6/50	842,338 C4072
2/1/53	923,213 C2923
3/11/55	1,010,138 C4475
27/1/58	1,094,124 C8268
29/6/61	1,191,358 C8212

Sheds and Works history

14/3/31	Old Oak
14/3/31	Swindon Works **ATC**
11/4/31	Weymouth
19/5/32	Weymouth shops **R**
27/8/32	St Philips Marsh
22/11/32	Swindon Works **I**
17/12/32	Old Oak
15/6/34	Swindon Works **G**
24/8/35	Worcester
21/9/35	Old Oak
17/3/36	Swindon Works **I**
2/12/37	Swindon Works **G**
2/8/39	Swindon Works **I**
6/1/41	Old Oak shops **R**
23/1/42	Swindon Works **I**
15/2/44	Swindon Works **G**
17/7/45	Old Oak shops **R**
10/5/46	Swindon Works **I**
22/5/47	Old Oak shops **R**
24/2/48	Old Oak shops **L**
4/5/48	Swindon Works **G**
6/7/49	Canton shops **U**
13/8/49	Reading
14/6/50	Swindon Works **HG**
19/4/52	Didcot
1/11/52	Reading
2/1/53	Swindon Works **HG**
10/11/53	Old Oak shops **LC**
25/10/54	Bath Road shops **U**
3/11/55	Swindon Works **HI**
3/6/57	Reading shops **U**
27/1/58	Swindon Works **HG**
24/4/59	Caerphilly Works **LC**
15/1/60	Wolverhampton Works **LC**
5/10/60	Reading shops **U**
29/6/61	Swindon Works **HI**
Transferred to LMR Book Stock 30/12/62	
15/12/62	Banbury
14/5/63	Banbury shops **U**

Tenders

From new	1823
18/4/34	2598
12/1935	2577
2/1936	2407
2/12/37	2654
2/8/39	2568
2/12/41	2718
8/12/43	2420
14/3/46	2437
28/7/47	2607
18/3/48	2535
24/7/50	2712
14/6/50	2620
2/1/53	2677
3/11/55	2598
7/9/57	4017
27/1/58	2702
8/10/60	2712
29/9/61	2660

Mileage 1,254,441

Withdrawn 22/10/63 Sold to G Cohen ltd Morriston 1/1/64

4998 EYTON HALL on the first right-hand curve after taking the Plymouth line at Aller Junction, about a mile before Stoneycombe Quarry. The train is running as a Class F goods; that means it has a set of vacuum fitted wagons behind the engine which increases the braking power and allows a higher average speed. The period is the mid-1950s in late winter or early spring; 4998's easy working suggests that, out of sight at the end of the train, will be a 51XX banker (see *The Prairie Papers*) that would drop off at Dainton summit. ColourRail

4998 EYTON HALL comes into Eastleigh station past the great Motive Power Depot (curiously empty, though it was often a bit like that – it was the rear yard that usually had lots more to offer) in the background – date not recorded. J. Davenport, Initial Photographics.

Still *plate intacta* at Oxford on 10 July 1963; it was withdrawn in October. Many oddities emerge when the background to many of these GWR names is examined. For this information of course we have the RCTS to thank. Eyton Hall turns out not to be even mentioned in GWR records, though there was one at Ruabon and another at Leominster, and at least six elsewhere so someone at Swindon had probably just noticed (an) Eyton Hall while out in the country one day! J.L. Stevenson, courtesy Hamish Stevenson.

4999 GOPSAL HALL

Built in 1931 to Lot no.268 at Swindon Works
To traffic 3/1931

Mileages and Boilers

From new	4489
8/12/32	82,936 C4489
30/4/34	151,585 C4489
27/2/36	243,961 C4412
30/9/37	339,749 C4412
20/5/39	418,937 C4977
27/8/41	492,173 C4977
31/8/42	526,399 C4960
17/6/44	577,912 C4960
29/5/46	643,212 C4990
21/7/48	717,274 C7222
11/3/53	895,484 R6211
26/7/55	991,302 C4964
3/10/57	1,077,195 C2813
22/1/60	1,167,156 C7209

Tenders

From new	2173
13/10/33	2253
14/3/34	2616
13/4/39	2628
10/6/41	2791
19/7/42	2260
17/6/44	2262
6/4/48	2550
17/5/52	2400
11/3/53	2864
26/7/55	2426
3/10/57	2808
31/3/58	2682
4/9/58	2558
22/1/60	2707

Mileage 1,262,589

Withdrawn 21/9/62 Sold to John Cashmore ltd Newport 25/8/63

Sheds and Works history

14/3/31	Old Oak
14/3/31	Swindon Works **ATC**
11/4/31	Weymouth
25/11/31	Reading shops **R**
8/12/32	Swindon Works **I**
17/12/32	Oxford
30/4/34	Swindon Works **I**
5/5/34	Old Oak
31/3/35	Worcester shops **R**
27/2/36	Swindon Works **G**
7/3/36	Newton Abbot
30/5/36	Laira
30/9/37	Swindon Works **I**
25/1/38	Laira shops **R**
13/9/38	Newton Abbot Works **L**
20/1/39	Laira shops **R**
20/5/39	Swindon Works **G**
24/6/39	Chester
27/8/41	Swindon Works **I**
31/8/42	Swindon Works **L**
9/1942	Oxley
18/8/43	Bath Road shops **R**
17/6/44	Swindon Works **I**
15/12/44	Wolverhampton Works **R**
29/5/46	Swindon Works **G**
15/6/46	Stafford Road
4/1/47	Tyseley shops **R**
21/7/48	Swindon Works **I**
3/12/49	Southall
22/5/50-11/6/50	Stored at Swindon
25/1/52	Penzance shops **U**
26/1/52	Penzance
14/6/52	St Philips Marsh
11/3/53	Swindon Works **HG**
26/7/55	Swindon Works **HI**
9/2/56	Southall shops **U**
16/6/56	Bath Road
3/11/56	St Philips Marsh
13/7/57	Canton
3/10/57	Swindon Works **HG**
5/3/58	Swindon Works **HC**
31/3/58	Swindon Works **LC**
4/9/58	Old Oak shops **U**
22/1/60	Swindon Works **HI**
28/1/61	St Philips Marsh
7/6/61	St Philips Marsh shops **U**
10/8/61	Caerphilly Works **LC**
23/1/62	Ebbw Jct shops **LC**
3/5/62	St Philips Marsh shops **U**

GW lined green on 4999 GOPSAL HALL at Weymouth on 11 October 1931. There had been Halls at Weymouth from the first, and up to half a dozen or more were there until transfer of the shed to the Southern. H.C. Casserley, courtesy R.M. Casserley.

4999 GOPSAL HALL with roundel on tender leaves Patchway Tunnel with a train out of Wales in April 1936; roundel on 4,000 gallon tender, lamps old style and not painted white. From the make up of the stock and boards it is a regular timetabled secondary express, therefore horsebox behind the engine; it is probably one of the regular through trains from North West England to Torbay and Plymouth. The first three coaches will be for Torbay, the restaurant car and six coaches going on to Plymouth. Halls were probably the usual motive power, because at this time Castles were still quite few on the ground and well spread round the system for the major express services. Even Cardiff Canton did not get Castles in numbers until 1930 onwards. See also 4977 for this remarkable location.

STOP LOOK LISTEN – 5900 Halls
coming soon... ColourRail